# The OLD WORLD
# AND AMERICA

## SIGNING THE MAGNA CARTA

Archbishop Langton and the English Barons force King John to sign this document which is the basis of English and American rights and liberties.

# The OLD WORLD AND AMERICA

## by Rev. Philip J. Furlong, Ph.D.

*Professor of History, Cathedral College, New York*

### TESTS AND EXERCISES
*by* BRENDAN BYRNE

TAN BOOKS AND PUBLISHERS, INC.
Rockford, Illinois 61105

Nihil Obstat:     Arthur J. Scanlan, S.T.D.
                  Censor Librorum

Imprimatur:    ✝ Patrick Cardinal Hayes
                  Archbishop of New York
                  August 2, 1937

Originally published by William H. Sadlier, Inc., New York, New York. Edition I—M & L.

Library of Congress Catalog Card No.: 82-51247

ISBN: 0-89555-202-7

Printed and bound in the United States of America.

TAN BOOKS AND PUBLISHERS, INC.
P.O. Box 424
Rockford, Illinois 61105
1984

# AUTHOR'S NOTE

This text, although based upon the author's "Old World and American History," is really a new book. The changes in content and in organization from the earlier book were dictated by classroom experience.

To the many teachers who contributed ideas for this text, the author is profoundly grateful. In a most real sense this book is theirs. The author is indebted to his colleague, Dr. Joseph Moody, for reading the manuscript and to Mr. Frank X. Sadlier and F. Sadlier Dinger for their help in preparing the book for publication. Mr. Brendan Byrne provided the teaching material. Wherever the book may have failed the blame must rest entirely with the author.

P. J. F.

* * * * * * * * * * * * * * * *

# CONTENTS

# I

# THE BEGINNINGS OF CIVILIZATION

# II

# OUR DEBT TO THE GREEKS

# III

# CONTRIBUTIONS OF ROME TO CIVILIZATION

# IV

## CHRIST AND HIS CHURCH

# V

## THE TRIUMPH OF THE CHURCH

# VI

## THE PEOPLE OF THE MIDDLE AGES

# VII

## THE IDEALS OF THE MIDDLE AGES

# *VIII*

## THE AGE OF NEW INTERESTS

# *IX*

## THE AGE OF CHANGE

# *X*

## THE AGE OF DISCOVERY

# *XI*

## SPAIN'S WORLD EMPIRE

# *XII*

## RIVALRIES IN EUROPE

# *XIII*

## THE FOUNDATIONS OF AMERICA

# I

## THE BEGINNINGS OF CIVILIZATION

### AIM

To understand that everything in the present comes from the past.

To realize that the earliest peoples knew how to do things that are useful to us in our daily lives.

To BLESS yourself you make the sign of the cross. The sign of the cross is a reminder of the most important facts in history, that Jesus Christ was born for us, lived and died for us, and rose from the dead the third day after His death. These all important events occurred nineteen centuries ago in the Old World. From this you can understand why it is quite necessary to study about the Old World and American History.

# I

## Part 1: THE FOUNDATIONS OF HISTORY

Everything in your life is connected with the past. The prayers that you say, the knowledge that you learn in school, the style of your clothes, and the sort of food that you eat, all are related in some way with the past.

THE UNITED STATES FROM MANY NATIONS. The motto of the United States is "E Pluribus Unum." These three Latin words mean "one from many." There is a good reason for having this motto, for our great country is one nation made up of many states But this motto might also tell us that our country is "one from many" nations. There are many things that prove this. Notice the names of the shopkeepers on the windows along the streets in your town. Look through the telephone book and see the different kinds of names there. These names may be seen: Italian, German, Irish, English, Polish and French. They are now the names of Americans.

Why are there such differences among American names? This is because America has drawn her population from the various European countries. Each of these countries in the Old World has had a share in the making of our wonderful nation.

THE DISTANT PAST. The influence of the Old World on America goes back many years. When people began to come to America, they brought with them much that was known in their own country. Thus the English settlers brought to

*Drawn expressly for "The Old World and America"*

## One From Many

People from over all the world have given themselves to America. They brought with them from their native lands gifts of useful knowledge.

America among other things certain important ideas about government and the law. The Spaniards introduced their religion. They also introduced their art and architecture and their way of farming. The European nations were many centuries learning the things that their early explorers and colonists brought to our shores.

B.C. AND A.D. You will often see on the cornerstone of an important building something like this, "A.D. 1900." That means that the building was put up in the year 1900. The letters A.D. stand for the Latin words "Anno Domini" which mean "In the year of our Lord." Whenever you see "A.D." linked with a date, it means that the event happened so many years after our Lord's birth. The meaning of "B.C." you can guess. These letters in connection with a date tell us that the event took place "before Christ."

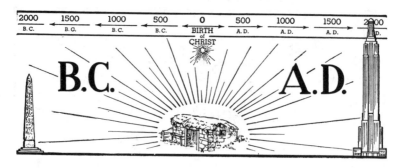

| 2000 B.C. | 1500 B.C. | 1000 B.C. | 500 B.C. | 0 BIRTH of CHRIST | 500 A.D. | 1000 A.D. | 1500 A.D. | 2000 A.D. |

## A.D. and B.C.

Count the years backward for "B.C."
Count the years forward for "A.D."

THE FOUNDATIONS OF HISTORY. Those who study history carefully will learn that the many wonderful things we enjoy come from the past in some way. For example, the radio, by which we are able to hear a concert given hundreds of miles away, is an invention of recent times. But the invention of the radio was possible only because of the knowledge the scientists of the past had given us concerning electricity and the air.

THE PAST THE TEACHER OF THE PRESENT. The present learns from the past somewhat in the manner in which a family might become wealthy after many, many years. Think of a man years ago working hard and saving a small fortune. He hands this on to his son who in turn labors very hard, saving money. This man in turn gives to his son the fortune he received from his father plus what he had earned himself. Suppose this went on for two hundred years. At the end of that time the fortune would be large. But it is large only because each generation added to what it had received, and passed along the increased fortune. So it is with civilization.

Each century receives the benefit of much that the earlier

centuries have done, it adds something of its own, and gives the enlarged treasure to the next century. However, there are times when nations lose or waste the gifts of preceding ages just as a person might waste the fortune handed down to him. You have heard of such a case in the story of the Prodigal Son. Although some nations have been wasteful of their inheritance, people in general have made use of the intelligence God has given them. Consequently, we of today owe a great debt to those who have gone before us.

PURPOSE OF THIS STUDY. We hope to learn something about the contributors to our country's greatness. We shall find that our study will lead us over all Europe and through many centuries. Is it not remarkable that the motto of the United States should be in Latin? Latin is no longer the language of any country. It was, however, the language of a great and powerful nation two thousand years ago. After all these years we go back to that country for words to tell the world about ourselves. Our country is great not only because she has received much from the past but particularly because she has used well what the past has given her. In this book we shall learn something about what the Old World has done for America.

## THE BEGINNINGS OF HISTORY

THE DAWN OF CIVILIZATION. God created the world. God created man and made man master of the earth. He told man to "rule it." And so man began to use his beautiful world that God had given him. In time there were many people living on the earth. Some were skilled in making iron and brass implements. We learn this from the Bible. (Genesis IV, 21, 22)

*Courtesy American Museum of Natural History*

## Before the Dawn of Civilization

Thousands of years ago great beasts roamed the earth. Nothing is left of them now but their bones. From these skeletons scientists are able to show us what they may have looked like.

Unfortunately man neglected God. The Bible tells us that "it repented God that He had made man." God then sent a great flood which destroyed all living things except those which Noah, by command of God, took into a great boat or ark.

## PRIMITIVE MAN

PRE-HISTORIC PEOPLE. There are no written records about some of the earliest people. But we know some things concerning them from what they left behind them. Thus we know that some people who lived long ago (sometimes they are called primitive people) dwelt in caves. As time went on men made other dwellings. Sometimes these were huts of wood or clay, sometimes they were made of stone. Men knew how to

*Courtesy American Museum of Natural History*

## One Way of Learning About the Past

Primitive man was a great hunter. He thought of game constantly. He even drew pictures of the animals he hunted and killed. Today we see his drawings on the walls of caves and from them learn how primitive peoples lived.

make fire and to use it in cooking their food, heating their homes, and frightening wild animals. We know that these people hunted and fished. Many of the stone implements that they used have been found in their caves and near them.

FIRST STEPS IN AGRICULTURE. People found that there were plants and trees that would supply them with food. Men learned to carry on simple farming. Thus foods became more varied. Men learned also that they could have help from the animal kingdom. By taming some animals they could have beasts of burden. Other animals provided them with food and clothing.

FARM IMPLEMENTS AND CARTS. The first farm implements were very simple. Little by little they were improved.

Putting wheels on a cart was a wonderful advance. Improvements were made in dwellings and in clothing. Women learned to weave cloth. Civilization, therefore, made great progress in many ways. We can learn about this progress from the written records that some peoples have left behind them.

CIVILIZATION AND NATURAL RESOURCES. Some peoples developed into great nations faster than other groups. That was partly because they were aided by natural advantages such as good rivers, fertile lands and healthful climate which help make people prosperous. Among the peoples of ancient times to whom we today owe a great debt were those who dwelt along three great rivers. These were the Nile in Egypt, and the Tigris and Euphrates in western Asia.

---

## OBJECTIVE TESTS

---

Test 1: Choice.

Copy the numbers 1 to 5 on a piece of paper. Write the best word or phrase in each of the following statements.

1. The motto of the United States is ("freedom forever," "one from many")
2. The English settlers brought to America (their idea of self-government, their system of farming)
3. The sign of the cross reminds us (that God created the world, that Jesus Christ lived and died for us)
4. The United States was settled (by many nations, by the Spanish and the English)
5. We know how the earliest people lived (from written records, from the tools they left behind them)

Test 2: Sequence of Events.

Arrange each event in the order of time.

Jesus Christ is born      Columbus discovers America
God creates the world      The radio is invented
Jesus Christ rises from the dead      The English come to America

Test 3: Historical Vocabulary.

Write the phrase which gives the best definition.

1. What does Deluge mean?
    a) a great famine          c) a great flood
    b) the coming of primitive  d) the Creation of the world
       men

2. What does "E Pluribus Unum" mean?
    a) "United we stand, di-   c) "God save our country"
       vided we fall"          d) "One from many"
    b) "Liberty and Equality"

3. What is history?
    a) a tale of fiction        c) a collection of facts
    b) the story of man and    d) a group of stories
       what he has done

---

## STRANGE FACTS

---

How many of the following facts can you explain?

1. The American Indian is the only true native American.
2. All white American citizens are immigrants or descendants of immigrants.
3. Americans acknowledge the birth of Christ whenever they write the date.
4. Caves teach us a great deal of history.

---

## QUESTIONS THAT MAKE YOU THINK

---

1. What is the difference between the meaning of B.C. and the meaning of A.D.?
2. Give one good reason for studying history.
3. What is the difference between history and a fairy tale?
4. Explain one way in which the Latin language shows itself in our country today.
5. Which of these words mean the same thing:
    agriculture, manufacturing, farming, hunting? Explain your answer.

6. "Today we owe a great debt to the people who have gone before us." Explain two of these debts.
7. Why do we have so many Italian, German, Irish, English, Polish, and French names in the United States?
8. "America owes a great deal to the Old World." Explain.

## ACTIVITIES

1. Look at the writing on a penny, five cent piece, dime, quarter, and a half dollar. Make a list of the mottoes you found.
2. From clay make a model of a primitive cave man.
3. From wood make a model of an ancient cart.
4. Make a list of 10 last names of your classmates. Next to each write the name of the country in the Old World from which the name came. Ask if you do not know.
5. Make a drawing of the Deluge and Noah's Ark.
6. Paste in your scrapbook pictures and clippings about primitive man.

## QUESTIONS THAT TEST YOUR CHARACTER

1. Why should Americans be kindly toward foreigners?
2. Why should we be interested in our ancestors?
3. "The story of the Deluge should teach all men a lesson." Explain.
4. "Our Country has used well what the past has given her." Make a list of five ways in which you can use well what your parents have given you.

## IMPORTANT WORDS

"one from many"
A.D.
B.C.
Bible
creation of the world

civilization
primitive man
Deluge
natural resources
Genesis

# I

## Part 2: OUR DEBT TO THE ANCIENT EAST

Three rivers helped in the development of civilization. These rivers were the Nile in Egypt and the Tigris and Euphrates in Western Asia. The important civilizations which grew up about these rivers are called the "river civilizations." The people of the river civilizations learned many things of value which the people of Europe learned in turn from them.

---

## THE EGYPTIANS

---

EGYPT, THE GIFT OF THE NILE. The Egyptians were the folk who lived in the valley of the Nile. This river is in Northern Africa. The Nile River deserves much of the credit for their success; indeed Egypt was called the "Gift of the Nile." The Nile provided a good highway, making travel easy. Of much greater importance was the way it helped the farmer. Once a year there are heavy rains in the mountains where the river has its source. This water floods down and on reaching the lower Nile valley overflows the river's banks. At that time much of the country is under water. During the dry season, the river returns to its channel but it leaves behind a deposit of the richest soil. The country on either side of the river is evenly coated with a fertile loam.

The farmer scattered seeds in this soft rich soil. Sheep were driven across the land which had been sown to trample the seed into the earth. It was easy for the farmer to obtain a bountiful harvest of beans, oats, barley, and wheat.

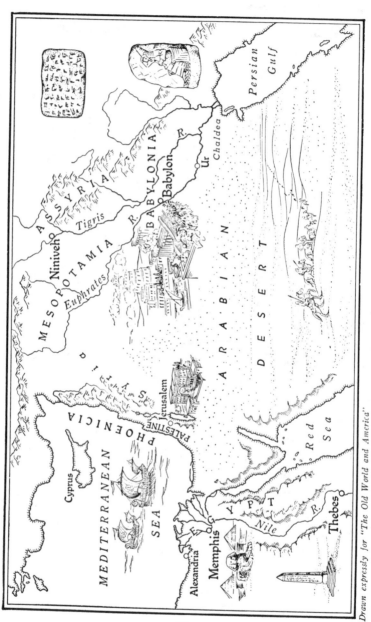

Map of The Early Civilizations

Drawn expressly for "The Old World and America"

12

## Egypt, "The Gift of the Nile"

The Nile overflows its banks today as it did for countless ages before the pyramids were built. Locate the Nile on the map on page 12.

EGYPTIAN ACCOMPLISHMENTS. The Egyptians were skillful builders. They constructed huge pyramids of stone as tombs for their kings. They also built large and beautiful temples, for they were religious people. They believed so firmly in life after death that the bodies of the dead were preserved as mummies.

Some of the useful things learned by the Egyptians were used centuries later by the people of Europe. The Egyptians were expert farmers. They understood the importance of the rotation of crops. They were skilled in methods of irrigation. The Egyptians understood surveying. Surveying was a matter of necessity for when the Nile overflowed boundary lines were often destroyed. The wise men of the Egyptians, by studying the stars, were able to make a calendar with a year of 365 days. This knowledge also helped them to calculate the time when the Nile would overflow.

EGYPTIAN PICTURE WRITING. Perhaps one of their most important accomplishments was their system of writing. The Egyptian way of writing had an influence on the alphabet we use. The earliest form of Egyptian writing is called hieroglyphics or picture writing; each picture stands for a word.

The Egyptians put some of their records on tall stone shafts called obelisks. Other records were written upon papyrus. This is a paper-like substance made from a plant that grew near the Nile. Scholars have learned to read these writings, finding out about Egyptian history, their religions, ideas, their belief in life after death, and other opinions which they held.

THE PHARAOHS. The Pyramids were constructed by the Egyptians as tombs for their Kings, or "Pharaohs." That is the name the Bible gives to the Egyptian Kings. The largest Pyramid was built by Pharaoh Khufu. Some centuries after Khufu another Pharaoh refused to give Moses and Aaron permission to lead the Jews out of Egypt.

---

## THE BABYLONIANS AND ASSYRIANS

---

THE RIVER CIVILIZATIONS OF WESTERN ASIA. As long ago as twenty centuries before the birth of Christ, great nations were to be found in the country about the Tigris and the Euphrates Rivers, in western Asia. Locate these rivers on map, page 12. The Babylonians were a famous people who lived in that section of the world. They remind us of the Egyptians. Like the Egyptians they were able to keep an account of events for they had a system of writing. It was not picture writing, however; instead of using pictures the Babylonians used wedge-shaped characters to represent their words.

## The Rosetta Stone

This famous stone was found by a French officer near the mouth of the River Nile. On the stone is written the same message in three ancient languages. One of them is Greek, another Egyptian hieroglyphics. Scholars were able to read the Greek message and from that were able to find out what the hieroglyphics meant. After that they could read the ancient Egyptian writing and learn about that ancient country.

© *Ewing Galloway*

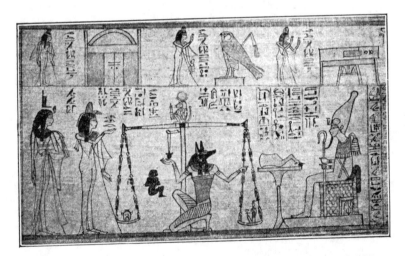

## Papyrus

This is the story of an Egyptian Princess which was written on the Egyptian paper called papyrus which was made from the plant of the same name.

*Drawn expressly for "The Old World and America"*

## Writing on Bricks

This was a clumsy way of writing but it had the advantage of being permanent so that today we can dig up these old tablets and learn what happened thousands of years ago.

Bricks were used instead of paper. The writing was done while the brick was still soft. When the writer had finished, he put the brick into the oven where it was baked hard.

THE BABYLONIANS AS BUILDERS. The Babylonians like the Egyptians were great builders. Their land was not well supplied with building stone so they had to make use of brick. Bricks were made of clay and then dried in the sun or in kilns. Perhaps the use of brick in building led the Babylonians to invent a way of roofing their buildings by means of arches or vaults. The Romans who came later, and who were great builders, probably learned the art of building arches and vaults from the descendants of the old Babylonians. The Babylonians learned how to use pulleys in lifting great weights. This helped them in their building operations.

THE GREAT KINGS OF BABYLON. The people of Babylon did not think of themselves as belonging to one large nation. They felt they belonged just to the city where they dwelt. If they lived in the country their ruler was a sort of king who reigned in the nearby city. However, several important kings ruled all Babylon. Sargon (2752 B.C.), a famous warrior, invaded and conquered this region making himself a supreme ruler.

Some centuries later Hammurabi (2081 B.C.), the great lawgiver, ruled. His Code of Laws is one of the most remarkable sets of laws for human conduct ever drawn up. To people of today many of Hammurabi's laws seem very harsh, but for his time they were a great improvement. Most important was the fact that these laws were written laws. When laws are written everyone can know the law and the law applies to all the people. As a rule people who have written laws are more civilized people than those whose laws are not written.

THE BABYLONIAN WEEK. The Babylonians reckoned the passing of time by making a seven day week. The Hebrews also had a seven day week. It seems most likely that the people of western Europe learned to use the seven day week from the Babylonians. They divided the hour into sixty minutes and we probably received our division of time from them.

THE ASSYRIANS AS THE LEADERS. The Babylonians had jealous neighbors on either side. The Assyrians in the north at one time overcame the Babylonians. Babylonia, however, regained her position when the great fortress city of Nineveh fell. The New Babylonian Empire, sometimes called the Chaldean Empire, then came into existence. The most famous figure in the history of the New Babylonian Empire was King Nabuchodonosor. His story is told in the Holy Bible.

*Drawn expressly for "The Old World and America"*

## The Hanging Gardens

They are called one of the seven wonders of the ancient world. With few tools and poor appliances these ancient people did marvelous work just by man power.

KING NABUCHODONOSOR. (604 B.C.) When Nabuchodonosor was king, Babylonia (Chaldean Empire) again became a mighty nation. Nabuchodonosor was a great soldier. He led an army against the Hebrews in Palestine and conquered them. Later Jerusalem, the great city of the Hebrews, was destroyed and its sacred temple ruined. Thousands of the Hebrews were taken captive to Babylon. The Bible tells of the cruelties of their exile. It was during this time called the "Babylonian captivity" that Daniel, the prophet, was cast into the lions' den, and Jeremias sang his beautiful lamentations. King Nabuchodonosor was known for his interest in building. To please his queen, he constructed the famous hanging gardens.

THE PERSIAN EMPIRE. After Nabuchodonosor's day, Babylonia became less powerful. Persia, the country to the

*Drawn expressly for "The Old World and America"*

## Phœnician Traders

The artist shows a Phoenician shipping clerk using the alphabet to make a list of goods to be traded. Do you think that this was one of the ways the alphabet was spread wherever the Phoenicians traded?

south, was an unfriendly neighbor. Babylonia was conquered by the Persians and so her proud rule came to an end.

---

## PHŒNICIANS AND HEBREWS

---

THE PHŒNICIANS. The Phœnicians lived in Western Asia. Their country was a narrow strip of land facing the Mediterranean Sea on the west and backed up on the east by tall mountains. These high mountains protected the Phœnicians, to some extent, from the more powerful people east of them. But the mountains to the east did not stop the Phœnician merchants on their trading trips. They were able to cross the mountains through the passes. On these trading trips they learned many things; for example they may have learned of an alphabet, a very imperfect one, used by the people in the East.

THE PHŒNICIAN TRADERS. It was almost natural for the Phœnicians to become great sea traders. They lived on the seashore and they were a progressive people, eager to learn. On their trading expeditions on land and sea they came in contact with various nations. They were quick to take advantage of any good idea they found among the nations with whom they traded. The Phœnicians were teachers as well as traders; they carried ideas as well as merchandise to the colonies they founded (see map, facing page 43).

THE ALPHABET. It is said that we got our alphabet from the Phœnicians. Their traders, we have learned, knew about an alphabet used in Syria. They also knew about the Egyptian system of picture writing but this system did not at all satisfy them. Although the Egyptians had made many improvements in their system of writing, the Phœnicians thought it too clumsy. The Phœnicians began by using a picture for each syllable. Finally a picture or character was used to represent a single sound just as our letters of the alphabet represent sounds. The Phœnicians gave their alphabet to the Greeks who in turn passed it on, with many improvements, to the Romans. It was from the Romans that our ancestors in western Europe learned to use the alphabet.

THE HEBREWS. The Hebrews, or Jews, were unlike the other peoples of Asia. They were not conquerors as were the Babylonians or the Persians nor were they great builders. They did not have magnificent cities made splendid by great public buildings. The Hebrews had a more important work. It was their mission to preserve the knowledge of the true God and His teachings.

THE BIBLE. The Bible, which is the "word of God," was written almost entirely by Hebrews. The saintly heroes about whom we read in the Bible, men like Joseph, Moses, Samuel,

*Drawn expressly for "The Old World and America"*

## Solomon's Temple

The Jews were a religious people. They put their best effort into building a beautiful temple to God. This picture gives an idea of how it may have looked before it was destroyed.

Daniel, and many others, were men of the Jewish nation. But the chief glory of the race is this: from it came the Messiah, Jesus Christ, the Son of God.

---

Egypt and the countries of Western Asia seem a long distance from America. They are far away not only in time and place but also in ideas. We must remember, however, that these were the first civilized countries. They had learned to do many useful things: Systems of laws, the art of writing, methods of reckoning time, surveying, building arches and domes and columns, sailing ships, all these and more the people of the river civilizations knew. What they had learned, another people in the *West*, the Greeks, were to learn from them. When, therefore, we study about the ancient Greeks we shall be learning about people who lived somewhat as we do and who have had a great influence on our life today. *Civilization moves West.*

---

## OBJECTIVE TESTS

---

TEST 1: Completion.

The great peoples of the ancient East were the Egyptians, Babylonians, Assyrians, Persians, Phœnicians, and Hebrews. In each of the following, write in the name of the people which matches the items mentioned.

| Contribution | People |
|---|---|
| 1. Huge pyramids | . . . . . . . . . . . . . . . . . . |
| 2. Obelisks | . . . . . . . . . . . . . . . . . . |
| 3. Brick buildings | . . . . . . . . . . . . . . . . . . |
| 4. 60 minutes in an hour | . . . . . . . . . . . . . . . . . . |
| 5. Hanging gardens | . . . . . . . . . . . . . . . . . . |
| 6. Knowledge of the true God | . . . . . . . . . . . . . . . . . . |
| 7. Spread the alphabet | . . . . . . . . . . . . . . . . . . |
| 8. Papyrus scrolls | . . . . . . . . . . . . . . . . . . |
| 9. Hieroglyphics | . . . . . . . . . . . . . . . . . . |
| 10. Wedge-shaped writing | . . . . . . . . . . . . . . . . . . |

TEST 2: Historical Vocabulary.

Select the correct phrase.

1. What is an obelisk?
   a) a metal disc
   b) tall figure of wood
   c) tall stone shaft
   d) a wedge-shaped character
2. What is a pyramid?
   a) Huge tomb of stone
   b) A triangle
   c) A compass for travelers
   d) A heap of stones
3. What is papyrus?
   a) An Egyptian drink
   b) A Babylonian flower
   c) A kind of ink
   d) A paper-like substance
4. What is a mummy?
   a) Egyptian monument
   b) An Eastern temple
   c) A preserved corpse
   d) An ancient ghost
5. What are hieroglyphics?
   a) A kind of picture writing
   b) Ancient laws
   c) Egyptian drugs
   d) The Phœnician alphabet

TEST 3 : Matching.

Copy Column A on your paper. Next to each name, write the number from Column B which matches.

|  | Column A | Column B |
|---|---|---|
| (  ) | Sargon | Jewish prophet |
| (  ) | Hammurabi | first strong king of Babylonia |
| (  ) | Nabuchodonosor | destroyed Jerusalem |
| (  ) | Daniel | code of laws |

## QUESTIONS THAT MAKE YOU THINK

1. Explain why the overflowing of a river is not always a disadvantage to a land.
2. Why was Egypt called the "Gift of the Nile"?
3. Just how do we know that the Egyptians believed in life after death?
4. "The Egyptians were expert farmers." Explain why we say this is true.
5. Point out two ways in which the Babylonians are like the Egyptians?
6. Why did the Babylonians use brick in building, when the Egyptians used stone?
7. Why did the Hebrews dislike the Babylonians?
8. Name the greatest contribution of the Hebrews. Explain your answer.
9. Name two Babylonians whom you consider great men. Give a reason for considering each great.
10. What are the advantages of the Phœnician system of writing over that of the Egyptians and Babylonians?

## STRANGE FACTS

How many of these can you explain?

1. The ancient Egyptians knew many secrets of chemistry which still puzzle scientists of today.
2. The Egyptians by their study of the stars could foretell the time the Nile would overflow.
3. Nabuchodonosor built the first pent-house.
4. The Hebrews paved the way for the coming of Christianity.

## QUESTIONS THAT TEST YOUR CHARACTER

1. Do you think it is good to have a written code of laws? Why?
2. "The Egyptians took advantage of the gifts of Nature." In what ways may we Americans profit by this lesson?
3. "The Egyptians were industrious people." Give an argument for, or against this statement.
4. "The Hebrews were not great conquerors, yet they were great people." Just why do we say this statement is true?

## ACTIVITIES

1. Make a chart, comparing the contributions of each people of the ancient East.
2. From soap make an obelisk.
3. From soap or clay make a pyramid.
4. From clay construct the "Hanging Gardens of Babylon."
5. Ask a Hebrew friend to tell you the achievements of his race of which he is most proud. Tell the class what he said.
6. Make a chart comparing (a) hieroglyphics, (b) Chinese characters, (c) modern alphabet.
7. Paste pictures in your scrapbook regarding the people of the ancient East.
8. Find on your map all the countries mentioned in the lesson.

## IMPORTANT WORDS

| | | |
|---|---|---|
| pyramid | "Gift of the Nile" | "hanging gardens" |
| obelisk | "Babylonian captivity" | life after death |
| hieroglyphics | fertile loam | alphabet |
| papyrus | rotation of crops | "word of God" |
| | Pharaoh | |

## II
### OUR DEBT TO THE GREEKS

### AIM

To learn how Greek civilization helped to prepare the world for the preaching of the Gospel.

To learn how the accomplishments of the ancient Greeks are of value to the modern world.

WALK DOWN any street in your city and study the ornamentation used on the buildings. In a number of instances you will be looking at ornaments that the Greeks originated. Many letters of our alphabet are the same as those found in the Greek alphabet. A number of the words which we use are of Greek origin. In grammar school or in high school, you study geography, geology, physics, geometry. These words are taken directly from the ancient Greek. But more important still is the fact that from the Greeks we have learned some ideas about freedom, the value of education, and the nobility of thinking. We are to learn something about the Greeks, therefore, because they have taught us many things that are helpful to us in our daily lives.

# II

## *Part 1:* THE GREEKS AND DEMOCRACY

No doubt you were surprised to learn that it is necessary to go back so many centuries to understand properly the history of the United States. Nevertheless, this is a fact. In the following pages, therefore, we shall study about the ancient Greeks who are near to us in everything except time. By studying about the ancient Greeks we shall be able to appreciate better our own history.

THE GEOGRAPHY OF GREECE. Before taking our first glimpse into the lives of the ancient Greeks, it will be necessary first to study the geography of Greece. Greece is located between Europe and Asia; it has a mountainous surface; and it has a coast of many bays and harbors. All this is important because it had an effect upon the history of the people who lived in Greece.

GREECE AT THE CROSSROADS. If you look at a map of the eastern part of the Mediterranean you will see that Greece is a peninsula. It is located on that great highway, the Mediterranean Sea. Greece is in an especially interesting spot at the crossroads between Europe and Asia. Now that is important because in ancient times, as you have learned, there was considerable civilization in Egypt and in that part of Asia which is quite near Greece. The Greeks, then, were in a position in Europe to receive the benefits of these ancient civilizations. Also, and this is useful to remember: the people living in

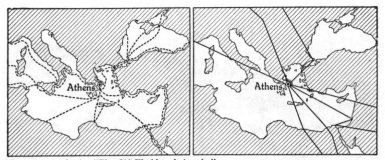

*Drawn expressly for "The Old World and America"*

## The Crossroads

Ancient Greece was at the center of the shipping routes of those days. Modern airplane routes show that Greece is still at the crossroads.

Greece were protected by the sea and the tall mountains which surrounded them from the less civilized people, those who lived in the west.

There are certain peculiar features about the land of Greece. The country of Greece is divided into small sections because of its many mountains and valleys. You can easily see that in such a country the people might come to live in small groups each cut off from the other. This would be especially true if these people were lovers of independence. The Greeks were unusually self-reliant. In time, there developed in Greece many little states which are called city-states. Indeed, when we study Greek history we shall not be studying the story of a single united nation. We shall be studying the history of a number of tiny countries, the Greek city-states.

THE LAND OF GREECE. In size ancient Greece was quite small. Many states in our country are as large as the whole of Greece, and some states, like Texas or California, many times larger. The Greek peninsula is surrounded almost entirely by water, and due to its irregular shape no part of Greece is far from the sea. The eastern coast has the best harbors; for that

*Drawn expressly for "The Old World and America"*

## Early Inhabitants

This young lady looks very modern. She really lived in ancient Crete perhaps four thousand years ago.

reason, the eastern part of Greece was more highly developed. The Greeks became sailors. This was due partly to the fact that they lived so close to the sea and partly because the soil was so poor that farming was unprofitable. But the spirit of adventure also attracted them to the sea. They loved the blue waters of the Ægean and the Mediterranean. The Greeks through their voyages were able to learn many of the good ideas that other nations possessed.

EARLY INHABITANTS. We are not going to learn much about the very first inhabitants of Greece. More than two thousand years before the coming of Our Lord, a race of people dwelt along the shores and on the islands of the Ægean Sea and in the land of Greece itself. We do not know so very much about them. We do know, though, that they had wonderful cities. The palaces of their kings were indeed magnificent, and they built about their cities strong walls to keep out their enemies.

On the island of Crete, 200 miles from Greece, had been built the city of Cnossus, one of the most wonderful cities of ancient times. There were also other splendid cities in Crete. The inhabitants of the cities of Crete made vases of gold and silver and porphyry, a hard red stone. Their craftsmen excelled as sword makers and armorers. Many of the fine things the people of Western Asia and the Egyptians knew how to do, the Cretans learned from them. Cretan civilization was therefore a combination of gifts from the river civilizations. This combination of gifts the Cretans were to hand on to yet another people, the Greeks, who followed them in this region. The story of the Greeks and all they accomplished is of the utmost importance in the history of the world.

THE GREEKS. The Greeks about whom we are to study did not come from Greece; they probably came from some place in central Europe. They were a pastoral people, that is, they lived by raising sheep and cattle. They were warlike, too. It is thought that they wandered south looking for new pastures for their flocks. At length, they came to Greece. Of course, they could not go any farther, except in ships, so they drove out the people they found on the peninsula, and took the country for themselves. Some of these wandering Greeks crossed the sea to the nearby islands and to the shores of Asia Minor. Soon the entire Ægean region was under their control. This was the beginning of Greek history.

THE BEGINNINGS OF GREEK HISTORY. These Greeks in their wanderings naturally traveled in groups. Each group was made up of so many families which were related one to the other. A single group of many families all related is called a tribe. After their arrival in Greece, each family group, or tribe, selected a place to dwell. Each tribe became independent and lived its own way. This fact led to the development of the city-states.

THE GREEK CITY-STATES. It is important constantly to remember that the history of the Greeks is the history of the city-states. Refer to the map. Locate Athens; now Thebes; point to Corinth; find Sparta south of Corinth. Each of these cities had its own independent life. Corinth was just as independent of Athens as we are of England. Indeed wars between the Greek city-states were frequent and there was always rivalry among the city-states. Each city-state had its own kind of government. Some city-states were more progressive than others. Some excelled in laws and art and learning; others were backward.

---

## THE GREEKS AND GOVERNMENT

---

THE LEADER. We can think that government among the Greeks developed somewhat in this way. In the group or tribe, there had to be a leader of some sort to act as chief. He was usually one of the older men of the village, who because of his years and experience was best able to give good advice. If war was the question before the tribe the office of leader was most important. You will notice that in the beginning the leader was chosen by the will of the men of the tribe. The men of the tribe or citizens believed that they were all equal. They were all descended from the same ancestor or hero whom they regarded as a god. They usually worshiped this ancestor and looked to him for protection. The chief was therefore only a leader among his equals.

THE KING. In time the leader of the tribe became more powerful. At first he was leader only. There are men, however, who are not content unless they can rule. Suppose such an

**Ancient Greece**   As you study your history lessons try to find out
what the little pictures represent.

ambitious man, who was also the best warrior in the tribe, were to become the leader. Soon he would probably become not only *leader* but *ruler* as well. The form of government under him would be called a monarchy; that means the rule of one. This sort of ruler could be called a king.

THE NOBLES. But while the office of king was being brought about, a new part of government was forming. The old tribe leader, you remember, was merely a leader among equals. Little by little, certain men of the tribe began to grow more wealthy than their neighbors. Instead of all men of the village being equally rich or poor, a few began to control the best land or the largest number of sheep or cattle. Naturally, such men being the most powerful in the village, would be closest to the king. They would have a great deal to say about how the village should be run. Out of this situation there developed the council. The king and the council, however, were not always free to act as they liked. In some city-states they had to consult the citizens, especially about such important matters as going to war or making a treaty. The citizens were summoned to the market place where the question was put before them. But although the citizens were important in most of the city-states in Greece, nevertheless as time went on the nobles became more powerful.

THE RULE OF THE NOBLES IN GREECE. Suppose that the influential men, or nobles, were to decide that they and not the king would rule the village. If the nobles succeeded in doing away with the king and getting control of the government for themselves, there would be a new form of government called an aristocracy. The government would be no longer in charge of just one; a group would control. This would be a government of a few for the few. The power which the nobles enjoyed sometimes passed on to their sons. In many places

**Monarchy**   One King governing many men.

**Aristocracy**   A few Nobles governing many men.

*Drawn expressly for "The Old World and America"*

**Democracy**   All men governing themselves.

in Greece the kings were overthrown. In their stead a group of nobles ruled the people. Of course, government by several men is some improvement over rule by one man alone. This form of government is by no means the best possible.

DEMOCRACY. The ideal form of government is that kind in which the people rule themselves. The government by the people is called democracy. The word democracy comes from two Greek words meaning the rule of the people. The Greek city of Athens had gone through the different stages of government; first monarchy, then aristocracy, and finally, democ-

*Drawn expressly for "The Old World and America"*

## The Law Giver

### The Greeks receive their first written laws from Draco.

racy, government by the people themselves. But Greek democracy while a great improvement over the government in other lands during ancient times was far from perfect. The Greeks did not understand the value of human life or the dignity of man. The world did not learn of these great truths until Our Lord taught them from the Cross.

LEADERS FOR DEMOCRACY. In the story of democracy, the names of Draco, Solon, and Pericles are important ones to remember.

Draco served the Athenians by giving them a written body of laws (621 B.C.). Before Draco's time the people followed custom. Custom is not as satisfactory as written law because customs sometimes can be changed easily. A set of written laws was much needed, but since Draco's laws were so severe, they left much to be desired. (You have already learned that Hammurabi's code of laws was published in Babylonia before 2025 B.C. The Egyptians probably had a code even before this.)

Solon greatly improved the lot of the ordinary Greek by his reforms. He gave even the poorest citizens a voice in the government.

Pericles was another outstanding figure in the history of Athens. He was a sort of political leader of the people. During the "Age of Pericles," 461-429 B.C., Athens was enjoying its *Golden Age*. In the time of Pericles some of the most beautiful of the Greek temples were built; the merchants enjoyed perhaps their greatest prosperity and the citizens enjoyed the greatest measure of freedom.

## OBJECTIVE TESTS

TEST 1: Historical Vocabulary.

Pick out the best definition in each of the following:

1. What is a democracy?
   a) Rule by the Democratic Party
   b) A country with a President
   c) The people rule themselves
   d) Rule by politicians
2. What is an aristocracy?
   a) Rule by a group of nobles
   b) Rule by a dictator
   c) The rich people rule
   d) The soldiers rule
3. What is a monarchy?
   a) Rule by the strong
   b) The nobles rule
   c) The king rules
   d) The president rules

4. What is a city-state?
   a) A town in a county
   b) A city which is independent
   c) A city which is the capital
   d) A city with a king
5. What is a tyrant?
   a) A weak king
   b) A ruler who rules by force
   c) A powerful noble
   d) The mayor of a city-state

TEST 2: Choice Test.

Write the correct phrase in each of the following:

1. From the Greeks we have learned ideas (about agriculture, about freedom)
2. Greece is located (between Europe and Africa, between Europe and Asia)

3. The Greeks are unusually (self-reliant, miserly)
4. The country of Grece was divided (into city-states, into nations)
5. The city of Cnossus is located (on the island of Crete, on the mainland)
6. The early Greeks lived (by trade, by hunting and fishing)
7. The Greeks have given us (a love for beauty, seven days in a week)
8. The best harbors of Greece are (on the eastern coast, on the western coast)
9. The Greeks have given us (the art of embalming, love of education)
10. Cretan civilization inherited (European civilization, Babylonian and Egyptian civilization)

---

## QUESTIONS THAT MAKE YOU THINK

1. Point out one thing in common among the following men: Draco, Solon, Pericles
2. Why are Draco and Hammurabi said to be alike?
3. Explain just how geography influenced Greek history.
4. Why did so many of the Greeks become sailors instead of farmers?
5. Which of the forms of government tried by the Greeks do you consider best? Give reasons for your answer.
6. Give a good definition of the "golden age" of Athens.
7. Name two ways in which your neighborhood shows the influence of the Greeks.
8. Give one disadvantage of Draco's laws.
9. Why was a written body of laws a gain for democracy?
10. Explain one weakness of Greek democracy.

---

## STRANGE FACTS

How many of the following can you explain?
1. The earliest Greeks did not come from Greece.
2. The ancient Greeks had every form of government which the world has today.
3. The laws of Draco were said to have been "written in blood."
4. The Greeks did not understand the value of human life.

5. The ancient Greeks never formed a Greek nation.
6. The Greek tribes worshiped their ancestors.

---

## ACTIVITIES

---

1. Make a chart, showing the influence of geography upon Greek history. In your chart include (a) valleys, (b) mountains, (c) harbors, (d) barren soil, (e) nearness to sea, (f) nearness to Asia.
2. Draw an outline map of Texas. Inside Texas, draw a map of Greece, showing the size of each.
3. Suppose you lived in ancient Athens. Write a short report of the kind of government Athens had.
4. Make a drawing of a tombstone for each: Pericles, Draco, and Solon Write on each stone the man's achievements.
5. Suppose you were one of the scientists who dug into the island of Crete. Write a report for a newspaper, telling what you found at the City of Cnossus.
6. From wood make a model of an ancient Greek ship.
7. Dress a small doll as an ancient Greek soldier.
8. Paste in your scrapbook pictures and clippings about early Greece.

---

## QUESTIONS THAT TEST YOUR CHARACTER

---

1. "The Greeks were self-reliant." In what ways should you be self-reliant?
2. "The Greeks did not appreciate the value of human life." In what ways are people of today guilty of this same defect?
3. "The Greeks showed that the idea of freedom could be abused." Explain how you have abused freedom in your life.
4. "The Greeks loved beauty." Explain this statement fully.

---

## IMPORTANT WORDS

---

| | | |
|---|---|---|
| city-state | crossroads | "golden age" of Athens |
| geography | pastoral life | peninsula |
| monarchy | aristocracy | river civilizations |
| code of laws | democracy | lovers of independence |
| self-reliance | tyranny | |

# II

## *Part 2:* THE GREEKS AND COURAGE

The Greeks had that kind of courage that enabled them to face danger bravely. This sort of courage is often called physical courage. It helped the Greeks to defeat a powerful enemy, the Persians. Greek civilization otherwise would have been destroyed. Courage also was characteristic of those Greeks who left their homeland to settle in different places about the Mediterranean Sea. Thus Greek ideas were spread. Courage also was the mark of the Greek soldiers who followed Alexander the Great when he conquered countries far distant from Greece. The Greek warriors taught people in those far-away lands Greek ideas and Greek ways of doing things.

THE DANGEROUS EAST. While the Athenians were learning to check the power of the nobles, building beautiful temples and writing splendid books, a grave danger was threatening. This danger was the desire of the great country of Persia to crush Athens. Persia was a powerful country in Asia. The country was ruled by a king who possessed untold riches. The king of Persia had thousands of servants to do his bidding, and he had a huge army to fight his battles.

PERSIA'S ENMITY TOWARD THE GREEKS. Some of the Greeks, seafarers, no doubt, had settled the Ionian islands along the coast of Asia Minor. They had built up splendid colonies, becoming wealthy through successful trading. However, these Greeks were not free. They had come under the power of the king of the Persians, whom they cordially hated. In an attempt to win their freedom, the Ionian Greeks revolted. Athens had been friendly with these Greeks and had done a great deal of trading with them. Though Athens helped the revolt failed. After the uprising had been put down the Persian king, Darius, determined to make the Athenians suffer for the aid they had given the Ionians.

The first attempt to destroy the liberty of the Greeks was not very successful. Darius had sent an army into the upper Greek peninsula and a fleet of Phœnician ships across the sea. He expected an easy victory, but a storm destroyed the ships upon which his army depended. The expedition had cost a great store of treasure and Athens remained untouched. The failure of the Persians only served to kindle the wrath of Darius.

THE SECOND ATTEMPT. Darius then fitted out a new expedition which sailed directly across the Ægean, landing near the plains of Marathon. Marathon was only twenty-six miles from Athens. The Persians were magnificently equipped. Besides they were very angry because of their first failure and were determined to crush the Greeks. Opposed to the vast Persian army was a little band of Athenians, in number nine thousand. With them were a thousand men from the city of Platæa. Sparta had promised aid but the promise was not kept. The odds were terribly against the Greeks.

MARATHON, 490 B.C. The Persians drew up their battle line along the seashore. The Greeks waited in the hills and when the signal was given, to a man they rushed upon the Persians. They cut through them and forced those nearest the sea into it to be drowned. After the victory of Marathon the Greeks sent a runner to Athens with the news. He ran the entire distance, reaching Athens just able to cry "Nike" (Nee-kay), victory; then he expired. The Marathon race of the present

*Drawn expressly for "The Old World and America"*

**Marathon**

> This was a victory of the Greek spear over the Persian bow and arrow, made possible by better Greek generalship.

day is a reminder of this great victory. So great was the glory of the victors that they were long remembered as the protectors of Greek freedom.

THE LAST PERSIAN ATTACK. Despite the setbacks the Persians suffered, they were not willing to give up the idea of conquering Greece. Darius, the king, had died, meanwhile, and was succeeded by his son, Xerxes. Xerxes was anxious to avenge the defeats suffered by his father. To be certain of the victory, he prepared for the new war long and carefully. He gathered together an immense army that was many times as large as the biggest army the Greek city-states could raise. Xerxes also built a great fleet of warships and when everything was in readiness, he renewed the war.

WAR ON LAND. The new war began in 481 B.C. The first battleground was in northern Greece. The Persians marched through the country without trouble until they came to the narrow pass between mountain and sea which is called Thermopylæ. As long as this pass could be held against the Persians, the southern part of Greece would be safe. But let the Persians once get through this pass and victory would be almost certain and easy. Once through the pass at Thermopylæ the Persians could go down to Athens, destroy it, and then attend to their other Grecian enemies. The pass was held by a brave band of Spartans under the leadership of Leonidas. The Spartans were famous for their courage. A Spartan mother, it was said, advised her son going off to war to return with his shield or on it. Indeed the Spartan soldiers were called "the walls of Sparta." But what could a little band of Spartans do against the mighty force of the Persians? The Persian hordes surged against the Greeks but to no purpose. Leonidas and his men beat them off with terrible losses. Southern Greece was still safe.

SPARTAN COURAGE. A traitor ruined everything. This wretch showed the Persians a winding path that would take them behind Leonidas. Suddenly Leonidas found himself attacked front and rear. The brave Spartans determined that the Persians should pay dearly for the victory and so Leonidas and his little band fought until the last man was killed. The Persians were now free to march south into Athens which they did, destroying the country as they marched. Those Athenians who could, fled to the nearby islands; the others perished.

THE ATHENIAN NAVY. One thing only remained that could save the Athenians from utter destruction: the Athenians had a good navy. The Athenians also had a fine statesman named Themistocles directing their activities. The Persians gave battle. The Greeks destroyed almost the entire Persian fleet at Salamis. This happened in 480 B.C.

*Drawn expressly for "The Old World and America"*

**Return of the Victors After Salamis**

> These Greek sailors deserved a great welcome. They saved Greece and therefore the civilization that Greece passed to later ages.

THE BATTLE OF PLATÆA. The Persian army now made a last attempt to conquer the Greeks. By this time, all the Greek city-states, realizing that they must unite or be conquered, came together in solid array and met the Persians at Platæa. The victory again went to the Greeks. Thus ended the last attempt of the Persians to conquer Greece.

THE IMPORTANCE OF THE VICTORY. Suppose we ask ourselves what would have happened had the Greeks been defeated by the Persians? As a conquered nation, many would have been sold into slavery. But more than this, all that the Greeks had done in art, in learning, and in government, and all that the Greeks were yet to do, would probably have been lost to later ages. The courage of the Greeks had won a victory for civilization.

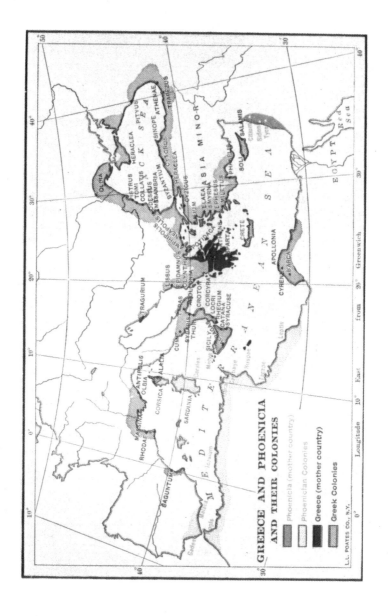

GREECE AND PHOENICIA
AND THEIR COLONIES

Phoenicia (mother country)

Phoenician Colonies

Greece (mother country)

Greek Colonies

L.L. POATES CO., N.Y.

## THE SPREAD OF GREEK CULTURE

**THE SPREAD OF GREEK IDEAS.** Greek ideas, Greek ways of doing things, so splendid in themselves, would have been of little use to the world if they had not gone to other lands. Fortunately Greek ideas were spread by colonization and also by conquest.

**GREEK COLONISTS.** The Greeks were really forced to found colonies because the soil in Greece and in the nearby islands was so poor that large crops could not be raised. As the population increased, larger and larger crops became necessary. Faced with a food shortage the Greeks had to find new homes, often in distant places.

**THE LOCATION OF GREEK COLONIES.** Greek colonies were located about the shores of the Black Sea; they were also to be found on the Island of Cyprus in the Mediterranean. To the .west, Greek colonies were located in Sicily, Italy, and Spain. When we study the history of the Romans, we shall learn about the Greek colony at Saguntum, in Spain. The French city of Marseilles is located where in ancient times a Greek colony was to be found. You can appreciate how widespread was the influence of Greece from the location of the Greek colonies.

A Greek colony was really a Greek city-state transplanted to some other part of the ancient world. These colonial cities were free. While they did not belong to any city-state in Greece, the people in the colony were Greeks. They had Greek ideas, Greek ways of doing things, and they spoke the Greek language.

**THE SPREAD OF GREEK CUSTOMS THROUGH CONQUEST.** The Greeks taught other peoples through conquest

*Drawn expressly for "The Old World and America"*

## The Golden Age

Much that we are so proud of in our art and culture can be traced back to the age of Pericles.

also. You may have heard that one of the world's greatest generals, Alexander, came from a land just north of Greece. Alexander by his conquests did a great deal to teach Greek customs to people in distant places. Before learning about Alexander, however, let us see what was happening in Greece after the Persian Wars.

GREECE AFTER THE PERSIAN WARS. After the Wars the Persians who could escape lost no time in getting out of Greece. They had been thoroughly defeated by the Greeks at Platæa. With the war over and the Persians out of Greece, the Greeks were free to look after affairs at home. As was to be expected, Greece continued after the wars to make further progress in the arts of civilization. As we have learned, the age of Pericles, named after the great Athenian statesman and covering the period from 461 to 429 B.C., is called the *Golden Age* by historians. It is so called because of the fine things done

by the Athenians in art, literature, learning, science, and government. Progress was made not by Athens alone; all the Greek
cities shared in the spirit of advancement.

WARFARE AMONG THE GREEK CITIES. Unfortunately
the Greek cities became jealous of one another. Soon they were
fighting fiercely among themselves. From 431 to 404 B.C. there
was warfare in Greece. In the end, some of the best of the
Greek cities had been quite ruined. All the Greek cities that
engaged in the contests were greatly weakened by the wars.
So weak were they, that shortly after the wars all Greece had to
surrender to the famous Philip of Macedon.

PHILIP OF MACEDON. The city-states of Greece were conquered by a man who came from a land to the north of
Thessaly. He was called Philip of Macedon. He appreciated
the accomplishments of his neighbors who lived in Greece to
the south, but he could not understand why they fought among
themselves. Nothing has been said thus far of Macedon (Macedonia) where Philip was king. Now, however, we must learn
something about this king. If you will look at the map, you will
see that Macedon is a mountainous country. The people who
lived there were a strong, hardy race. They spent their time
hunting or making war.

PHILIP'S AMBITION. Philip decided to be master of all
Greece instead of being merely king of Macedon. So he got
together an army which was generally successful and in the
battle of Chæronea, 338 B.C., he made himself master of the
entire Greek peninsula. In that battle King Philip defeated the
last force the city-states of Greece could send against him.
Philip had in mind a campaign into Persia to return the visit
made by the Persians at the time of Marathon, but he was murdered and this plan was never carried out by him. However,
he had a son who was equally anxious to be a conqueror. In

*Drawn expressly for "The Old World and America"*

## Philip and Alexander

> Philip tells young Alexander of his plans to conquer the Persians.

due time this son, Alexander, undertook to carry out his father's plan for the conquest of Persia.

ALEXANDER THE GREAT. Philip's son, Alexander, had all his father's genius. Indeed, he was a greater man than his father in many ways. If you had to name the greatest generals of all time, your list would include the name of Alexander. Many think he was the greatest general that ever lived. Of course he enjoyed many advantages too; for example, Aristotle, who was one of the wisest of men, was his teacher.

THE CONQUESTS OF ALEXANDER. Alexander left Greece in 334 B.C. to begin his career as conqueror. He took revenge upon the Phœnicians by destroying their cities because they had aided the Persians during the first Persian war. He next turned his attention to Egypt where again he was successful. Then Persia was put under the Greek yoke, to punish the

*Drawn expressly for "The Old World and America"*

**No More Worlds to Conquer**

Alexander with the sea before him and the desert at his back wept because he had conquered everything.

Persians for their invasion of Greece. Alexander drove his armies as far east as India. All this had been done by his thirty-second year.

THE CONQUEST OF GREEK IDEAS. Alexander's conquests were not conquests of arms only; his were also conquests of ideas. The Greek language went wherever Alexander's armies went. Greek was made the official language of the conquered country. Alexander remodeled old cities and built new ones, all according to the Greek plan. Alexandria, a city in Egypt named after Alexander, was built to order on the Greek plan by Greek architects. Greek teachers were sent for to provide the territories now under the power of Greece with Greek education. The effects of his conquests Alexander did not live to see. He was stricken with a fever from which he died (323 B.C.). After his death the effect of his conquest of *arms* passed away; but the effect of his conquest of *ideas* lived on. All through the East where Alexander had led his army, Greek ideas, Greek opinions, and Greek customs became common. When people thought alike and did things in the same way they began to have a feeling of union.

---

## ORAL DRILL

---

1. What kind of government had Persia?
2. Of what country was Darius king?
3. Who won the battle of Marathon?
4. Where did Leonidas come from?
5. Name a famous naval battle of this time.

---

## OBJECTIVE TESTS

---

TEST 1: Matching Test.

Copy the names under Column A. Next to each write the number that best matches from Column B.

|      Column A       |     Column B                              |
| ------------------- | ----------------------------------------- |
| (  ) Alexander      | 1. defeated at Salamis                    |
| (  ) Philip         | 2. code of laws                           |
| (  ) Aristotle      | 3. philosopher, and teacher of Alexander  |
| (  ) Pericles       | 4. conquered Greek peninsula              |
| (  ) Leonidas       | 5. "Golden Age" of Athens                 |
| (  ) Themistocles   | 6. directed Athenian navy                 |
| (  ) Xerxes         | 7. Battle of Thermopylæ                   |
| (  ) Draco          | 8. marched to India                       |

TEST 2: Description Test.

Pick out the word or phrase which best describes each man:

1. Darius: Indian king; king of Egypt; great soldier; king of Persia.
2. Leonidas: stupid; fearless; slow; jealous
3. Themistocles: Athenian king; Persian general; Athenian statesman; great artist

4. Alexander: military genius; admiral; rich; poetic
5. Philip: ruler of Philippines; statesman; king of Macedon; king of Persia

TEST 3: Order of Time.

Pick out the oldest item in each:

1. (a) Cretan civilization, (b) battle of Salamis, (c) "Golden Age" of Athens, (d) invasion by Darius.
2. (a) Alexander conquers east, (b) Ionian islands revolt against Darius, (c) battle of Marathon, (d) defeat of Leonidas.
3. (a) Philip conquers Greece, (b) death of Alexander, (c) Draco's code, (d) rule of Pericles.
4. (a) spread of Greek culture in Asia, (b) wars of Alexander, (c) murder of Philip, (d) invasion of Greece by Darius.
5. (a) "golden age" of Athens, (b) battle of Marathon, (c) reforms of Solon, (d) battle of Chœronea.

## QUESTIONS THAT MAKE YOU THINK

1. List four important events during the wars with Persia. Tell why each is important.
2. Give two causes of the Persian invasion.
3. Why were Spartan soldiers called the "walls of Sparta"?
4. "The Greek victory over the Persians was a victory for civilization." Explain this statement.
5. Give a good reason why the Greeks founded a great number of colonies.
6. Why did the Greeks never want to become a single nation?
7. Was Alexander a great man? Explain your answer.
8. Explain how the Greeks were able to defeat the great forces of Persians.
9. Was Leonidas a hero? Explain your answer.
10. Show how Alexander's victories helped Greek civilization.

## STRANGE FACTS

How many of these can you explain?
1. The battle of Marathon has given its name to a race in the Olympic Games of today.

2. The training of a boxer today is somewhat like that of a Spartan soldier.
3. Alexander conquered the civilized world of his day.
4. Alexander's conquests were conquests of ideas as well as arms.

## ACTIVITIES

1. Make a monument to the bravery of Leonidas and his Spartans. Use soap, wood or clay or pencil and paper.
2. Make believe you were a soldier in Alexander's army. Tell the class of your journeys.
3. Dramatize: the runner tells of the victory at Marathon.
4. Make drawings of the three kinds of Greek columns. Copy them from the picture in your book.

## QUESTIONS THAT TEST YOUR CHARACTER

1. Did Leonidas have courage? Explain.
2. Why should we all have courage? Give an example of courage today.
3. Name two good qualities of character which the runner of Marathon has.
4. Alexander was a man of action and a lover of learning. What lesson does this carry for us?

## IMPORTANT WORDS

Spartan courage
colonies
Marathon
invasion

conquest of ideas
conquest of arms
Greek ideas
Salamis

transplanted

# II

*Part 3:* THE GREEKS AND LIFE

Our chief interest in Athens or Corinth, or in the other city-states of ancient Greece, is due to the fact that what they did has had an influence upon our lives at the present time. For example, the Greeks made statues that we can still admire. Ornaments the Greeks used on their buildings we sometimes copy for use on our own buildings. Books that the Greeks wrote are still read by students over all the world. Some ideas they had about government, about the state, about living, we find helpful in one way or another. It is because of these things that we study the history of the ancient Greeks.

THE GREEKS AND RELIGION. The ancient Greeks lived before the coming of Our Lord, consequently they could not know about the life and teachings of Christ nor about the Church which He founded. The Greeks worshiped many gods and goddesses. They believed that Mount Olympus, the highest mountain in Greece, was the dwelling place of the gods. Here the gods directed the fortunes of men and determined the fate of cities.

Zeus was the father and leader of the gods. Poseidon ruled the sea; he was an important god for the Greeks who knew the sea so well and depended upon it. Zeus, the Greeks believed, had a son, Apollo, the sun god. He was the god of poetry and music. Apollo, they believed, spoke to the people through the Oracle at Delphi where hundreds came asking for advice. Athena, the goddess of wisdom, was also related

*Courtesy Metropolitan Museum of Art*

**The Temple at Delphi.**

People from all parts of the Greek world came to consult the Oracle at Delphi where they believed the priestess received messages from Apollo as answers to questions.

to Zeus. To the Athenians, she was the most important goddess. Of course each city-state had its own special god who was the common ancestor of all the people.

THE GREEK TEMPLE. The importance of religion in Greek life led to the building of temples some of which were of very great beauty. The most famous of the Greek temples were to be seen in Athens—the remains or ruins of them are there to this day. These famous structures were built on the Acropolis. This is an oblong table of rock or natural platform. The top of the Acropolis was reached by a flight of magnificent stairs. On the Acropolis was the beautiful Parthenon, the temple of Athene, goddess of the Athenians. There were other

© *Underwood & Underwood*

**The Acropolis of Ancient Athens.**

As an artist pictured it for us in all the glory of Greece at its best.

buildings equally wonderful. On all sides were statues, the work of Phidias and possibly Praxiteles. The statues fashioned by these and other Greek artists are among the very best ever carved by man.

GREEK ORNAMENT. We shall find it very interesting to examine the ornaments that the Greeks originated. Suppose we study the way they beautified their columns. A column is a stone post or pillar that supports a crosspiece. Now a column at first was perfectly plain: the Greeks thought it could be improved by fluting, that is by carving little channels down the side of the column. They thought that a stone cushion or "capital" could be placed between the top of the column and the crosspiece. This idea they may have borrowed from the Egyptians. The Greeks had three methods or orders for making these capitals attractive. The Doric order makes use of a plain stone cushion for a capital. The Ionic order is

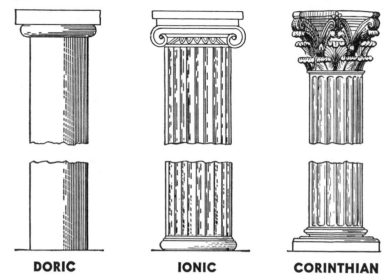

**DORIC          IONIC          CORINTHIAN**

The three orders of Greek Capitals.

more elaborate than the Doric. Scrolls or "volutes" are carved down the ends of the capital in the Ionic order. The Corinthian order is the most ornate of all. It was developed, however, long after the Doric and Ionic orders.

THE GREEKS AND BEAUTY. The word "beautiful" seems to describe perfectly most of the works of art which the ancient Greeks produced. Indeed the very word "beautiful" was loved by the Greeks. In architecture they understood that beauty and usefulness must go together. Beauty is not a quality that is added to a thing; it must be a part of it. Perhaps the fact that the Greeks insisted that the beauty of an object grew out of its usefulness was due in turn to the fact that the Greeks had learned to reason.

GREEK BOOKS. The Greeks wrote books on all sorts of subjects. There were books of poetry like the *Iliad* and the

*Courtesy New York Public Library*

## The Wooden Horse of Troy

Homer tells us the story of the siege of Troy. It was finally captured by a trick. The Greeks built a great wooden horse as a gift to the Trojans. Inside of the horse were hidden some of the best Greek soldiers. The Trojans took the horse into their city, the Greeks came out at night, opened the gates, and the city fell.

*Odyssey* of Homer. These famous books tell us of the early times in Greek History but do not always report the facts exactly as they happened. The Greeks wrote about the stars and the heavenly bodies. One of their historians, Herodotus, is called the "father of history." Hippocrates is called the "father of medicine." Today many young doctors before beginning to practice medicine take the so-called "Hippocratic oath." One of their great mathematicians was Euclid. The study of geometry is sometimes named for him. In fact, you could make a fine library of the books written by Greek scholars and fill it with books on philosophy, or wisdom.

THE PHILOSOPHERS. There was a class of men who studied how men should act and more particularly, how they should think. These men spent their whole lives seeking wisdom. Such men are called philosophers. Socrates was one of the most famous of the Greek philosophers. His maxim, "know thyself," was the subject of endless discussions. Aristotle was another famous philosopher. He is regarded by many as one of the greatest thinkers of all times and wise men nowadays believe in many of his ideas. You will remember that Alexander was his pupil.

THE GREEK THEATER. The Greeks in ancient times had as much interest in the theater as most people today have in the movies. But the theater the Greeks attended was not like ours. It had no roof; it was hardly a building. The plays were given under the open sky in an enclosure at one end of which was a stage. The people sat on stone benches which were raised one above the other somewhat like a grandstand. Instead of being built above the ground like most of our stands, the Greeks saved labor by building their stand on the side of a hill. There was no scenery in the Greek theater. A few principal actors wearing masks carried on a conversation and a chorus added its part to the entertainment. In the beginning the plays were simple but after a time the Greeks came to write plays that still interest us.

GAMES AMONG THE GREEKS. Nowadays, every four years, the athletes from the different countries of the world meet to compete for prizes. We call this meeting the Olympic Games. You have probably heard that for some years past the athletes of the United States have won many of the track and field events. The modern system of Olympic Games is copied after the Olympic Games of ancient Greece. The games in

*Courtesy of the New York Public Library*

## Greek Games

> The Greek youth was always in training. If victorious he was richly rewarded with banquets and gifts and in Athens, granted free board for life.

ancient times were held in honor of Zeus, father of the gods. They took place at Olympia in the city-state of Elis. All the city-states of Greece sent athletes to these games and while they were in progress none of the Greek city-states could be at war—at least among themselves.

THE EVENTS AND THE PRIZE. There were events of various kinds including short dashes, long runs, jumping, discus throwing, boxing, and wrestling. The victors in the events were rewarded with crowns of wild olive. The winners were regarded as heroes. The Olympic Games were the most important games held in Greece and they helped to give the people from different parts of the country a feeling that all Greeks had something in common. This feeling was strengthened by the fact that only Greek athletes could compete. Outsiders were excluded. The Olympic Games, however, were not the only ones held in Greece. There were games going on in all parts of

*Drawn expressly for "The Old World and America"*

## A Greek Home

Is this house like an American home? How does it differ?

Greece most of the time. Athletics came into the daily life of every Greek. The average Greek citizen would not dream of missing his daily exercise at the gymnasium.

THE MARKET PLACE. After the Greek citizen left the gymnasium, he probably strolled to the market place. This was one of his favorite haunts. Here he could meet his friends and here he discussed politics and the questions of the day. But his exercise at the gymnasium and his visit to the market place came only after the day's work was over. For the Greeks were an industrious people who believed in hard work.

A DAY IN ATHENS. The ordinary citizen of Athens was an active fellow. He rose early in the morning, often before dawn, and after a frugal breakfast of coarse bread and a little wine went off about his work. If he had a farm in the country he rode to see it on horseback or on a donkey. If, however, he was a shopkeeper or craftsman his shop or store was usually part of his house.

GREEK HOMES AND HOME LIFE. A Greek house was a very plain dwelling indeed. The house was not more than two stories high. The part which faced the street was perfectly plain without windows. Usually each house had a single door for entrance and exit. Built about an open court, each house had an abundance of light and air. Inside everything was of the plainest. Very little furniture was to be seen and none of the conveniences which we regard as so necessary were to be found. The only artificial light was supplied by oil lamps which were seldom used because almost everyone went to bed soon after sundown. Water was drawn from a well which was often used by all the families in the neighborhood.

THE GREEK WORLD. The Greeks who lived so simply nevertheless had much to teach the people who came after them. Fortunately their accomplishments became widely known throughout the Ancient World. Greek civilization had helped to prepare people for the coming of Christ by providing a unity of thought. You remember that when Our Lord was crucified in Palestine the inscription, "Jesus of Nazareth, King of the Jews," was attached to the cross. This inscription was written in a Hebrew tongue, in Latin, and in Greek. This shows how widely Greek influence had spread.

---

## OBJECTIVE TESTS

TEST 1:  Similarities Test.
    In each of the following there are two items which are alike in some way. Pick out the two which are most alike. Be able to explain how they are alike.
1. Phidias, Praxiteles, Poseidon    3. Alexander, Athena, Philip
2. Zeus, Hippocrates, Apollo        4. Darius, Aristotle, Socrates
                    5. Iliad, Parthenon, Odyssey

TEST 2:   Historical Vocabulary.

1. What is philosophy?
   a) a kind of mathematics
   b) a system of art
   c) love of wisdom
   d) a religion
2. What is meant by a Greek capital?
   a) a carved border
   b) the base of the pillar and the crosspiece
   c) the column itself
   d) a stone cushion between the column and the crosspiece
3. What is meant by an oracle to-day?
   a) one who gives advice
   b) an old man
   c) an Eastern bird
   d) a public speaker
4. What is geometry?
   a) study of the earth
   b) a branch of poetry
   c) a branch of mathematics
   d) science of eye-glasses

TEST 3:   Matching Test.

Copy the names in Column A. Next to each write the number from Column B that best matches it.

| Column A | Column B |
|---|---|
| ( )  Phidias | 1. famous oath |
| ( )  Athena | 2. geometry |
| ( )  Acropolis | 3. simple style |
| ( )  Corinthian | 4. ornate style |
| ( )  Ionic | 5. famous hill |
| ( )  Doric | 6. wisdom |
| ( )  Euclid | 7. Olympic Games |
| ( )  Zeus | 8. scrolls or volutes |
| ( )  Hippocrates | 9. poetry |
| ( )  Homer | 10. sculpture |

---

## QUESTIONS THAT MAKE YOU THINK

1. Why was Poseidon an important god for the Greeks?
2. "The geography of the country helped the Greeks appreciate beauty." Explain.
3. Point out one thing in common possessed by Hippocrates and Herodotus.
4. The word "theater" in Greek means "hall of the gods." Give the reason for this meaning.

5. Prove that the Greeks were eager to keep themselves physically fit.
6. Compare the "movies" of today and the Greek theater of long ago.
7. Why do we say the Olympic Games helped bring about peace?

## ACTIVITIES

1. From soap make one of the following: Ionic column, Corinthian column, Doric column.
2. Write a diary, telling of a day in old Athens.
3. Make a "peep-box" with colored glass. Inside the box place a picture or drawing of the famous Parthenon.
4. From soap try to make a model of the Parthenon.
5. Write a letter to a sports-editor of a newspaper. Ask him to explain the origin of the Olympic Games. Read the reply in class.
6. Visit a modern gymnasium and make a list of the different activities you observe. Which of these do you think were practiced in ancient Athens?
7. Make a drawing of an ancient Greek home.

## QUESTIONS THAT TEST YOUR CHARACTER

1. Were the Greeks superstitious? Explain your answer.
2. Are you superstitious? Explain your answer.
3. State one good point in Greek life which you admire. State one bad point.
4. Show how you can help to make (a) your own home more beautiful; (b) your school; (c) your classroom; (d) your neighborhood.
5. The Greeks believed in moderation in all things. Do you agree or disagree? Why?

## IMPORTANT WORDS

| | | | |
|---|---|---|---|
| deity | column | volutes | Parthenon |
| temple | athletics | philosophy | Olympic Games |
| architrave | capital | gymnasium | market place |

# III

## Contributions of Rome
## to
## Civilization

### AIM

To show that civilization through the Romans moved
westward into Europe.

That the modern world owes to Rome notions of law,
order, and learning.

Rome is in Italy. Italy, like Greece, is a peninsula. If you
think of the outline of "a boot with a high heel" you will
have a fair idea of the shape of Italy. Italy, like Greece, is
mountainous, but the mountains of Italy just form a back-
bone. They do not divide the country into small sections.
Rome was located on this peninsula. In time Rome ruled not
only Italy but also the entire Mediterranean basin and western
Europe. At that time, India and China were civilized countries, but they had a different sort of civilization. It is well to
remember that the Greeks had made settlements in southern
Italy. The inhabitants of Italy learned much from these Greeks.
From them they may have learned the alphabet, methods of
warfare, and trading.

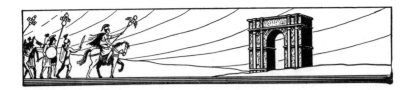

# III

## *Part 1:* THE ROMAN PEOPLE

The letters S P Q R were deeply respected by the ancient Romans. The letters stand for the Latin words *Senatus Populusque Romanus,* which means "the Senate and the Roman People." The proud Romans believed that they far surpassed all other races. When you study the accomplishments of the Roman People you will understand why. You should also be able to see how the accomplishments of the ancient Romans have had an influence upon our lives today.

THE CITY OF ROME. The city of Rome is located on the Tiber River in the western part of Italy, about half way up the "boot." This spot was a good location for a city because it was near enough to the sea to enjoy the advantages of a harbor city. Yet it was far enough inland for its inhabitants to be safe from pirates. At that time there were different groups of people in Italy, each having its own language and customs. As Rome was situated in the center of Italy, her inhabitants could trade with the tribes to the north and to the south. The seven hills on which Rome was built made a natural fortress easy to defend.

THE FIRST ROMANS. To begin our story, we must go back perhaps about eight centuries before the birth of Christ. At that time, one of the Latin tribes from central Italy saw the advantages offered by the seven hills. These people also thought that it would be good to be close to a river which soon reached the sea. This tribe decided to settle there on the **River Tiber.**

*Drawn expressly for "The Old World and America*

## Map of Italy

Notice the position of Rome. Trace out the great Roman
roads leading to it. Locate the Appian Way. Locate
Carthage. It is easy to see that one or the other of these
great cities, Rome or Carthage, had to control the Mediterranean Sea.

And so on the spot which later was called Rome a settlement was made. Thus began Roman history.

Shortly thereafter, another tribe joined the first one and still later on a third tribe came to settle. Soon all seven hills were occupied. The people belonging to these three tribes were the original Romans. They called themselves Patricians, thinking that they were far better than other tribes who later took up their abode in Rome.

OCCUPATIONS OF THE EARLY ROMANS. The Romans, in the beginning, cared very little for commerce. Their chief occupation was farming. They also raised cattle; indeed a man's wealth could be reckoned in terms of cattle. The Roman word for money was derived from the Latin word which meant flocks. There were few other occupations. A small number of mechanics supplied the weapons for warfare or the very simple farm tools which the people required. In their early days the Romans did not follow the sea as did the Greeks; nor were they interested in planting colonies.

EARLY ROMAN HISTORY. A number of accounts of the early days of Roman history have come down to us but not all these accounts are to be trusted. Of few points we can be sure. It is fairly certain that in the early times, the Romans were ruled by a king. After the year 509 B.C., however, it seems that the last king of the Romans was driven from the throne and Rome became a Republic.

THE EARLY REPUBLIC. When the Romans got rid of their king they went on to change the different offices of the government. The chief power was now in the hands of two men called consuls. The consuls were elected by all the men who had the right to vote. The consuls were assisted by other officers. The Senate, which was an advisory body, was made up of the older

*Drawn expressly for "The Old World and America"*

**The Two Consuls**

Do you think two consuls were better than one king?

and more important men of the city. The Senate had great influence.

PATRICIANS AND PLEBEIANS. The history of Rome from the year 509 B.C., when the last king was put away, until the year 287 B.C., contains many accounts of the struggle between the Patricians and the Plebeians. You remember how the three tribes who first settled Rome called themselves the founders of Rome and therefore kept for themselves many privileges. These three tribes and their descendants were the Patricians. Those who came into Rome later were known as Plebeians.

THE STRUGGLE BETWEEN PATRICIANS AND PLE-BEIANS. The Patricians wanted to keep all the offices of government for members of their own class. They were the wealthiest among the Romans and owned the best land. The lot of the Plebeians was hard. However, the Plebeians had no intention of remaining in subjection to the Patricians. The Plebeians struggled for their rights. In 287 B.C. the Plebeians succeeded in obtaining for themselves many privileges which formerly had been enjoyed by the Patricians alone. This victory of the Plebeians was made possible by one they gained more than one hundred and fifty years earlier. This was when the Laws of the Twelve Tables were published.

THE LAWS OF THE TWELVE TABLES. At that time the Plebeians demanded that the laws be written down so that every one would know what was the law. The Plebeians did not know the law. They did not know what their rights were nor whether they were receiving justice from the magistrates, who were Patricians. The Patricians had to yield to the demand that the laws be written down. The laws were engraved on twelve stone tables. The Laws of the Twelve Tables are the foundation of all Roman law. The victory of the Plebeians arose from the fact that all could now know the law and that the law was the same for all.

## ROME'S CONQUEST OF THE WORLD

THE BEGINNINGS OF ROME'S CONQUEST. Such a sturdy race as the Romans could not help but be successful in war. In those days warfare was an everyday matter and a nation had to conquer or be conquered. Little by little Rome succeeded in conquering Italy. The Romans sometimes made friends and allies of their former foes. By keeping a number of her soldiers in the newly conquered territory, to teach Roman ideas and methods, Rome joined to herself the greater part of Italy.

CARTHAGE THE RIVAL OF ROME. Rome pushed her power north and south in Italy, thus getting the whole peninsula

*Courtesy B. F. Williamson*

**Naval Battle**

> The Romans were new to sea fighting but soon became good sailors. They built a winning navy.

under her control. At the same time, a great nation in northern Africa was preparing to destroy her. This was Carthage, a city founded by Phœnician traders, in the ninth century before Christ (see Map p. 64). Larger in size of territory, greater in numbers of people, richer in resources and wealth, this rival, Carthage, seemed to have every advantage over Rome.

CAUSES OF THE RIVALRY. Rome had undergone many changes since the early days. The city was no longer a collection of mud huts. People lived in better houses and possessed greater wealth. Nor were the Romans any longer content with the cultivation of rude farms. They had come to look upon war as a profitable venture. War increased Roman territory. Stores of gold were sometimes taken from the conquered peoples. By making slaves of the captured soldiers, the Romans obtained laborers to do their work for them. Roman businessmen began to think of trading as a new way to wealth and influence.

WEALTH FROM TRADING. Now trading was practically the only source of wealth that Carthage had. If the Romans were to engage in commerce, it would mean that both the Romans and the traders from Carthage would be rival traders with the same cities. The ship owners and merchants of Carthage did not like to see the traders from Rome taking away their business. And the Roman traders when they realized how much money could be made in commerce had no intention of giving up.

THE PROSPECTS OF CARTHAGE. Rome feared Carthage with good reason. Carthage controlled almost all of the coast of north Africa. Besides this she had other holdings that were near enough to Italy to cause fear at Rome. Much of Spain was under Carthaginian rule, as well as a strip of the French coast that is nearest Italy. In addition to this Carthage had a foothold in Sicily. Besides controlling all this land Carthage had immense resources in money. Finally, Carthage had a splendid fleet and skillful sailors to man it. Rome had neither sailors nor ships. However, an abandoned ship was dug from the sand. It served as a model for the Romans when they began to build their own ships. War was certain to come. The long struggle began in 264 B.C.

## THE PUNIC WARS

THE FIRST PUNIC WAR (264-241 B.C.). The series of wars between Rome and Carthage are called the Punic Wars from the Latin name for Carthaginians. Carthage made the attack. The Carthaginians hoped to cripple Rome before Rome could get ready. Although the war was fought at sea, Rome defeated Carthage. This was a great feat because the Romans knew less about ships than their rivals. The Romans won wars not only because of their courage but also because they knew how to invent war machines. And so after twenty-four years of fighting the Romans defeated the Carthaginians at Mylæ. This victory brought to a close the First Punic War.

THE SECOND PUNIC WAR (218-202 B.C.). For a quarter of a century there had been peace between Rome and Carthage. Trouble commenced anew. The trouble this time centered about Saguntum which was a Greek colony in Spain (see map opposite page 43). The Carthaginians were besieging Saguntum expecting to take it and so to get control of some silver mines in that neighborhood. The people of Saguntum sent to Rome for aid. The Romans were willing to help. An expedition was fitted out, but too late to save Saguntum. It fell into the hands of the Carthaginians.

HANNIBAL. Other successes followed this first victory because the Carthaginians were led by a brilliant general named Hannibal. When Hannibal was a little boy, his father, Hamilcar, made him take an oath that as long as he lived he would hate the Romans and do all in his power to injure them. This promise Hannibal meant to keep. It seemed as if he might do so for Hannibal had great ability and was a remarkable general.

CROSSING THE ALPS. Hannibal led an army into Spain. After putting down opposition in Spain, he decided to attack Italy. During the winter Hannibal crossed the Alps with a large force of men. This was a great feat in itself and the report of it greatly discouraged the Roman allies in northern Italy. But the stories about his army did even greater harm. Hannibal had a great train of elephants, "beasts bigger than houses," and a swarm of brown-colored soldiers. We can imagine the terror-stricken allies when they saw Hannibal's force.

*Drawn expressly for "The Old World and America"*

## Hannibal Crossing the Alps

Even today an army would find it hard to cross the Alps.

THE BATTLE OF CANNAE. Hannibal met the Romans at Cannae in 216 B.C. where the Romans suffered a severe defeat. So complete, indeed, was Hannibal's success that final victory for Carthage seemed to be assured. Strange as it may seem the victory of Hannibal at Cannae proved to be the turning point in Rome's favor. Hannibal's success had cost him a big price. He had lost many of his best soldiers. Those who were left needed rest; they were unfit for immediate fighting. Hannibal wanted more men and fresh supplies very badly. Unfortunately for him, he could get neither. The longer Hannibal remained in Italy, the worse his position became.

ZAMA. 202 B.C. Hannibal got back to Carthage as fast as he could. Carthage was now on the defensive. The battle fought near there at Zama, 202 B.C., paved the way for the complete destruction of the power of Carthage. Carthage passed out of history as a world power after the Third Punic War (B.C. 146).

**THE MEDITERRANEAN, A ROMAN LAKE.** It was good for civilization that Carthage was defeated by Rome. The Carthaginians were good for making money but for little else. Their government was a rich man's government. The Carthaginians had no laws worth talking about. What Rome had to teach the world about law and government was saved for us by the defeat of Carthage. By defeating Carthage, Rome came into possession of all the land that Carthage had controlled. The great trade that Carthage had enjoyed now became Roman trade. Rome's success made her the sole power in the Mediterranean, for Greece, in the meantime, had come under the control of Rome. The Mediterranean could be called a "Roman Lake."

**CHANGES AFTER THE WARS.** Wars such as we have been studying bring about great changes in the countries that are engaged in fighting. Some of the greatest changes occurred after the wars in the lives of the Romans and in their occupations. Even the character of the Roman citizens was affected. The wonderful Roman army was made up of free men who in peace times worked their small farms. When the call to war came, these farmers left their few acres. After the Punic Wars, the soldiers returned to their farms, which in the meantime, had been almost ruined. You can picture a soldier, broken in health perhaps, returning to his neglected farm and trying to get up enough courage to begin anew. This condition would have been bad enough had all men shared the same fate. But it was the poor man who suffered most while the wealthy escaped.

**THE GRACCHI BROTHERS.** The few truly patriotic men among the wealthy Romans realized that the poor must be given a chance to make a living, otherwise disaster would come

*Drawn expressly for "The Old World and America"*

## The Gracchi Brothers

They gave their lives in an attempt to make Rome a better place for the poor.

upon Rome. Among the better minded Romans must be mentioned the Gracchi brothers. They tried hard to have laws passed so that a rich man could have only a limited amount of land. According to their plan a rich man who owned much more land than he needed would be made to turn some of it over to the poor. This plan would give all men a chance. Unfortunately, the Gracchi brothers were killed by their enemies before their plans could be put into effect.

THE DRIFT TOWARD ONE-MAN GOVERNMENT. The common people lost their good friends and protectors when the Gracchi brothers were killed. The lot of the poor man grew steadily worse. As years went on, several ambitious men, one after another, tried to get control of affairs in Rome. At last a man arose who actually made himself master of the whole Roman world. The man was Julius Cæsar.

## ORAL DRILL

1. Which is larger, Italy or Greece?
2. Who were the Patricians?
3. Did a king rule the Romans in their early or later history?
4. Who were the Plebeians?
5. Why were the laws of the Twelve Tables so important?
6. Who were the Gracchi?
7. Who founded Carthage?
8. Where did the Romans defeat Hannibal?
9. Who won the Punic Wars?
10. What can you say about the army and navy of Carthage?

## OBJECTIVE TESTS

TEST 1: Completion Test.
   Fill in the missing word or words in each of the following:
1. The ................ brothers tried to help the poor man in Rome.
2. The wars with Carthage are called the ................ Wars.
3. Hannibal surprised Rome by crossing the ........ in winter.
4. Rome is located on the ............. river.
5. The opponents of the Patricians were called ............
6. After the wars with Carthage the ............... Sea became a Roman lake.
7. The chief power in the Roman republic was in the hands of the two men called ..................
8. The body of important older men in Rome was called the ..............
9. The chief occupation of the early Romans was ............
10. The laws of the ................ are the foundation of all Roman law.

TEST 2: Order of Events.
   Arrange the following events in order of time:
      Hannibal is defeated at Zama.
      Julius Cæsar comes to power.
      Rome is ruled by a king.
      First Punic War is declared.

TEST 3: Historical Vocabulary.

1. Who were the Plebeians?
    a) rich Romans
    b) Roman farmers
    c) common people
    d) Roman nobles
2. What is a republic?
    a) a government ruled by a strong man
    b) rule by nobles
    c) rule by Senators
    d) people elect men to rule them
3. What is a consul?
    a) a general
    b) advises the government
    c) an elected official who heads the government
    d) a dictator
4. Who were the Patricians?
    a) the Roman people
    b) those who settled in Rome
    c) original tribes of Rome
    d) the great merchants

---

## QUESTIONS THAT MAKE YOU THINK

---

1. Compare the influence of geography   a) upon Greece
                                         b) upon Rome.
2. Compare the occupations of the early Romans and the early Greeks.
3. Explain how Roman and Greek government differed.
4. Why do the Twelve Tables remind you of Draco?
5. Give one cause of the wars between Carthage and Rome.
6. Why did Rome fear Carthage?
7. What was the greatest achievement of Hannibal? Explain your answer.
8. Why were the Gracchi popular with the poor Romans?
9. Show how the wars with Carthage helped Rome.
10. Show how these wars had a bad effect upon Rome.

---

## QUESTIONS THAT TEST YOUR CHARACTER

---

1. Was Hannibal a great man? Give reasons for your answer.
2. Were the Gracchi right in their demands? Explain.

3. What lesson should you draw from the effects of the wars with Carthage upon the Roman farmers?
4. In what ways should you imitate the early Romans?
5. What mistakes of the early Romans should you avoid?

## ACTIVITIES

1. Dress a doll as a Roman soldier.
2. Draw a picture showing Hannibal and his army traveling in the Alps.
3. Write "Hannibal" like this:

H
A
N
N
I
B
A
L

Let each letter stand for the first letter of a word, describing the man's character.
4. Do the same for "Gracchi."
5. Make a drawing of the famous Twelve Tables. Alongside these draw a picture of the Ten Commandments.
6. Make a "peep box." In it place a list of the chief events in the wars with Carthage.
7. From wood make a Roman or a Carthaginian ship.
8. Paste in your scrapbook pictures and sketches of early Rome.

## IMPORTANT WORDS

| | | |
|---|---|---|
| consul | Mediterranean | plebeians |
| senate | Punic Wars | Tiber |
| patricians | republic | tribe |

# III

## Part 2: THE ROMAN EMPIRE

Rome at first was a City-State. Later, Rome's control extended over the entire peninsula of Italy. Finally, Rome became an empire by acquiring territory beyond the confines of Italy. The story of this Roman Empire is bound up with certain leaders. Perhaps first in importance among those who helped to build the greatness of the Roman Empire was the Roman general, Julius Cæsar.

---

### JULIUS CÆSAR

---

CÆSAR'S OPPORTUNITY. Fifty years before the birth of our Lord, there was much quarreling among the different groups in Rome. It seemed likely that any leader who was strong enough and popular enough to control the army could make himself master of the Roman world. The man who took advantage of this troubled state of affairs was Julius Cæsar. He came from one of the fine old Roman families. Although a rich man, Julius Cæsar believed in making the lot of the poor man more bearable. He not only supplied the poor of Rome with food, but also frequently had circus performances for their amusement.

CÆSAR AS A YOUNG MAN. Julius Cæsar was greatly interested in politics. Indeed he became a politician, that is, he made politics his business. As he was very popular with the

*Drawn expressly for "The Old World and America"*

## The Surrender of Vercingetorix

Vercingetorix was a powerful Gallic chief. Taken in battle, he stood thus before Caesar, conquered but unafraid.

common people, he found no great trouble in being elected to office. He held all the positions in the government a man could have. Finally, Julius Cæsar was elected Consul, the highest office in Rome.

CÆSAR'S AMBITION. Cæsar wanted to have great power. It is said that when he was a young man, in company with some friends, he took a trip into northern Italy. One day coming upon a tiny village, one of his companions jokingly asked him how he would like to be the first man in that small place. Cæsar replied that he would rather be first in a small village than second in Rome. Cæsar now took a long step towards becoming first in Rome. He led a victorious army across what is now France and beyond into England. This move helped Cæsar's own fortunes and it also had an effect upon later history.

THE GALLIC WARS. An important date is 58 B.C. That year Cæsar led an army into Gaul, which is now France. Why is this date important? Until now we have said almost nothing about western Europe. Notice that the countries thus far studied are located in the Mediterranean basin. Civilization before Cæsar's time was to be found principally in southern Europe and in Asia Minor. After Cæsar's time we find western Europe making great progress in civilization.

THE INHABITANTS OF WESTERN EUROPE. It seems hard to believe that in Cæsar's day, the British Isles and western Europe were inhabited by tribes of half-civilized men. These barbarians roamed over the country at will, spending much of their time fighting and hunting. Their few wants were easily supplied. They hardly bothered with farming. Cattle raising was their most useful occupation. Cæsar thought he would conquer these tribes, thus advancing Rome's power and adding to his own influence. This he finally succeeded in doing and so Roman civilization was brought to western Europe.

CÆSAR'S CONQUESTS. The best account of these conquests is given by Cæsar himself. He wished to appear to be very modest about his exploits. He therefore used the pronoun "I" only three times. When you go to high school you will have the chance to read about Julius Cæsar's campaigns from the book written by himself.

RESULT OF THE CONQUESTS. The Romans by their victories gained a large extent of fertile land. A new center for commerce was opened to Rome. The Gauls received the benefits of Roman civilization. Indeed, shortly after this, some of the best schools in the Roman Empire were to be found in Gaul. That part of Britain or England which the Romans had conquered also received the benefits of Roman civilization. The

*Drawn expressly for "The Old World and America"*

**Building Hadrian's Wall in Britain**

  This wall was built by the Romans to keep the warlike Picts and Scots out of Roman Britain.

influence of Rome upon England as well as upon western Europe continues to this day.

JULIUS CÆSAR, MASTER OF ROME. Julius Cæsar was a popular man with the common people in Rome. The gifts, circus performances, and entertainments he had given had won him many friends. Cæsar's very great success in Gaul made him a man to be feared. Among the powerful men of Rome, especially in the Senate, Cæsar had many enemies. These men had a decree passed by the Senate declaring that Julius Cæsar must give up the command of the army before a certain day.

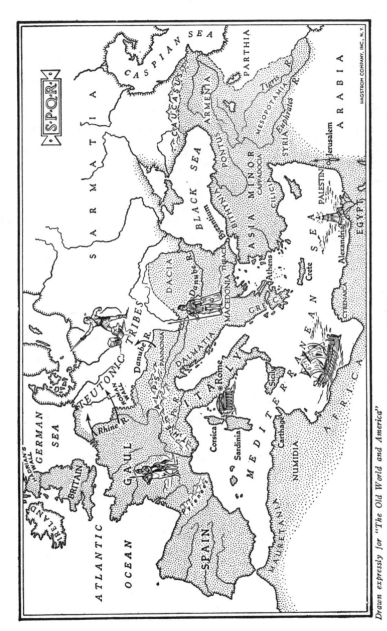

*Drawn expressly for "The Old World and America"*

**The Roman Empire at its Greatest Extent**

Cæsar realized that once he lost the army, his power would be gone. Then his enemies might succeed in having him banished. So Cæsar decided on a bold move.

CROSSING THE RUBICON. There was a small stream in northern Italy called the Rubicon. This stream marked the dividing line between Italy and the northern provinces. For a general to lead his troops across this stream in the direction of Rome, without the permission of the Roman Senate, would be regarded as an act of war. Cæsar said, "The die is cast." He crossed the Rubicon at the head of his troops. He knew that his soldiers loved him. Their loyal support with their splendid courage, he felt, would overcome all opposition. Julius Cæsar therefore marched into Italy, confident of the outcome. Soon he was master of Italy. But there was one man in particular who still opposed him. His name was Pompey. Cæsar defeated the army which Pompey had collected. Thus a serious rival was put out of the way.

FURTHER VICTORIES AND FINAL DEFEAT. Cæsar added to his power by further victories. He planned a campaign into Egypt and another into Asia Minor. In these campaigns he was successful. One of his great victories he describes to the Roman senate in three words: *"Veni, vidi, vici,"* which means, "I came, I saw, I conquered."

Cæsar's enemies at Rome were not at all willing to give up. They resolved that Cæsar should be destroyed because they felt that he had too much power. A group of conspirators plotted his death. They gathered about him in the Senate in Rome. They pretended that they wished to ask him a favor. When the signal was given, they rushed upon Cæsar and stabbed him to death.

THE ROMAN EMPEROR. Cæsar had shown that one man rule in Rome was possible. There were two men who were

*Drawn expressly for "The Old World and America"*

**Caesar Carried in Triumph**

The Eagles of his Legions and the standards of the lesser troops are held by the soldiers.

anxious to succeed Julius Cæsar. One of these men was Octavian, Cæsar's nephew and heir. The other, Marc Antony, was a close friend of Cæsar. Marc Antony had been close to Cæsar for some years and understood Cæsar's ideas and methods. Octavian and Antony went to war to see which one was to be the sole ruler of the Roman Empire. In a decisive battle Antony was killed. His rival, Octavian, or Augustus as he was called, was made emperor. His power was unlimited. In 14 A.D., the Roman emperor was worshiped as a god.

---

At this very time, in Palestine, our Lord was helping St. Joseph in the carpenter shop at Nazareth.

## ORAL DRILL

1. Why was crossing the Rubicon a warlike step?
2. What was the feeling between Pompey and Cæsar?
3. What relation was Octavian to Cæsar?
4. Was Cæsar poor or rich?
5. Were the Gauls civilized or barbarians?
6. Why was Cæsar slain?
7. What is an empire?

## OBJECTIVE TESTS

TEST 1: Choice Test.
1. Julius Cæsar lived (before, after) the birth of Christ.
2. Julius Cæsar was (a lawyer, a politician).
3. Julius Cæsar conquered (Sicily, France).
4. The great enemy of Cæsar was (Augustus, Pompey).
5. Julius Cæsar was killed (by conspirators, by the police).

TEST 2: Similarities Test.

Two items out of each three are alike in some way. Select the two and be able to explain how they are alike.
1. Rubicon, Asia Minor, Tiber.
2. Octavian, Augustus, Gracchi.
3. Consul, Senator, deity.
4. Herodotus, Cæsar, Hannibal.
5. Gaul, Egypt, Greece.

TEST 3: Order of Time.
Arrange the following events in the order of time.

Cæsar crosses Rubicon
Octavian defeats Antony
Cæsar conquers Gaul
Cæsar conquers Asia Minor
Cæsar is master of Rome

## QUESTIONS THAT MAKE YOU THINK

1. Give two reasons for the success of Julius Cæsar.
2. Why was Cæsar very popular with the common people?
3. "Julius Cæsar became consul." Just what does this mean?
4. Explain the effect of Cæsar's conquest upon Gaul.
5. Why was it easy for Cæsar to conquer Gaul?
6. Was Cæsar wise in crossing the Rubicon? Explain.

7. What did Cæsar mean when he said, "The die is cast"?
8. Show how Cæsar increased the power of Rome.
9. "Cæsar was not only a great soldier, but a good author." Explain this statement.
10. Why did the Senate oppose Julius Cæsar?

## ACTIVITIES

1. Draw a tombstone for Julius Cæsar. Upon it give the chief events of his life.
2. Dramatize: Marc Antony's speech over the body of Julius Cæsar.
3. Hold a meeting of the Roman Senate, discussing the victories of Cæsar in Gaul.
4. Have a debate on the question, "Who was greater, Hannibal or Julius Cæsar?"
5. Make a large colored map of the Roman Empire on a piece of cardboard. In the map draw original pictures and print other interesting information.
6. Write the name of Cæsar like this:   C
                                        A
                                        E
                                        S
                                        A
                                        R

   Let each letter of his name begin a word describing his character.
7. Paste in your scrapbook pictures and clippings about Julius Cæsar.

## QUESTIONS THAT TEST YOUR CHARACTER

1. Was the killing of Cæsar a good act? Give reasons.
2. What lesson is there for you in the violent death of Cæsar?
3. Was Julius Cæsar a great man? Give reasons.
4. Explain one defect in the character of Julius Cæsar.
5. Was Julius Cæsar a truly modest man? Explain.

## IMPORTANT WORDS

| | | |
|---|---|---|
| ambition | decisive battle | Roman Empire |
| popular | Emperor | "The die is cast!" |

# III

*Part 3:* ROMAN ACCOMPLISHMENTS

The modern world would owe a great debt to Rome for preserving the accomplishments of the Greeks. But the Romans were not mere copyists, they were originators as well. The language of the Romans is the foundation of that spoken in France and in Italy, in Spain and in Portugal, and in most of the countries on the great continent of South America. The world is indebted to Rome for Roman law. Our calendar is partly of Roman origin. Julius Cæsar improved the Egyptian calendar. The Roman or Julian calendar was changed to our present calendar many centuries later (1582) by Pope Gregory. The world is also indebted to the Romans for valuable ideas about order and government.

---

## LIFE AMONG THE ROMANS

---

ROMAN RELIGION. Religion was an important matter in every Roman home. Indeed each household had its own gods, for each family worshiped its own ancestors. This fact placed the father of the family in a place of special importance. In every Roman home the doorway through which the family entered, the niche where the food was kept, and the fire which cooked the food, were all held sacred. The Romans also had public official worshipers, the Vestal Virgins, and the Roman priests.

ROMAN HOMES AND HOME LIFE. In the early days Roman homes were severely simple. Later they became quite

*Courtesy Metropolitan Museum of Art, New York*

**A Roman Court**

> A room in the Metropolitan Museum of Art, New York, has been arranged to resemble a Roman courtyard. However, in Rome the courtyard would have been open to the sky.

elaborate. The plan of the house depended to a great extent on its location, and of course upon the means of the owner. Houses in the country were usually low and covered a large piece of ground. In the city of Rome, where land was expensive, the houses were several stories in height. After a time the height was limited. The Emperor Augustus issued a decree limiting the height of city houses to seventy-five feet. So you see the Romans had their zoning problems, too. In the center of each house there was usually an open court. All the rooms opened into it except the storerooms. Some modern conveniences, such as good artificial light and electric refrigeration, were missing yet the wealthy Romans had many comforts. In the colder parts of the Roman Empire heating plants were installed. From a central furnace in which charcoal was burned, warm air was circulated throughout the house by a series of tiled ducts.

ROMAN OCCUPATIONS. The occupations the Romans engaged in were various. The Roman citizens in the days of the Empire were usually either very rich or very poor. If the Roman were wealthy, he probably made his money by trading, banking, or the cultivation of a great farm. The rich Roman rarely took an active part in the carrying on of the business; this was left to the freedman whom he hired or sometimes even to a slave.

THE POOR CITIZEN. The very poor citizen often avoided work and did nothing. When possible he attached himself to some wealthy patron on whom he depended for shelter and food. Honest labor was held in contempt. All work was done by slaves. The wealthy Romans looked down even on shopkeepers. Labor, therefore, was not respected. Rich and poor alike spent their days in idleness or watching the brutal and degrading shows at the amphitheater.

ROMAN EDUCATION. The Romans in later times were careful to provide their children with an education. Even Roman girls received an education. In this practice the Romans differed from the Greeks, among whom the education of the girls was neglected. The education given Roman girls, however, was not the equal of the training which the boys received. Boys studied reading, writing, and some mathematics. They were expected to know Greek. If a boy wanted a finished education, especially in public speaking, he went to Greece to study. Cicero, the famous Roman orator, went to Rhodes, an island inhabited by the Greeks, to complete his education.

THE SCHOOL. The Roman boy did not go to public school, nor did all boys get their education in the same way. In some

*Courtesy B. F. Williamson*

**A Chariot Race in Ancient Rome**

Do you think an automobile race is as exciting and dangerous as a chariot race?

instances boys went to the homes of schoolmasters where they received instruction. The boys paid the schoolmaster for teaching them. Frequent whippings were a regular part of the training. Some Roman boys did not need to leave their homes to go to school, for when the time came to begin schooling, a Greek slave was purchased who could give the necessary instruction at home.

## ROMAN AMUSEMENTS

THE CIRCUS. The Romans were fond of various kinds of spectacles. The circus was a favorite attraction. At the circus the Romans could witness thrilling chariot races. A chariot is a light, two-wheeled wagon drawn by two, four, or six horses. Several chariots were entered in each race. The length of the course was about four miles. To cover the course, the charioteers had to drive their horses around the track seven times. Racing about the track at breakneck speed, and trying to be on the inside at the turn, demanded great daring on the part

*Courtesy B. F. Williamson*

**Thumbs Down**

The victorious gladiator looks to the spectators for the sign of mercy, "thumbs up"; but the sign is "thumbs down."

of the drivers. Frequently there were spills, when horses and charioteers were seriously hurt.

THE GLADIATORS. Many Romans, however, were not satisfied with chariot races. They wanted to see spectacles that were even more dangerous. Performances where a human life was almost certain to be taken became a favorite form of amusement among the Romans. For this kind of entertainment they went to the amphitheater to see men called gladiators fight with deadly weapons until one of them was mortally wounded. Sometimes two bands of gladiators fought instead of a single pair. When a gladiator was so seriously wounded that he could no longer fight, his conqueror would look up at the spectators to see whether his poor foe was to live. The onlookers signaled with their thumbs. Thumbs down meant death.

For their spectacles the Romans built huge structures. The Circus Maximus in Rome was famous through the ancient world. The Colosseum, a great stone grandstand or amphitheater, circular in form and seating perhaps 50,000 people, was the scene of the deadly combats between gladiators. There, too, many of the Christian martyrs died for their faith.

THE ROMAN BATHS. The Romans, like the Greeks, insisted on the care of the body. In place of the Greek gymnasium, the Romans had the baths. These were more than mere bathing places. Attached to the baths were rooms for taking exercises, and usually a park was close by, where the Roman gentleman could meet his friends. Barber shops and other conveniences were located at the baths also. The bath served the important Roman as a social and athletic club.

## ROMAN ACCOMPLISHMENTS

THE ROMANS AS BUILDERS. Although Roman buildings are less beautiful than Greek buildings they are often more practical. For instance, the system of roofing used by the Romans shows what practical people they were. The Romans considered wooden roofs unsatisfactory for large buildings. Such a roof cannot be very strong. It is liable to take fire, and a fire in an ancient city was a serious matter. The cities had neither good fire engines nor a high-pressure water system. Therefore, the Romans used a roof of brick or concrete wherever possible.

THE ARCH AND THE DOME. The Romans found that by using a system of arches, a permanent roof could be built. If the Romans wished to cover an oblong space they made a wooden form upon which stone arches were built in the shape of a half barrel. This device is often called a barrel vault,

**The Pantheon**

> The front of this Roman temple shows Greek influence in design but the domed roof is entirely Roman.

because the roof, when seen from below, looks like the half section of a barrel taken lengthwise. Our stone bridges are built in this fashion.

Of course, a barrel vault would not do for covering a large square area. However, covering a square area was not too great a problem for the Romans to solve, for they knew how to build domes. Very likely Roman soldiers learned how to build arches and domes while on military campaigns in the East. Later ages in turn learned this art from the Romans.

Brick was a favorite material with the Romans. Concrete, which is so important to us today, was also in general use. It is evident that the Romans improved upon the Greek builders in two ways: they used new types of building construction and they made use of a greater variety of materials.

THE ROMAN FORUM. The finest buildings in Rome were built about the Forum. Originally this was the market place

**The Forum**

A modern idea of what this famous part of Rome looked like. Have you seen modern buildings like these?

and the trading center of the city. It soon became the site of the shrine of Janus. The door of the shrine of Janus was kept open during periods of war. The temple of Vesta was located in the Roman Forum as well as other splendid public buildings. At either end of the Forum were triumphal arches, erected in memory of great Roman victories. Nearby was the Colosseum.

ROMAN AQUEDUCTS. A large city must have a constant and plentiful supply of pure water. Rome was a large city. How could water be supplied to Rome's numerous population? The Romans obtained their water supply by going out into the country, sometimes great distances, and bringing the water to Rome through a system of aqueducts.

The aqueduct itself was simply a covered brick channel. The water had to flow to the city of Rome, and the country between the source of supply and the city was far from level. Therefore the Romans were forced sometimes to tunnel hills or in other places to raise the aqueduct above ground to keep the proper grade. To have the aqueduct at the right height when crossing low or marshy ground called for great engineering skill on the part of the builders. The difficulty was overcome by supporting the water pipes on a series of arches.

The city of Rome could not have grown to such a size, unless the Roman engineers had been capable of solving the problem of Rome's water supply. A part of this splendid system, after two thousand years, is still able to be used.

ROMAN ROADS. We are justly proud of our state roads. The Romans were likewise proud of their system of public roads. When a new territory was acquired, the Romans set to work to see that it could be reached easily. The saying that "All roads lead to Rome," was a fact. The Roman roads reached out into every part of the Empire, and so well built were they that some of them are still used.

THE LATIN LANGUAGE. The Latin Language was the language of Rome. Our own language makes use of hundreds of Latin words or words of Latin origin. Latin is used today by scholars and scientists over all the world. For example, men who study about plants, botanists, will give a plant a Latin name. Then a botanist in Italy or in France or in the United States will know just which plant is meant although in the language of each of these countries the plant will be called a different name. Latin is the language of the Church. Doctors use it. Lawyers employ Latin for legal terms. Many great educators believe that one must study Latin to have a thorough education.

ROMAN WRITERS AND PHILOSOPHERS. The Romans wrote books but their books were probably not as many nor as fine as those written by the Greeks. The Romans liked to write history and to tell of the glorious past of the city. Roman writers were especially boastful about Rome's military history. Cæsar wrote a splendid account of the conquest of Gaul. Tacitus tells us much about the Germans. It seems as though the Romans were determined that the world should know of Roman valor, hence the number of historians. The Romans liked speech-making. For them, the ideal man was the orator. Cicero was the most famous of their orators. Virgil and Horace were their best known poets.

ROMAN LAW. Boys and girls sometimes imagine that the "law" means merely that one must not walk on the grass when there is a sign that says "Keep off." The law does refer to such things but it means a great deal more. Law is the foundation of society. It enters into all the business we do; in fact, it covers most of our dealings with our fellow citizens. As civilized men living in what we call organized society, law is so necessary that without it we would become savages.

Many scholars think that we ought to remember the Romans chiefly for the system of law they gave us, because everyone benefits by Roman law in some way. A number of our most important ideas about contracts have come down from the Romans.

THE ROMAN IDEAL OF GOVERNMENT. The vast expanse of the Roman Empire was successfully ruled by a single city. That is, next to their system of laws, possibly the greatest accomplishment of the Romans. Have you not noticed the name of the Roman Emperor, the Cæsar, as he was called, in the Gospels? It is indeed remarkable that the Cæsar who lived in Rome a long, long distance from Palestine should be mentioned in the pages of the Gospels. This is because Palestine was under the control of Rome somewhat as India today is under the

**The Age of Augustus**

Art and architecture flourished. Splendid buildings and fine roads were constructed. Literature held a high place but most important of all, during this reign Our Lord was born in Bethlehem.

control of England. That Rome should have ruled her enormous empire without great injustice was one of her greatest achievements.

GREEK ACCOMPLISHMENTS AND ROMAN IMPROVEMENTS. The Greeks had some fine ideas about democracy. They believed in the rule of the people,—though not the rule of all the people; for the Greeks had slaves. Their state, however, was small—the Greek city-state. Citizenship in the Greek city-state was a matter of birth and family. The kind of government which flourished in the city-states of Greece was narrow. The Roman Empire, on the other hand, was able to unite under a single government the peoples from Britain to

Arabia. The Roman Empire lasted long enough to teach the world the importance of law, order, and unity. As Greece had prepared the world for the coming of Our Lord by teaching men to think alike on certain subjects, Rome prepared the way in another manner by providing a single government.

ROMAN ACCOMPLISHMENTS. Most of the splendid achievements of the Greeks, the Romans preserved for future ages. Rome, though a conqueror, was not a destroyer. The Romans were both preservers and builders of civilization. In doing practical things, no nation has quite surpassed the Romans. They were great soldiers, lawyers, builders. It is true, there is much in Roman history that is unattractive and even hateful. But the world owes much to Rome. Above all else, Rome has this glorious boast: the whole world was at peace under the undisputed rule of Rome when our Lord came. Thus was the way prepared for the preaching of the Gospel. *"And it came to pass that in those days there went out a decree from Cæsar Augustus; that the whole world should be enrolled." "And the Word was made Flesh and dwelt amongst us."*

---

## ORAL DRILL

1. How did the Romans regard their ancestors?
2. How was building regulated in Rome?
3. What feelings had the Romans towards labor?
4. For what was Cicero famous?
5. What was one of the principal purposes of Roman roads?
6. Were Roman girls educated?
7. What kind of treatment did the pupils receive in Roman schools?
8. What did the Romans have resembling our modern club?
9. What was the language of Rome?

## OBJECTIVE TESTS

TEST 1: Choice Test.
Select the best answer in each:
1. The Roman religion was one of (no gods, many gods)
2. The Latin language is the foundation of (German, French)
3. The Vestal Virgins were (priestesses, school teachers)
4. Roman boys studied (German, Greek)
5. (Charioteers, Jockeys) raced in the Circus Maxims

TEST 2: Similarities Test.
Pick the two items in each of the following which are alike. Be able to explain how each is alike.
1. Circus Maximus, Colosseum, Forum
2. dome, arch, concrete road
3. Julius Cæsar, Cicero, Pope Gregory
4. Augustus, Virgil, Horace

TEST 3: Historical Vocabulary.
Pick out the best definition in each of the following:
1. What was an aqueduct?
   a) a race track
   b) an athletic field
   c) a covered brick trough
   d) a Roman garden
2. What is meant by a gladiator?
   a) a professional fighter
   b) a lion-tamer
   c) an amateur runner
   d) a Roman soldier
3. What was the Colosseum?
   a) an amphitheater
   b) a Roman lake
   c) a Roman statue
   d) a Roman palace
4. What was the Circus Maximus?
   a) an aqueduct
   b) a great tent for animals
   c) a Roman road
   d) an athletic field

## QUESTIONS THAT MAKE YOU THINK

1. Name two Roman contributions to civilization.
2. "Our modern calendar shows the influence of Julius Cæsar." Give a reason for agreeing, or disagreeing.
3. Compare the Roman and Greek religion.
4. How was the Roman home different from your own home?
5. "All work was done by slaves." State one bad effect of this practice.

6. Why did some Romans study in Greece?
7. Define "gladiator."
8. Describe the amusements of the Romans.
9. Show how Roman roads helped the Empire.
10. "The Romans were great lawgivers." Explain fully.

## ACTIVITIES

1. From wood make a Roman triumphal arch.
2. From wood make a model of a Roman aqueduct.
3. Draw a sketch of sports at the Circus Maximus.
4. Suppose you had a dream about a thrilling chariot race. Tell the class about it.
5. In your diary write about "A Day in Old Rome."
6. Draw a tree entitled "Latin Language." Label the various f r u i t "Italian Language," "Portuguese Language," "French," "Spanish." Label the leaves with original titles, showing the influence of Latin today.
7. Make a chart comparing Greek and Roman accomplishments. Decorate each item with original pictures or sayings.
8. Have a little pageant in class to illustrate "Our Debt to Rome."
9. Tell the class about a "movie" you saw about ancient Rome.
10. Paste in your scrapbook pictures and clippings about Roman civilizations.

## QUESTIONS THAT TEST YOUR CHARACTER

1. Is a gladiator's fight very much different from a modern boxing bout? Explain.
2. Was it wise for Romans to despise labor? Explain.
3. Mention two bad habits of the Romans; two good habits.
4. Give one lesson which the life of the Romans teaches you.
5. What does the Roman expression mean, "a sound mind in a sound body"?

## IMPORTANT WORDS

| | |
|---|---|
| dome | Julian calendar |
| arch | Roman law |
| aqueduct | Latin language |
| Colosseum | Circus Maximus |

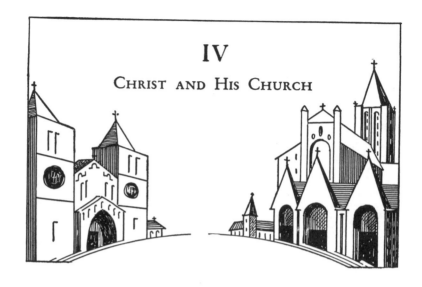

# IV

## CHRIST AND HIS CHURCH

### AIM

To understand that Christ in the world is the most important fact in history.

To understand that the Catholic Church is the mystical Body of Christ.

MORE THAN 1900 years ago, Jesus Christ the Son of God, came upon earth to save mankind. After His atoning death on the cross He rose glorious and immortal. Before leaving this world to go to the Father, Our Lord founded the Catholic Church and gave to that Church the command to "teach all nations." The life and teachings of Jesus Christ and the existence in the world of the Catholic Church which is His mystical Body has changed the whole story of mankind and will continue to affect society "until the consummation of the world."

# IV

## *Part 1:* THE SAVIOUR OF THE WORLD

The coming of Christ into the world is the central fact in all history. For long years before this great event took place, the knowledge that a Saviour was to redeem the world had been carefully guarded by the Chosen People. At length, just as the prophets had foretold, Jesus was born "in Bethlehem of Juda."

THE SAVIOUR'S LIFE. The wonderful life of the Son of God is known to us from the gospels. We have often heard how "He went about doing good"; "He became like to us in all things save sin." The Life of Our Lord may be divided into three parts; the hidden life, the public life, and His Passion and death. The hidden life of Our Lord was spent in Nazareth with His mother and with Saint Joseph. When Our Lord was thirty He began His public life.

THE PUBLIC LIFE. During His Public Life Our Lord journeyed up and down Palestine. He worked many miracles; the most awful diseases vanished before His divine power; He raised the dead to life by a mere word. Then having taught men the truths they ought to know for salvation and having trained His apostles, He was ready to die for mankind. And so the public life was concluded with the passion and death of Our Saviour.

THE RESURRECTION. After Our Lord died, He was taken down from the cross and placed in the tomb. Here He remained

**Public Life of Christ**

**Death on the Cross**

*Drawn expressly for "The Old World and America"*

**Resurrection of the Saviour**     **Spreading Christ's Church**

102

three days, until Easter Sunday when He arose glorious and immortal. The Resurrection of Our Lord is certain proof that He is God. Our Lord then spent forty days upon earth before His ascension. During His last days on earth, He taught His Apostles in every particular the work they were to do. They were told to "teach all nations"; to "preach the gospel to every creature." Our Lord promised that He would be with His Church until the end of time. When it was time for Him to leave, He called His Apostles about Him and having blessed them, He ascended to His Father.

THE BIRTH OF THE CHURCH. From a human standpoint the Apostles were badly fitted for success. But Our Lord knew what they lacked and He promised to send them the Holy Ghost who would "teach them all things." This promise of Our Lord was fulfilled on Pentecost Sunday, which was the fiftieth day after the Resurrection of Our Lord. On Pentecost the Apostles received the Holy Ghost. Pentecost, therefore, is the birthday of the Church.

## OBJECTIVE TESTS

TEST 1: Completion Test.
   Write the numbers 1 to 10 on a sheet of paper. Next to each write the missing word or words.
   1. Jesus was born in the town of . . . . . . . . . . . . . . . . . . . . . . . . . . . . .
   2. The Life of Our Lord may be divided into . . . . . . parts.
   3. The hidden life of Our Lord was spent with . . . . . . . . . . . . . and with . . . . . . . . . . . . . . . . . . . . . . . . . . . .
   4. When Our Lord was . . . . . . . . . years of age, He began His public life.
   5. During His Public Life Our Lord journeyed up and down the country called . . . . . . . . . . . . . . . . . . . . . . . . . . . . . . . . . . . . . . . .
   6. The twelve specially chosen followers of Our Lord were called the . . . . . . . . . . . . . . . . . . . . . . . . . . . .
   7. The Resurrection of Our Lord took place on . . . . . . . . . . . . .
   8. The Resurrection is proof that Jesus is . . . . . . . . . . . . . . . . .

9. Before His Ascension Our Lord spent . . . . . . . . . . . days on earth after His Resurrection.
10. The birthday of the Church is . . . . . . . . . . . . . . . . . . . . . . . .

TEST 2: Sequence of Events.
   Arrange each event in the order of time:
      Our Lord's Resurrection
      Our Lord's Life in Nazareth
      Three Wise Men come from the East
      Our Lord works many miracles during His Public Life
      Our Lord is Crucified
      Our Lord is Scourged
      Our Lord ascends to His Father
      The Feast of Pentecost
      Our Lord is placed in the Tomb

## QUESTIONS THAT MAKE YOU THINK

1. Why do we call Jesus Christ "Our Saviour"?
2. Why should we read the Gospels?
3. We say "Jesus Christ is God." How did He prove that He is God?
4. Why is Easter Sunday an important day?
5. Our Lord promised He would be with His Church "until the end of time." Why is this promise very important?
6. "The birthday of the Church was on Christmas Day." Do you agree? Give a reason for your answer.
7. Make a list of five of Our Lord's miracles.
8. Why do Catholics pray to St. Joseph to ask God for the blessing of a happy death?
9. Why is Good Friday an important day for Christians?
10. Prove that Jesus Christ is God.

## QUESTIONS THAT TEST YOUR CHARACTER

1. Make a list of five virtues of Jesus which every boy and girl should try to copy.
2. Give one lesson you should learn from the coming of the Holy Ghost to the Apostles.
3. Name two virtues of St. Joseph which every boy and girl should admire.
4. Why do we say the Holy Family was a perfect family?

## ACTIVITIES

1. Draw a picture of the Holy Family at Nazareth.
2. Use the name Saint Joseph to describe his character. Thus:

S acred Protector
A lways Watchful—and so forth
I
N
T

J
O
S
E
P
H

3. Make a wooden Cross to hang in your bedroom. Try to imitate the cross in your parish church.
4. Get 12 little dolls. Dress them as Twelve Apostles. Put the name on each.
5. Make the Stations of the Cross. Then, make a small copy of one of these Stations from soap, or wood. Others in the class can make other Stations.

## WORD LIST

| | |
|---|---|
| Saviour | ascension |
| apostle | miracle |
| gospels | Easter Sunday |
| immortal | Pentecost Sunday |

# IV

## *Part 2:* THE CATHOLIC CHURCH

After having received the Holy Ghost the Apostles feared nothing. The world became the "vineyard of the Lord" to the Apostles. Each Apostle expected to bring the knowledge and love of Christ to the people of the district under his charge.

SAINT PETER AND ROME. When Our Lord founded the Church, He made St. Peter the head of it. St. Peter journeyed to Rome which was made the headquarters of the Church. St. Peter was, of course, the first bishop of Rome. The Pope who lives in Rome today is his direct successor. He represents Christ just as St. Peter did. St. Peter was martyred at Rome, 67 A.D.

THE APOSTLE OF THE GENTILES. Soon after the Apostles began their work of bringing people into the Church a remarkable man was converted to Christ. This man was Saint Paul whose name originally was Saul. Saul was a Jew. He was sincerely devoted to his Jewish religion. When he saw many among the Jews becoming Christians, he determined to use all his energy to stop what he then thought was a terrible act of disloyalty. But by a miracle Saul learned how mistaken he had been. Thereafter he became deeply attached to Our Lord declaring "for me to live is Christ." His name was changed to Paul. As Paul the Apostle he made long and dangerous journeys to various parts of the Roman Empire converting the pagans to Christianity. Most of the Epistles you have read at Mass on

*Courtesy B. F. Williamson*

## To the Lions

The Christian martyrs make a holiday for pagan Rome.

Sunday have to do with churches founded by Saint Paul. Like Saint Peter, Saint Paul died at Rome, a martyr for Christ.

THE ZEAL OF THE APOSTLES. The extraordinary zeal of the Apostles, with the good example of the early Christians, brought many converts into the Church. Our Lord had told His Apostles "to teach all nations." This commission they and their successors did their best to accomplish. But the success of the Apostles was bought at a great price. Souls that were bought were paid for in martyrs' blood. At different times Christ had told the Apostles that they would be persecuted and this is exactly what did happen to them. Often they were imprisoned and finally they all suffered martyrdom except St. John. He was saved from death only by a miracle.

After the death of the Apostles the Church continued her efforts to win souls for Christ. The success of Christianity did not escape the attention of the Roman emperors. Gradually they began to see that this new force in the world was utterly

**The Catacombs**

> In these underground passages lie the bones of countless martyrs. Here the early Christians sometimes worshiped.

opposed to the unholy lives of the Romans. They also began to believe that Christianity was opposed to the Roman Empire. "The Christians must not be," they decreed. For three centuries Christianity had to fight for its very existence.

THE SUFFERINGS OF THE EARLY CHRISTIANS. The courage of the early Christians was amazing. Tens of thousands remained true to Christ in spite of the most terrible tortures. Thousands of Christians were brought into court. There the Roman judge and other officials gave them the choice of worshiping a false god or undergoing torture and even death. The true Christian always chose to suffer for Christ. Not only men and women, but even boys and girls gave up their lives for Christ. Little St. Agnes was beheaded. St. Tarsicius was beaten to death whilst protecting the Blessed Sacrament. Many Christians were thrown to the wild beasts in the Colosseum. "The

Christians to the lions!" became a familiar cry in many places throughout the Roman Empire.

THE CATACOMBS. A wonderful monument to the loyalty of the early Christians is still to be seen in the catacombs. These were long passageways dug below the surface of the earth. The length of those in Rome is said to exceed nine hundred miles. In times of persecution, the Christians sometimes met there to hold divine service. Their dead were often buried in the catacombs. The bodies of countless martyrs lie there. Interesting inscriptions are on the walls telling us of the great faith of these Christians. You will find there some beautiful sayings about Our Lord, His holy Mother, the Blessed Sacrament, and other truths of the Catholic faith.

THE EFFECT OF THE PERSECUTIONS. "The blood of the martyrs is the seed of the Church." This truth was clearly seen in the progress made by Christianity. In spite of terrible persecution the Church continued to grow. An early writer says that "the Christians are everywhere, in all classes of society, in the palace, the Senate, the Forum, and the camps of the Empire, everywhere,—except in the temples."

THE EDICT OF MILAN. The miraculous spread of Christianity continued. Then a wonderful thing happened. Constantine, a famous soldier, was declared emperor by his soldiers. However, his claim was disputed by another leader. Constantine had heard of the God of the Christians and resolved to place all his faith in Him. Then he fought a critical battle which he won. Not long after, in the year 313, Constantine issued a decree, called the Edict of Milan, by which the Christians were given full liberty to practice their religion. Before his death Constantine became a Christian.

## OBJECTIVE TESTS

TEST 1: Historical Vocabulary.

1. What were the catacombs?
    a) Roman race tracks
    b) ancient estates
    c) underground passage-
       ways
    d) palace of the emperor
2. Who were the Gentiles?
    a) ancient Hebrews
    b) a Jewish tribe
    c) a Roman religion
    d) people not Jews

3. What is an edict?
    a) an official decree
    b) a newspaper article
    c) a patriotic song
    d) any statement
4. What is an epistle?
    a) a law
    b) part of the Gospels
    c) a letter
    d) wife of an apostle

TEST 2: Sequence of Events.

Write the event in each group which happened the *longest time ago.*

1. (a) Edict of Milan, (b) conversion of Constantine, (c) Constantine declared emperor, (d) Constantine gives full liberty to Christians.
2. (a) Pentecost, (b) Easter Sunday, (c) death of St. Peter, (d) death of St. Paul.
3. (a) Saul persecutes Christians, (b) St. Paul converts pagans, (c) St. Paul founds churches, (d) St. Paul writes letters to his churches.
4. (a) St. Peter made head of Church, (b) St. Peter becomes bishop of Rome, (c) Edict of Milan, (d) death of St. John
5. (a) martyrdom of St. Paul, (b) Passion of Our Lord, (c) Christians build catacombs, (d) Holy Ghost comes to Apostles.

TEST 3: Cause and Effect Test.

Select the correct cause on each group.

1. Liberty to Christians: (a) jealousy of pagans, (b) edict of Milan, (c) desire to win votes, (d) influence of Jews.
2. The Pope represents Christ: (a) St. Peter, bishop of Rome, (b) St. Peter died at Rome, (c) Pope is elected, (d) Church must have a head.
3. Catacombs excavated: (a) Christians given toleration, (b) Constantine becomes Christian, (c) persecutions by pagans, (d) pagans become Christians.

4. Christians thrown to lions: (a) Christianity opposed to unholy pagan living, (b) Romans desired sport, (c) Christianity spread rapidly, (d) hatred of foreigners.

---

## QUESTIONS THAT MAKE YOU THINK

1. Describe (a) one likeness in the lives of St. Peter and St. Paul, (b) one difference.
2. Why is St. Paul called an Apostle?
3. Why do many people visit the catacombs today?
4. "The blood of the martyrs is the seed of the Church." Explain the meaning of this statement.
5. Why do we say the Pope is the Head of the Church?
6. "St. Peter was the Prince of the Apostles." What does this mean?
7. Why is Constantine said to have helped early Christianity?
8. Explain the effect of persecution upon the Church.
9. Why did early Christians welcome the Edict of Milan?
10. Outline the spread of the Church from Pentecost Sunday to the Edict of Milan (313 A.D.).

---

## QUESTIONS THAT TEST YOUR CHARACTER

1. Make a list of the great qualities of St. Peter.
2. Why is St. Paul regarded as a great man?
3. Do you think Constantine was a great Emperor? Give reasons for your answer.
4. Were the early Christians better people than Christians of today? Explain your answer.
5. Explain one reason why persecution failed to destroy Christianity.

---

## ACTIVITIES

1. Tell the class of some story you read about the early Christians.
2. Dramatize "the Emperor and the Edict of Milan."
3. Dress dolls like early Christians. Show that they were in all classes of the Empire.
4. Draw a picture of the catacombs.
5. Describe an imaginary visit to the catacombs.

6. Suppose you were an eye-witness of the early persecutions. Tell the class what you saw.
7. Using the letters of his name to begin a different adjective, describe the character of St. Paul.

S

T

P

A

U

L

8. Read one of St. Paul's Epistles to the class. Explain what it means. Use your own words.

## TOPICS FOR DISCUSSION

1. St. Paul did more for the Church than St. Peter.
2. Constantine was a pagan, not a Christian.
3. The persecutions really helped the Church.
4. The rapid spread of Christianity was a miracle.

## WORD LIST

| | |
|---|---|
| martyr | persecution |
| St. Peter | catacombs |
| St. Paul | epistle |
| Pope | edict |
| Gentiles | Constantine |

# IV

*Part 3:* SHEPHERDS OF THE FLOCK

Our Saviour had warned His followers to "beware of false prophets" for He knew that in every age there would be false teachers. These false teachers would try to coax people to give up the Catholic religion. The Church had the help of wise men called Fathers and Doctors to combat the wrong ideas.

FATHERS AND DOCTORS OF THE CHURCH. The Church had her champions who defended the truth of her teachings. These leaders have been called the Fathers of the Church. Some were given the special title, Doctor of the Church. Many of the Fathers and Doctors of the Church lived in Rome and in the western part of the old Roman Empire. Some, like Saint John Chrysostom (347-407), dwelt in Constantinople, or in the eastern portion of the Roman Empire. All of the Fathers of the Church were learned men and most, though not all, were bishops. Upon those writers who were especially learned, the Church has bestowed the title Doctor of the Church. The title Doctor of the Church has also been granted to certain great teachers who lived after the first centuries of the Church's existence.

SAINT AMBROSE (340-397) AND SAINT AUGUSTINE OF HIPPO (354-430). Saint Ambrose and Saint Augustine were Doctors of the Church. Saint Ambrose was bishop of Milan but his influence, because of his writings, extended far

*Courtesy B. F. Williamson*

**St. Monica and St. Augustine            St. Jerome**

beyond the limits of that city. Augustine, a young lawyer from Hippo, in North Africa, went to Milan to teach. There he met Saint Ambrose who baptized him. From that time all Augustine's great talents were given to the service of the Church. He wrote various books including a famous text which has the title, *The City of God*. This great book answers the objections of the pagans against Christianity. He made it clear that the decline of Rome was due to paganism although many pagan Romans had tried to blame Christianity.

SAINT JEROME (340-420) AND THE BIBLE. Saint Jerome, another Doctor of the Church, lived in many places in the Roman Empire. He visited Rome but his heart was in the East. Some time after his ordination, Jerome decided to retire to Bethlehem. Here he spent the last years of his life collecting the books of the Bible, arranging them in proper

*Titian*

## CHRIST'S LESSON IN PATRIOTISM

"Render unto Caesar the things that are Caesar's, and unto God the things that are God's." These words spoken by our Saviour mean that we must be loyal to our Country and true to our God.

order, and translating many of these books into Latin. Saint Jerome's edition of the Bible is called the Vulgate.

THE PROGRESS OF THE CHURCH. The Emperor Constantine through the Edict of Milan, in 313, had freed the Church from serious persecution within the confines of the Roman Empire. The Doctors and Fathers of the Church by their influence and by their learning were helping the Church to grow strong. In the meantime, outside the boundary of the Roman Empire, a danger to the Church and to civilization was threatening. Tens of thousands of barbarians were ready to invade the Roman Empire. Except for the fact that Christianity had come into the world, the great civilization of the ancient world would have been destroyed.

THE POWER OF CHRISTIANITY. The power of Christianity to save civilization is one of the contributions of the Church to the world. There are other outstanding benefits of Christianity which, as students of history, we should know.

(1) Christ taught that all men are equal before God. This teaching is the foundation of political equality. The freedom we now enjoy is based on it.

(2) Our Lord was a poor laboring man. When He came into the world, labor and poverty were despised. His example taught men to respect honest toil.

(3) When Christ came, the happiness of people was based almost entirely on the pleasures of the world, some of which were most degrading. Christ taught men how to enjoy a happiness that is based on being good. That is the only true happiness.

(4) Before Our Lord's coming, womanhood was held in low esteem. His love for His Blessed Mother, and the esteem in which she is held by the Church, did more than anything else to raise womanhood to its proper dignity. The beautiful ex-

ample of the Holy Family taught people the great importance of good family life.

(5) Our Lord had taught the absolute necessity for all men to love one another. Following Christ's commands the Church established hospitals for the sick, homes for the homeless, and shelters for little children whose parents no longer could take care of them. This is sometimes called the social mission of Christianity.

---

## OBJECTIVE TESTS

---

TEST 1: Cause and Effect.

In column A is a list of causes. Pick out 2 items in column B which are the effects of each cause.

| Column A | Column B |
|---|---|
| (1) All men are equal before God | ( ) respect for womanhood |
| | ( ) the secret of real happiness |
| (2) Our Lord was a poor laboring man | |
| | ( ) the basis of democratic freedom |
| (3) Men should help others and do good | ( ) respect for honest work |
| | ( ) necessity for living wage |
| (4) Christ loved His Blessed Mother | ( ) love for parents |
| | ( ) pleasures of the world are not enough |
| | ( ) human beings have the right to a fair trial by jury |

TEST 2: Completion Test.

1. The Church calls certain very learned writers . . . . . . . . . . . . of the Church.
2. St. Ambrose was Bishop of . . . . . . . . . . . . . . . . .
3. St. Augustine wrote the famous text called . . . . . . . . . . . . . . . .
4. . . . . . . . . . . . . . . . . . . . . was the author of the Latin Vulgate edition of the Bible.
5. The Emperor . . . . . . . . . . . . . . . . . . . . freed Christians from serious persecution within the Empire.
6. St. . . . . . . . . . . . . . . . . . . . answered the objections of the pagans to Christianity.

7. The great leaders of the early Church have been called
. . . . . . . . . . . . . . . . . . . . . . . . . . . . . . of the Church.
8. St. Augustine was baptized by . . . . . . . . . . . . . . . . . . . . . . .
9. St. John Chrysostum dwelt in the City of . . . . . . . . . . . . ..
10. St. Augustine came from the town of . . . . . . . . . . . . . . . . . .

TEST 2: Matching Test.

1. Apostle of Gentiles           (   ) St. Jerome
2. Eastern portion of Empire     (   ) St. Augustine
3. Northern Italy                (   ) St. Ambrose
4. A young lawyer in his youth(   ) St. Paul
5. Translated Bible into Latin   (   ) St. John Chrysostom

## QUESTIONS THAT MAKE YOU THINK

1. What is the difference between the title of "Doctor" and "Father"?
2. Name one great contribution of St. Augustine.
3. Why did the Church need champions during the early centuries?
4. Does the Church need champions today? Explain your answer.
5. Compare the work of St. Jerome and St. Augustine.
6. How did the Fathers and Doctors help the Church grow?
7. Our Lord was a poor laboring man. Why is it important to remember this?
8. Mention two great benefits of Christianity to civilization.
9. Make a list of four great leaders of the early Church. State the contribution of each.
10. "Christianity saved civilization." Explain this statement.

## QUESTIONS THAT TEST YOUR CHARACTER

1. Should we respect the weak? Explain.
2. Why should we respect womanhood?
3. "Our Lord's life showed that he loved the working man." Tell why this is true.
4. "Christ taught the equality of all men before God." Why is this idea important?
5. "St. Augustine was a real fighter." Why is this true?

## ACTIVITIES

1. On a large piece of cardboard make a list of the great contributions of Christianity.
2. Read a few lines from the *City of God* to the class. Try to explain them to the class. Your teacher will gladly help you, if they are too hard.
3. Draw a picture of the Latin Vulgate edition of the Bible.
4. Dramatize the conversion of St. Augustine.
5. Interview your teacher, priest, or parent on the topic: "What does the Church teach about the rights of the worker." Tell the class about it.

## TOPICS FOR DISCUSSION

1. The Church is the friend of the worker.
2. The early Church saved civilization.
3. St. Augustine is the greatest of the Doctors of the Church.
4. It is not so necessary today to defend the Church as it was in the early centuries.

## WORD LIST

| | |
|---|---|
| Father | political equality |
| Doctor | poverty |
| City of God | happiness |
| Vulgate | dignity of womanhood |

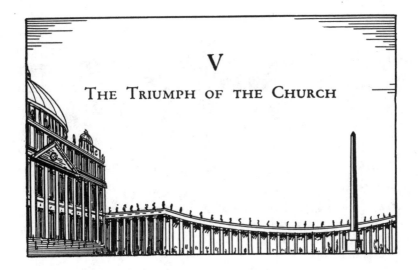

# V

## THE TRIUMPH OF THE CHURCH

### AIM

To show how the Teutonic peoples acquired the gifts of the Romans.

To show how the church saved western civilization after the fall of the Roman Empire.

THE mighty Roman Empire decayed and finally came to an end in Western Europe. Meanwhile the German tribes for various reasons crossed into the Roman Empire. The tribes would probably have completely destroyed the civilizations of Greece and Rome except for the Church. The Church converted these tribes. Great kings rose to help the Church in the struggle against disorder.

# V

## *Part 1:* THE AGE OF INVASIONS

The Roman Empire was slowly but surely growing so weak that it was only a matter of time when a more powerful people would conquer it. The people who were to do this were the Germans who were Teutonic barbarians of northern Europe.

---

## THE GREAT THOUSAND YEARS

---

THE TEUTONIC PEOPLES. You remember that Julius Cæsar had great difficulty in conquering the people who lived east of the Rhine and north of the Danube. These folk were the Teutons or Germans. There were many thousands of them. They lived in groups or tribes. You must not think they were the same as the people who live in modern Germany. It is true that the inhabitants of Germany are descendants of this race. But the Teutonic peoples we are to study about spread over most of Europe in later times. Their descendants form a goodly part of the population of practically every country in western Europe or what was once the Roman Empire. For this reason we say that the Teutons succeeded or took the place of the Romans.

QUALITIES OF THE TEUTONIC PEOPLES. The Romans always spoke of the Germans as barbarians, but they were a sturdy race. The men were big and strong and handsome. They

*Courtesy New York Public Library*

**The Teutons in their Forest Home**
The Warrior took first place among these people.

had fair hair and blue eyes, quite in contrast to the dark Italians. Brought up in the forests and accustomed to hardships from their earliest years, the Teutons were trained to fearlessness. Their religion also had an effect upon their character. It was the religion of a warlike people. We are reminded of their gods by some of the names of the days in the week. Wednesday is named for Woden, the king of the gods, while Thursday is named for Thor, the god of thunder.

THE TEUTONS IN THEIR FOREST HOME. The Teuton homes were very unlike the homes of the people in the Roman Empire. The houses of the Teutons were merely huts. One style resembled somewhat an Indian wigwam but in place of a covering of skins, the Teutons used thatch. A more elaborate type also was in use. For this a stone wall was built, circular in form; then a roof of thatch was placed above it. Perhaps the commonest form of dwelling was a simple hut made of logs.

Each hut was usually surrounded by a small patch of cleared land. Huts were built in clusters forming villages. Beyond the circle of huts was the common pasture land belonging to the village. The villages of the Teutons were usually not permanent for the warriors moved about too much.

OCCUPATIONS OF THE TEUTONS. The Teutons cultivated some grain and corn but perhaps their main occupation was cattle raising. Their wealth they reckoned in terms of cattle. To provide more food and also to obtain materials for clothing the Teutons hunted in the forest for wild boar, deer, and antelope. Except for hunting they had few amusements. The Teutons prided themselves upon their ability as warriors. They were unusually determined. They had a desire for liberty and respect for women. But they had vices. They frequently gambled, even gambling their freedom. Sometimes they drank to excess intoxicating liquors. They were often brutal and coarse.

TEUTON GOVERNMENT. The Teuton government was simple in form and under the control of all the freemen of the village. Their slaves, of course, had no rights. All the warriors were equal. They had kings or leaders but a man could hold such a position only because the freemen permitted it. All matters concerning the welfare of the tribe were discussed in a meeting held in the open air. If the warriors approved of a measure urged by the king or one of the chiefs, they made a loud noise by striking their shields with their spears or battle axes. They showed their disapproval by shouting. While each village managed its own affairs a certain number of villages banded themselves into a larger unit called a "hundred." The clan or tribe was composed of "hundreds."

THE ENTRANCE OF THE TEUTONS INTO THE ROMAN EMPIRE. For some years Teutons or Germans had been

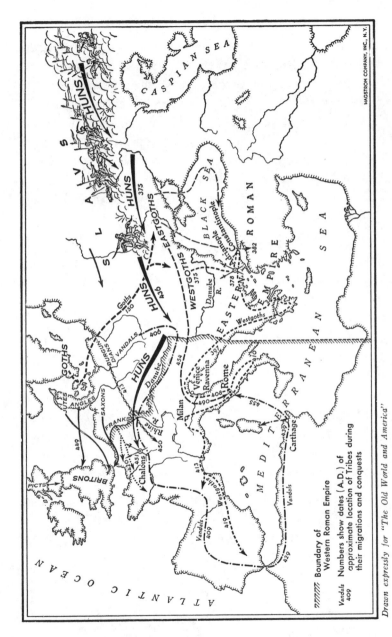

*Drawn expressly for "The Old World and America"*

**Map of the Teutonic Invasions** Refer to this map as you read about the various tribes.

employed as soldiers in the Roman army. When the Teutonic tribes who lived across the Rhine decided to move into the territory of the Roman Empire there was nothing to stop them. Their own kinsmen who were fighting in the Roman army could not be expected to repel these invaders. The Romans had to allow some Germans, as they called them, to cross the borders of the Roman Empire. Gradually the number of Germans in the Roman Empire became very great. At one time or another they would have taken possession of a large part of it. But taking possession of the Roman Empire was forced upon them perhaps sooner than they expected.

THE HUNS. More and more the Teutons felt forced to invade the Roman Empire to save themselves. In the fourth century a fierce race of men from Asia, called Huns, moved in behind the eastern Teutonic tribes. The Huns were the most terrible invaders Europe ever saw. Wherever they went they left a trail of destruction. They rode into battle carrying on their long lances the heads of enemies, as if to tell their foes what was to happen to them. Even the Teutons were afraid of the Huns. Teutonic tribes in eastern Europe called Goths, had to face the Huns. Some of the Goths, especially the East Goths, surrendered to the Huns. The West Goths feared the Huns far more than they feared the Romans, so they resolved to invade the Roman Empire, thus getting away from the Huns.

THE BATTLE OF ADRIANOPLE. The Teutons swarmed across the borders of the Roman Empire. The Romans, unwilling to permit this invasion, gave battle. The struggle between the Romans and the Goths took place at Adrianople. The Romans met defeat and their Emperor, Valens, was killed (378). Thus the Goths saved themselves from the Huns. The Huns, however, had not finished with Europe. We shall meet them later. Meanwhile we shall follow the Goths.

*Drawn expressly for "The Old World and America".*

### The Huns on a Raid

Is it any wonder this fierce tribe was dreaded by everyone?

THE RESULT OF THE BATTLE OF ADRIANOPLE. The next Roman Emperor, Theodosius, by name, made peace with the Goths. He gave them some territory south of the Danube on condition that they remain there peacefully. The Goths, however, preferred fighting to farming. While Theodosius was alive they kept to the bargain; after his death the Goths rose against the Romans. The Romans had no leader, while the Goths had a good one. He had been trained by the Romans themselves, for he had been a Roman soldier. His name was Alaric.

Alaric led the Goths on various expeditions and finally decided that he would march into Italy and capture Rome. Alaric, the barbarian, at the head of a band of plundering Goths, captured Rome, the mistress of the ancient world!

THE SPREAD OF THE TEUTONS OVER EUROPE. The success of Alaric and the Goths in Italy was repeated by other Teutonic tribes in many different parts of Europe. Spain and

France were conquered by Teutonic tribes. Africa was visited by the Teutons and also England. Often Teutonic tribes gave their names to territories or whole countries which they conquered. Thus, Lombardy in Italy, Jutland and Denmark in northern Europe were named for Teutonic tribes. Burgundy and Normandy in France have Teutonic names. This is also true of France and England. France takes its name from the Franks, England from the Angles.

THE TEUTON CONQUEST OF BRITAIN. You remember that Julius Cæsar conquered Britain for Rome. It was inhabited by a Celtic people called the Britons. Since the time of Cæsar's conquest, a part of the island had been under the control of the Romans. To enforce order and to protect the Britons from the wilder tribes in the north, the Romans had kept soldiers in Britain. When Alaric was besieging Rome (410) these Roman soldiers had to be recalled to protect Rome. Now, the Britons were a prey to their enemies from the north. The Britons then sent to Europe for aid. Their appeal was answered by a number of warriors belonging to a tribe of Teutons called Jutes. Under their leaders, Hengist and Horsa, the Jutes crossed the channel. They not only helped defend the Britons but took possession of a part of the island. Later, fighting men from two other Teutonic tribes, called Angles and Saxons, crossed over into Britain. England is named after the Angles, who called it Angleland. Thus the Teutons settled in Britain.

THE REAPPEARANCE OF THE HUNS. Let us now see what happened to the Huns, those fierce fighters from Asia. For a time they were satisfied to stay on the lands that belonged to the East Goths. This quiet life did not suit them. A cruel man named Attila became their chief. Thereafter the Huns became more dangerous each day. Attila moved westward. Nothing could stay him. It seemed as though the Huns

© *William H. Sadlier, Inc.*

## The Pope and the Huns

St. Leo the great Pope overawes Attila the "Scourge of Europe."

would overthrow both the Teutons and the Romans. Fortunately in the year 451 A.D., the Huns were severely defeated at Chalons, France. Attila, however, was not crushed. He then turned south into Italy. Hearing of his approach, some of the people in northeastern Italy fled to a group of islands just off the coast. This settlement became Venice, the city that has canals for streets.

ATTILA AT ROME. Attila's idea in entering Italy was to capture Rome. There is no doubt that he could have done this easily. The people defending Rome could scarcely resist so strong an invader. Rome was saved through the courage of Pope St. Leo. He went to the Hun camp where his very presence so awed the terrible Attila that he agreed to leave Italy. Thus Italy was saved from utter ruin. The Huns went away and troubled Europe no more.

THE END OF THE ROMAN EMPIRE, 476 A.D. The Teutons became very active in Italy after the Huns left. The power of old Rome was almost gone. In the year 476 A.D. a remarkable thing happened. The Roman Emperor Augustulus was deposed. His place was taken by a Teuton chief, Odoacer. This change of emperors marks the end of the old line of Roman Emperors in the West. In the East emperors continued to rule in Constantinople, but the Roman Empire was ending. This change, sometimes called the "Fall of the Roman Empire," did not take place suddenly in the year 476. The change was gradual but the year 476 is a convenient date to remember.

THE MEANING OF THE CHANGE. The fall of the Roman Empire in the West, 476 A.D., changed the course of the history of the world. Now, the ruler of the Roman Empire is not a Roman; he is a Teuton. The vast territory that formed the western part of the old Roman Empire is held by Teutonic tribes. The Teutons had actually taken the place of the Romans. One of the greatest people in history have been pushed aside. To regard this change as a great misfortune, would be a serious mistake. What Europe needed was a new race of men who would be guided by the teachings of the Catholic Church. The coming of the Teutons supplied this need.

THE BEGINNING OF THE MIDDLE AGES. The invasion of the Roman Empire by the Teutonic peoples and what is called the Fall of the Western Roman Empire, is an historical landmark. The great change just described marks the end of the ancient period. It is the beginning of a new period in the world's history, known as the Middle Ages. This period lasted for about one thousand years and so it has been called the Great Thousand Years. It was a period when the Church did great things for civilization. *Everything of value to humanity that was accomplished during this time was the result of the influence of the Catholic Church.* The first care of the Church, naturally, was to bring a knowledge of Christ and His teachings to the people of Western Europe. The Church did this through her monks and missionaries, but even while this was being accomplished a new danger threatened Western Europe. This was the spread of a pagan religion, Mohammedanism. It is named after Mohammed, the man who originated it.

## MOHAMMEDANISM

MOHAMMED, THE "PROPHET." Mohammed was an Arab. His birthplace was Mecca. As a boy, he earned a living by driving a camel in one of the many caravans that made trips across the deserts of Arabia. Camel driving is dull work; it requires little effort. As Mohammed had little else to do, he spent his spare time thinking about religions.

Young Mohammed was also interested in business and was most successful at bargain hunting. Soon he was promoted from the position of a mere camel driver to that of superintendent of an entire caravan. Then he got possession of the caravan by marrying the rich lady who owned it. Now he had his longed-for chance to make up a religion. When he was camel driving he came in contact with various religions. He knew just a little about the true religion, for he had met Christians. So he took ideas from different sources and made them into a new religion. Mohammed called his religion Islam.

THE RELIGION OF ISLAM. God is called "Allah" in the Mohammedan religion. Mohammed sums up his religion thus: "Allah is God and Mohammed is his prophet." Mohammed himself is a very important figure in this religion. The book of the Mohammedan religion is called the Koran. The Mohammedan church building is the mosque. There is one important

*Drawn expressly for "The Old World and America"*

## The Check of the Spread of Mohammedanism

Charles Martel on the morning following the victory at Tours receiving the thanks of the Christians.

teaching of this religion, namely, that those who die fighting against those who are not Mohammedans will live in their pagan heaven.

MOHAMMED AS A PREACHER. Mohammed began to preach in Mecca but he was expelled from the town. He then fled to Medina. This happened in 622 A.D., an important date. The Hejira, as his flight was called, proved to be the turning point in his career. Thereafter Mohammed was wonderfully successful. After getting a sufficiently large number of followers to make an army of good size, he began the conquest of Arabia, which was not difficult. He converted Arabia by conquering it. Mohammed died ten years after the Hejira, in 632, but the work of conquest did not stop. His generals formed a plan to conquer Europe.

THE SPREAD OF MOHAMMEDANISM. Mohammed's followers believed, as he did, that Islam should be spread by the sword. The Holy Land fell under the power of the unbelievers. Many years later (1097-1274 Christian warriors from Europe called Crusaders fought to recapture the Holy Land from the Mohammedans.) The Mohammedans then moved across north Africa, conquering it, and settling there. One of the Mohammedan generals followed the route of Hannibal through Spain. Next the Mohammedans attempted to take possession of France. In 732, the Mohammedans were beaten near Tours, in France, by the Frankish leader Charles Martel. How terrible would it have been had the victory gone to the unbelievers! It is significant that this battle was fought deep in Western Europe, in France. You can judge how successful the Mohammedans had been. They were not entirely driven out of Europe, however, for many centuries. Some, but not many, were still living there a hundred years after Columbus discovered America.

THE CHECK OF MOHAMMEDANISM. The defeat of the Mohammedans at Tours relieved Europe of a fearful danger. Meanwhile the Church had been converting the old barbarian Celtic peoples who lived in Ireland and in parts of England, as well as the Teutons, and teaching them the arts of civilization.

---

## OBJECTIVE TESTS

---

TEST 1: Selection Test.
1. The winner of the Battle of Tours was: (a) Charles Martel, (b) Attila, (c) Alaric, (d) Mohammed. . . . . . . . . . . .

2. Hengist and Horsa were the leaders of: (a) Angles, (b) Saxons, (c) Huns, (d) Jutes.  ............
3. The city of Venice was founded as a result of: (a) Mohammedan invasion, (b) invasion of the Huns, (c) a great plague, (d) the end of the Roman Empire.  ............
4. The people who lived east of the Rhine and north of the Danube were called: (a) Austrians, (b) Romans, (c) Teutons, (d) English.  ............
5. England was conquered by: (a) Goths, (b) Huns, (c) Angles, (d) Mohammedans.  ............
6. The Romans had conquered Britain under: (a) Augustus, (b) Julius Cæsar, (c) Emperor Valens, (d) Theodosius.  ............
7. The Goths made a treaty with: (a) Valens, (b) Julius Cæsar, (c) Attila, (d) Theodosius.  ............
8. Rome was saved from the Huns by: (a) Pope St. Leo, (b) St. Paul, (c) Mohammed, (d) Charles Martel.  ............
9. The Mohammedans believe in: (a) Blessed Trinity, (b) leadership of the Pope, (c) Allah, (d) many gods.  ............
10. Another word for Teutons is: (a) Franks, (b) Goths, (c) Germans, (d) Swedes.  ............

TEST 2: Matching Test.

In column "B" write the correct numbers from column "A." Write these on a piece of paper.

| Column A | | Column B |
|---|---|---|
| 1. Valens | ( ) | defeated at Chalons. |
| 2. Charles Martel | ( ) | made peace with Goths. |
| 3. Attila | ( ) | fled from Mecca. |
| 4. Romulus Augustulus | ( ) | stopped Mohammedans. |
| 5. Pope St. Leo | ( ) | sacked Rome. |
| 6. JuliusCæsar | ( ) | German god. |
| 7. Mohammed | ( ) | invaded Britain. |
| 8. Alaric | ( ) | saved Italy from the Huns. |
| 9. Theodosius | ( ) | defeated at Adrianople. |
| 10. Woden | ( ) | deposed by Germans. |

Test 3. Character Test.
Select the correct word to describe the character of each.
1. Attila: gentle, cruel, refined, pious.          . . . . . . . . . .
2. Teutons: well-educated, peaceful, crude, rich.          . . . . . . . . . . .
3. Theodosius: war-like, pious, peaceful, timid          . . . . . . . . . . .
4. Pope St. Leo: scheming, clever, rude, brave.          . . . . . . . . . . .
5. Alaric: ambitious, slow, poor, old.          . . . . . . . . . . .

Test 4: Sequence of Events.
Arrange the following events in the order of time.
1. battle of Adrianople          (          )
2. Goths cross into Empire          (          )
3. Julius Cæsar killed          (          )
4. end of Roman Empire in West          (          )
5. Hejira          (          )
6. battle of Tours          (          )
7. Crusades          (          )
8. Goths sack Rome          (          )
9. Attila at Rome          (          )
10. Battle of Chalons          (          )

## QUESTIONS THAT MAKE YOU THINK

1. Compare the religion of the Teutons with that of the Romans.
2. "The Teutons had a capacity for liberty." Explain.
3. Why were the Huns feared by the Goths?
4. "England is named after the Angles." Explain.
5. Why is Pope St. Leo remembered as a great man?
6. Why do writers speak of the "Great Thousand Years"?
7. In what way are each of the following alike: (a) mosque;
(b) Hejira; (c) Islam; (d) Koran?
8. Why is Charles Martel remembered as a great man?
9. Give *one* reason for the quick spread of Mohammed's new religion.
10. "The year 476 A.D. is said to mark the end of the Roman Empire." In your own words tell just what this means.

## QUESTIONS THAT TEST YOUR CHARACTER

1. "The Germans were unusually determined." Just what does this mean? Is this a good quality for you to develop? Give a reason for your answer.

2. Name *two* good and *two* bad qualities of the ancient Germans.
3. Name three good and three bad qualities of Mohammed.
4. Why should we admire Pope St. Leo?
5. Which of these men would you prefer to be: (a) Attila; (b) Mohammed; (c) Alaric; (d) St. Paul. Give a reason for your answer.

## ACTIVITIES

1. Dramatize Pope St. Leo meeting Attila.
2. Dress dolls like Roman and Teuton soldiers.
3. Hold a pageant to show what the Romans gave civilization
4. Imagine yourself Attila. Write a diary. In it describe your invasion.
5. From wood make a copy of a Teuton's hut.
6. Make an imaginary trip to Europe. Tell the class of your visit to: (a) Chalons; (b) Rome; (c) Tours.
7. Paste in your scrap-book pictures of ancient Germans and Romans.

## TOPICS FOR DISCUSSION

1. The Teuton invasion of Roman territory was a good thing for civilization.
2. The English of today are really Teutons.
3. The Franks saved Christianity at the battle of Tours.
4. Pope St. Leo was a great statesman.
5. The Teutons were pagans.

## WORD LIST

| Teutons | "hundred" | clan | Mecca |
|---------|-----------|------|-------|
| Goths | Islam | tribe | Thor |
| self-reliance | Woden | Allah | Franks |
| | freemen | Hejira | |

# V

## *Part 2:* SUCCESSORS OF THE APOSTLES

The Conversion of the pagans in Europe was the chief work of the Church. Some of the pagans believed in the gods of Rome, others, like the Irish, in the Celtic gods, while the Teutons worshiped their own gods. To convert these people the Church had services of the monks who followed the rule of Saint Benedict. It had also the zeal of great missionaries like Saint Patrick, Saint Augustine, Saint Boniface and Saints Cyril and Methodius.

SAINT BENEDICT. The family to which Saint Benedict belonged was a prominent one in Rome. Benedict could have been a man of importance in the affairs of the city of Rome. However, he decided that it was more important to imitate the life of Our Lord. He therefore left the world to dwell alone. Since the time of Christ many men, and women also, had done this. So many men admired Benedict and his way of life that they asked him to be their leader. He agreed to this and founded a community on a high hill in Italy called Monte Cassino. Here, in 529, he published a rule of life for the monks. This date is a most important one in European history because during the following centuries the monks of Saint Benedict did a great deal to make Christians of the people of Europe and to civilize them.

THE BENEDICTINE RULE. Saint Benedict believed that those who wished to serve God by leaving the world ought to live in a special dwelling called a monastery. There they could spend their days in prayer and could labor with their hands and with their minds. Thus prayer, work, and study were to be part of the daily life of the monks. Their days were to be passed, not according to the wishes of each individual monk in the monastery, but according to a rule which bound all.

The head of the monastery was an abbot who was elected by the monks. The abbot's term lasted during his life. Each monastery was independent and managed its own affairs. In time other monasteries would be founded and these too would be ruled over by abbots chosen by the monks themselves. Saint Benedict in drawing up his rule was teaching lessons of civilization.

THE IMPORTANCE OF THE BENEDICTINE RULE. First of all Saint Benedict insisted upon prayer as the foundation of a good life. He knew there can be no worthy civilization where people do not acknowledge God and obey His commandments. Saint Benedict commanded labor. Thus he taught men the dignity of work at a time when labor was despised and regarded as something for slaves to do. The rule of Saint Benedict taught people the importance of order at a time when Europe was in fearful disorder. Finally the Benedictine rule by providing for the election of the abbot pointed out a method of self-government and democracy.

## ST. PATRICK AND THE IRISH

IRELAND AND THE IRISH. Ireland is an island that lies west of England. The inhabitants, the Irish, are a Celtic people. They belong to the same race as the Gauls and Britons whom Cæsar conquered. While Ireland was never conquered by the Romans nor was Roman civilization forced upon Ireland, the

*Drawn expressly for "The Old World and America"*

### St. Patrick

**The Irish welcome him who was to become their Patron saint.**

Irish were by no means uncivilized. Indeed, when Europe was in the greatest disorder, the Irish schools were overcrowded. Scholars flocked to Ireland from everywhere and Ireland in turn sent her teachers over all Europe. The Church had much to do with the splendid things done by the Irish. What glory is due St. Patrick for carrying the Faith to Ireland!

ST. PATRICK. St. Patrick, who converted the Irish, was not born in Ireland. He was taken there as a slave. When a boy, he was captured by pirates who sold him to an Irish chieftain. Patrick was put to work tending swine. He worked many long hours each day; at night he often slept under the stars. Although his life was very hard Patrick did not complain for he was not thinking of himself. He was, however, greatly concerned about the Irish because they were pagans. They did not realize that Our Lord had died for them. Patrick longed to tell the Irish about Christ. An opportunity came to escape

and Patrick fled from Ireland. He did not mean to leave Ireland
for good. He set about preparing himself for the mission to
which he felt God had called him. Patrick attended the best
schools in Europe. After finishing his studies, he was ordained
a priest. Then the Pope gave him a commission to preach to
the Irish. Overjoyed at the prospect, St. Patrick set out for
Ireland in the year 433.

THE CONVERSION OF THE IRISH. It was no easy task
to convert a whole nation but with God's help St. Patrick meant
to do it. Success at length crowned his labors to such a degree
that Ireland has been called "the Isle of Saints and Scholars."
We to-day in America can actually see the fruit of his labors.
Indeed the sons of Ireland have carried the faith and Christian
civilization to the farthest parts of the earth. This they have
been able to do because as a people the Irish have been true to
their religion. In spite of dungeon, fire and sword they have
kept the Faith.

THE IRISH AND CIVILIZATION. Catholicity brought new
life to Irish civilization. Ireland became a new place, a world
in itself. There were splendid schools at Armagh and on Iona
Island. Indeed the Irish in the fifth, sixth, and seventh centuries
succeeded in building up a truly marvelous system of education. There were over thirty well-known schools at this time.
The whole scholastic system in Europe combined could not
then equal the splendid schools of Ireland.

When you study the history of Europe during the fifth
sixth, and seventh centuries you will learn in what a dreadful
state Europe then was. These were the centuries of ceaseless
warfare and widespread destruction. The Huns, the Mohammedans, the Norsemen, each in turn left a trail of ruin behind
them. The Church, aided by the Irish monks, was working all
during this time to bring back civilization to Europe.

THE IRISH MONKS IN EUROPE. By the sixth century the Irish monks had built their monasteries in France, Switzerland, and Italy as well as in England and Scotland. During the next three centuries they came to the continent in great numbers; says St. Bernard, "like bees from a hive." The mission of the Irish was to preserve and to restore civilization. "From Egypt in the East to Iceland in the North, hardly an acre can be found that has not been consecrated by the ceaseless strivings, the sweat and blood of the men of Ireland."

ST. GREGORY AND THE "ANGELS." The conversion of the English was due in part to the great pope, St. Gregory. When Gregory was only a simple monk he happened to be passing the slave market in Rome. There he noticed some handsome boys who were for sale. Attracted by their fine faces, he asked to what people they belonged. "Angles," was the reply. "No!" said St. Gregory, "not Angles but Angels," and, according to the account, he added: "The praise of God will yet be sung in their land, so that their fair souls may become angels in Heaven." Some years later this monk, Gregory, was called to the chair of Peter as Pope Gregory I. He remembered the handsome boys in the slave market and resolved to bring their people to the knowledge of the true God.

ST. AUGUSTINE AND THE FORTY MONKS. To convert the Angles in Angleland, or England, Pope Gregory sent St. Augustine with forty companions. St. Augustine made a landing in the southeastern part of England, in 597. The task before Augustine and his companions was a great one. Through the wife of the English king, Bertha, who was a Catholic, St. Augustine was given a hearing. King Ethelbert insisted that the meeting be held in the open air. He was afraid that these strange men had some power that could bring great harm upon him. St. Augustine so impressed King Ethelbert that he became a Catholic. He gave the missionaries permission to preach. Their labors bore fruit. Soon they had succeeded in converting

*Drawn for "The Old World and America"*

**St. Augustine at Canterbury**

The Britons eagerly accepted baptism in the Catholic church.

many to Christianity. Canterbury was made the headquarters of the Catholic Church in England. And thus Saint Augustine became first archbishop of Canterbury. He lived almost two hundred years later than the great Father of the Church, St. Augustine of Hippo. Civilization began a new life in England for the monks taught many of the people how to read and write, how to build, and other things that are part of civilized life. Religion was so important in England that the country was called "Our Lady's Dower."

ST. BONIFACE. Another name that stands for heroic zeal is that of St. Boniface. St. Boniface was of a noble English family. His parents were anxious that he take up a career in the world but Boniface felt called to higher things. He became a monk, and then, with the permission of his superiors, undertook the conversion of the Germans. His labors led him into the forests of Germany to preach to the fiercest of the German tribes. St. Boniface was utterly fearless. On one occasion he cut down an oak that was held sacred by the Germans. St. Boniface told the Germans he needed the timbers from the oak for a Christian chapel. The zeal of St. Boniface brought

*Drawn expressly for "The Old World and America"*

## St. Boniface

The patron saint of Germany destroys the sacred oak of the pagans. The tribesmen admired his fearlessness.

success. Great numbers were converted to Christianity and the Faith was firmly established. His life ended gloriously, for he won the crown of martyrdom.

PEOPLE OF EASTERN EUROPE. After reading the history of Greece and Rome, we became interested in two other great European peoples, the Celts and Teutons. We remember that the Gauls, Britons and Irish are Celts. The Teutons, we saw, were the peoples who took possession of the old Roman Empire in western Europe. We must tell of yet another people who help make up the population of Europe, the Slavs. The Slavs are divided into various branches, just as there are divisions of the Celts and Teutons.

SAINT CYRIL AND SAINT METHODIUS In north-central Europe lie Poland, Lithuania, and Czecho-Slovakia. The whole

*Drawn expressly for "The Old World and America"*

**John Sobieski**

King of Poland and defender of Europe against the Turks.

eastern part of the continent is occupied by Russia. All these countries are inhabited by Slavs. The people of Poland, Lithuania, and Slovakia were converted to the Catholic Church from paganism several centuries later than the peoples of western Europe—that is to say after the year 800. Once converted, they remained loyal to the Faith with remarkable constancy. The conversion of some of the Slavic peoples was due to the zeal of two Greek monks. Their names were Cyril and Methodius. Cyril spent about ten years among the Slavic peoples. His brother Methodius served as a missionary for almost thirty-five years, until his death (885). Besides preaching Christianity these heroes, Cyril and Methodius, brought civilization to eastern Europe. The people could not read nor could they write for they had no alphabet. St. Cyril taught them to use an alphabet. The Slavs also learned the other skills and accomplishments of civilized people.

POLAND, EUROPE'S DEFENDER. The loyalty of the Slavic people to their Christian Faith during later centuries is a splendid story. This is especially true of the Polish people whose bravery enabled them to fight the Turks who were infidels and enemies of European civilization. Later, we shall learn more about this common enemy; for the time being, it will be enough to remember that for centuries Poland acted as one of the strongest defenses against the Turks. As late as the close of the seventeenth century, Europe was threatened from this quarter, and was saved largely by the courage of John Sobieski and his soldiers who fought for "Faith and Fatherland."

---

## OBJECTIVE TESTS

---

TEST 1: Selecting the Odd Item.
   Three items are alike. Select one which is not like the other three.
   1. Patrick, Ethelbert, Augustine, Boniface.    . . . . . . . . . . . .
   2. Monastery, convent, church, palace.    . . . . . . . . . . . .
   3. Poles, Lithuanians, Slovaks, Germans.    . . . . . . . . . . . .
   4. Cyril, Methodius, Bertha, Benedict.    . . . . . . . . . . . .
   5. Canterbury, Rome, Monte Cassino, Tours.    . . . . . . . . . . . . 5.

TEST 2: Matching Test
   Select the number from Column "A" which matches each item from Column "B".

| Column A | | Column B |
|---|---|---|
| 1. Pope St. Gregory | ( ) | Armagh |
| 2. famous school | ( ) | Monte Cassino |
| 3. Benedictine rule | ( ) | St. Boniface |
| 4. welcomed St. Augustine | ( ) | Bertha |
| 5. martyred | ( ) | England |

TEST 3: Selecting the Correct Item.
   Select the correct item in each.
   1. St. Boniface: (a) daily labor, (b) marriage, (c) warfare, (d) disorder.    . . . . . . . . . . . .
   2. St. Patrick: (a) Germans, (b) Celts, (c) Swedes, (d) Slavs.    . . . . . . . . . . . .

3. St. Methodius: (a) Irish, (b) French, (c) Slav, (d) English. . . . . . . . . . . .

4. St. Cyril: (a) scholar, (b) Greek monk, (c) French bishop, (d) English missionary . . . . . . . . . . . .

5. John Sobieski: (a) Poland, (b) Ireland, (c) Italy, (d) Russia. . . . . . . . . . . .

## QUESTIONS THAT MAKE YOU THINK

1. What is meant by the Benedictine Rule?
2. Why is it true to say that democracy existed in each monastery?
3. "The Benedictine monks helped preserve learning." Show why this is true.
4. Name two great achievements of St. Patrick.
5. Why was Ireland called the "Isle of Saints and Scholars"?
6. Explain two contributions of the Irish monks.
7. Why was the conversion of Poland a great achievement?
8. What do St. Cyril and St. Methodius have in common?
9. What is an abbot? Why was it important that he be a learned and holy man?
10. Why is Canterbury regarded today as the religious center of England?

## QUESTIONS THAT TEST YOUR CHARACTER

1. "St. Boniface was a real hero." Explain fully.
2. Name three great qualities of St. Patrick.
3. Tell how you can profit by a study of the lives of the great missionaries.
4. Name five qualities which a good missionary should have.
5. "The missionaries led lives of adventure." Give two reasons for the truth of this statement.

## ACTIVITIES

1. From soap or wood make a model of a Benedictine monastery.
2. Dress dolls like: (a) an abbot, (b) an Irish monk, (c) an English king.
3. Imagine yourself St. Augustine. Write a letter to the Pope telling of your work in England.

4. Dramatize: St. Augustine meets King Ethelbert.
5. Make a series of "minute-movies" entitled "The Life of a Monk." Use pencil and paper.
6. Deliver a talk, "What the Monks Did for Civilization."
7. On an outline map of Europe, draw sketches of the missionaries of each country.
8. Write a letter to a Benedictine monk of today. Ask him to write you, telling of his daily life. Read his letter to the class.
9. Draw a picture of St. Patrick.
10. Paste in your scrapbook pictures and clippings of monks and missionaries.

## TOPICS FOR DISCUSSION

1. The Benedictine Rule was very easy.
2. St. Patrick was not a true Irishman.
3. The Irish Catholics did not recognize the Pope as their leader.
4. The Irish monks preserved learning.
5. The Poles saved Christianity.

## WORD LIST

| | | | |
|---|---|---|---|
| Benedictine rule | missionary | monastery | conversion |
| dignity of labor | abbot | democracy | monk |

# V

## Part 3: GREAT KINGS

The brave missionaries who made Christians of the fierce Teutons had also helped to civilize them. In the course of time several great kings by ruling wisely also helped to make their people better and more civilized. Two kings are especially famous. Charlemagne was the name of one. He ruled over a large part of the continent of Europe. Another famous king was Alfred who ruled over the people of England.

CHARLEMAGNE'S RISE TO POWER. Charlemagne came from a family of soldiers and heroes. His grandfather was a great general who had defeated the Mohammedans in a critical battle fought nears Tours, 732. His father, Pepin, also was a great leader. Charlemagne succeeded his father, Pepin, as king of a Teutonic tribe called the Franks. From the beginning Charlemagne made a splendid king. His secretary gives us a fine description of him. Charlemagne, he says, was "large and robust, of commanding stature and excellent proportions, for it appears that his height measured seven times the length of his own foot."

CHARLEMAGNE AS A MILITARY LEADER. Charlemagne began his reign by making himself master in his own country, or roughly speaking, what is now France. Then he turned his attention elsewhere. He led armies into Germany and into Italy. Everywhere he was successful. He put a real

*Courtesy New York Public Library*

### Coronation of Charlemagne

Charles the Great is crowned in St. Peter's, Rome, Christmas Day, 800 A.D., and the Holy Roman Empire is founded.

check on the power of the Mohammedans in Europe. By the year 800 A.D., he was undisputed master of a large part of western Europe.

THE CORONATION OF CHARLEMAGNE. Charlemagne went to Rome where he met Pope Leo. On Christmas day, 800 A.D., while Charlemagne was attending Mass at St. Peter's, the Pope placed a crown on his head calling him "Emperor of the Romans." Thus was a new empire founded. It differed from the old Roman Empire in very important points. This new empire was Teuton; it was Christian; it was entirely of western Europe. It was called the Holy Roman Empire and it lasted down to modern times.

CHARLEMAGNE AND EDUCATION. Strange as it may seem, although Charlemagne was a very important man he did not know how to write. He felt this handicap very keenly and tried so hard to learn that he kept writing materials under his pillow that he might practice. Charlemagne did everything possible to bring education to his subjects. He started a model school in his own palace for the sons of the Frankish nobility. The most famous scholar of the time was the Englishman, Alcuin. Charlemagne brought him to France as director of the Palace School. Charlemagne, or Charles as he is sometimes called, built up a splendid system of laws for the people. When he died, in 814, there was grief among his people.

THE DIVISION OF THE KINGDOM. Charlemagne probably suspected that after his death his sons would quarrel over the division of the territory. As an emperor Charlemagne ruled over an extensive territory for an empire consists of the original country plus lands which are added to it by conquest or treaty. To avoid trouble over the division of his large empire Charlemagne made a will. According to the will, each of his sons received a fair share of the land. Unfortunately, his sons would not agree to do as the will said. They began to fight. Some of the grandsons began to fight also. Bloody wars were fought over the division of the land. The quarrel was patched up twice, at Verdun, in 843, and again in 870, at Mersen.

THE TREATY OF MERSEN, 870. The treaty signed at Mersen contained some important matters. The great empire of Charlemagne was again divided. This time the parts represented more nearly the three modern countries of France, Germany, and Italy. Italy was marked off from Europe by natural boundaries. In the case of France and Germany the natural boundaries were not as noticeable.

*Drawn expressly for "The Old World and America"*

## The Norsemen Attacking Paris

These terrible sea rovers were feared over all Europe.

THE BEGINNINGS OF MODERN LANGUAGES. The treaty took into account the growing differences in language between the people in the western part of Europe and those in eastern Europe. The Franks who lived in what is now France were already speaking the language that was to become French. The eastern part of the Empire was purely German in both people and language. The division of Charlemagne's empire laid the foundation for France and Germany of today. However, the treaty of Mersen did not bring peace to Europe. Once more Europe was to be invaded by barbarians.

THE NORSEMEN. The barbarians who invaded Europe after the time of Charlemagne were a Teutonic people called Norsemen. These folk came from the northern part of Europe or what we call the Scandinavian countries. The Norsemen were fierce sea-rovers. In their wild sea excursions they went as far east as Russia and as far west as America. It is thought that America was visited by them about the year 1000.

THE EFFECT OF THE NORSE INVASIONS. To appreciate the effect of these invasions we must know what sort of people the Norsemen were. They were not civilized. Up to this time they had never attended school nor had they ever seen a book; they did not know anything about Christianity. These fierce sea rovers or Vikings made their trips in light, swift boats which were painted black; a carved dragon stood out from the ship's prow. Along the sides of the Viking ship the shields of the warriors were hung. The sail usually had a picture of a dreadful monster painted upon it. When the Norsemen reached the end of their journey, they landed and laid the country in ruins. Nothing was spared. Churches, homes, and schools shared the same fate. The people were killed or enslaved.

THE INVADED COUNTRIES. England suffered terribly from these cruel invaders. Ireland also was a prey to them. This was·a great misfortune because Ireland had, at this time, a high degree of civilization. The Norsemen visited France with such regularity that the weak French king offered them a large piece of French territory if they would cease making war in other parts of France. The offer was accepted and the Norsemen settled in a place called after them, Normandy. Soon they learned to speak French and to follow French customs. Some of the Normans excelled as architects; others became splendid scholars. Many, however, continued to prefer fighting. A body of Norman warriors led by their leader, Duke William of Normandy, invaded England, in the year 1066. William made himself king of England, calling himself King William I; to most people, however, he is best known as William the Conqueror. To understand the story of the Norman leader, William the Conqueror, and his invasion of England, we must first learn something about what happened in England after the Romans went away.

BRITAIN OR ENGLAND UNDER THE ROMANS. You remember how the Roman general Julius Cæsar tried to conquer the island which we call England. Other Roman generals came to England. In time most of Britain (England) became a Roman province and was ruled by Roman officials. The people enjoyed the benefits of Roman law and Roman civilization. Indeed, the remains of some of the old Roman structures in England still exist. The Romans gave names to places we think to be purely English. For example, Chester is the name of an English town. This name comes from *castra,* the Latin word for camp. There are also other traces of Roman influence.

THE DEPARTURE OF THE ROMANS. The Romans could not remain in Britain because the Teutonic tribes were taking possession of the Roman Empire. The city of Rome itself was not safe. While Rome's safety was threatened, the Roman authorities could not afford to keep soldiers in England. The order was given for the Roman soldiers to leave. From this time on (410) England was at the mercy of every foreign invader. The Teutonic peoples began to invade England. The Jutes, the Angles, and the Saxons came over from the continent of Europe and the Danes followed. England now had a mixed and quarrelsome population. Warfare was continuous. Fighting lasted for four hundred years and more. The different peoples would have destroyed one another had not a great man come upon the scene. This man was Alfred who well deserves the title "Great."

Drawn expressly for "The Old World and America"

**England, from Alfred the Great to William the Conqueror**

ALFRED THE GREAT. Alfred, who was born in 849, was the son of King Ethelwulf. When Ethelwulf began to reign, his kingdom was small. But by good generalship he made himself ruler of a large part of England. Warfare ceased for a time. While the country was at peace Ethelwulf went to Rome, taking his young son Alfred with him. In Rome they met the Pope who was most kind to them. Alfred was greatly impressed by what he saw. On his return to England he resolved to spend all his spare time studying, thus preparing himself to be a useful man.

ALFRED AS KING. Alfred's brother had become king. He did not reign long; the Danes, who were again at war with the English, killed him. Alfred then became king at a time when the English were in a desperate way. Alfred was king in name only, because the Danes were in possession of the whole country. The Danes sought Alfred's life. Alfred was compelled to hide in the woods and swamps. Whenever he could, he gathered together a band of English to train them to fight the hated Danes. The Danes at length were thoroughly defeated in a battle fought at Wedmore (Wet Moor). They agreed to live at peace with the English and to remain in a certain district called Danelagh (Dane Law). This is the section north of the Thames River and extending along the east coast.

ALFRED AND THE CHURCH. Next to defeating the Danes, Alfred's ambition was to bring education to the English. This was brought about by giving all the support possible to the Church. Quite properly, Alfred believed that the spread of learning depended on the spread of the Church. So missionaries were sent to the Danish parts of England and wherever else the Gospel had not yet been preached. Many of the churches and monasteries had been destroyed during the wars. Alfred directed that they be rebuilt.

*Drawn after a picture in the New York Public Library.*

**King Alfred in the Monastery School**

This good King realized that religion and learning could not be separated.

THE FATHER OF ENGLISH LITERATURE. Alfred is called the father of English Literature because he did much to advance the study of English. In his day the learned men spoke and wrote in Latin. Alfred desired that more interest be taken in English. He translated a "History of the World" from Latin into English. Alfred wanted his country's history to be known. Accordingly he had the "Anglo-Saxon Chronicle" written, which tells what happened in England during these early years.

ALFRED THE GREAT. Alfred's greatest ambition was to be a just king. He did everything possible to see that justice existed in all parts of his realm. Wrong-doers were speedily punished. The poor were protected from oppression. To secure justice for all he had a set of laws drawn up. There was a just punishment for those who broke the laws. To protect his people from invasion he had a fleet of ships built. These could be used for trading or to keep off an enemy. For his interest in building up a fleet he has been called "the Father of the English Navy." The English grieved deeply, when, in 901, King Alfred the Great died.

THE DANISH KINGS. Alfred did not entirely succeed in expelling the troublesome Danes from the kingdom. They still controlled a large part of England. Their influence was so great that after Alfred's death England had Danes for kings. The Danish line of kings lasted nearly one hundred and fifty years. Canute was the greatest of this line. His two sons reigned after him but they were bad men and bad kings. The last Danish king, a son of Canute, died in 1042. Then Edward the Confessor, an Englishman, was made king. Upon his death an event of great importance to English history occurred. This was the Norman conquest.

WILLIAM, DUKE OF NORMANDY. The Norman conquest took place in 1066. It was an invasion of England by Northmen from France. They were called Normans. You remember that the French king gave the Northmen a province in France which came to be called Normandy. William was the duke, or leader, of the Normans at the time Edward was king of England. He was Edward's cousin. William of Normandy insisted that Edward had promised him the English crown upon Edward's death. In the course of time, Edward the Confessor, king of England, died. After the death of Edward the question arose concerning his successor. Edward had no son. The choice of the Witan, or committee of England's leading men, fell upon Harold. Harold was a fine warrior and a good man. The Witan never even considered William.

*Drawn expressly for "The Old World and America"*

## Battle of Hastings

Harold was killed by an arrow. William, Duke of Normandy, then made himself king of England as William I.

THE NORMAN CONQUEST. William had no intention of abiding by the decision of the Witan. He claimed the throne of England. Then to enforce this claim, he collected an army, sailed across the Channel and made ready to invade England. Harold with an army met William and his force near Hastings. A fierce battle ensued. Harold was killed. William was master of England, for there was no one to prevent it. He became king of England as William I. (See map, page 152).

THE EFFECT OF THE CONQUEST ON ENGLAND. The Normans (Northmen) having lived in France for several generations had become Frenchmen. They had French manners and customs; they spoke the French language. The Normans brought their language and customs with them when they took up their abode in England. Thus Norman architecture was taken into England where it was used in the construction of cathedrals and castles. New words and phrases were added to the English language.

A change also took place in the way the country was governed. William realized that he was king of a people who were not united. William knew, therefore, that he could rule successfully only if all parties in England respected his authority and feared his anger. He built castles in different parts of England. These he placed in charge of trusted friends. In this way the whole country was put directly under the king's control. Thus the king became supreme master. This fact after some years helped to make the English people into a united nation.

## OBJECTIVE TESTS

TEST 1: Completion Test.
1. .................... succeeded his father, Pepin, as king.
2. Pope Leo crowned ........... "Emperor of the Romans."
3. The director of the Palace School was the famous scholar,
   ................... .
4. The Holy Roman Empire at Mersen was divided into France, Germany, and ................ .
5. The ............... were fierce sea rovers.
6. Normandy is in what is now of the country of ............ .
7. William, the Duke of Normandy, conquered the ......... ... in 1066.
8. Words ending in "chester" show the influence of the ............ in England.
9. Alfred, the Great, waged war against the ............... .
10. ............... is called the father of English literature.

TEST 2: Character Test.
   Select the correct word for each man.
1. William: holy, warlike, respectful, rich.          ............
2. Edward, the Confessor: pious, fighting, jealous, strong.                                         ............
3. Alfred: just, corrupt, old, weak.          ............
4. Vikings: peaceful, ferocious, learned, gentle.          ............
5. Alcuin: honest, rich, reverent, learned.          ............

TEST 3: True-False Tests.
   Write the numbers 1 to 10 on a piece of paper. Next to each write the word "true" or "false."
1. By 800 A.D. Charlemagne ruled a large part of western Europe.                              ............

2. Charlemagne encouraged learning. . . . . . . . . . . .
3. Charlemagne's empire was divided among his sons. . . . . . . . . . . .
4. England was not invaded by Norsemen. . . . . . . . . . . .
5. William the Conqueror became king of England. . . . . . . . . . . .
6. Alfred was the son of Canute. . . . . . . . . . . .
7. Alfred drove the Danes out of England. . . . . . . . . . . .
8. Canute was the "Father of the English Navy." . . . . . . . . . . .
9. Harold won the battle of Hastings. . . . . . . . . . . .
10. William introduced Saxon architecture into England. . . . . . . . . . . .

TEST 4: Sequence of Events.

Select the event in each group which happened the longest time ago.

1. (a) Charlemagne becomes Emperor, (b) Treaty of Verdun, (c) Treaty of Mersen, (d) battle of Hastings. . . . . . . . . . . .
2. (a) Angles and Saxons invade England, (b) Normans invade England, (c) Danes invade England, (d) Norsemen invade France. . . . . . . . . . . .
3. (a) Canute rules England, (b) Alfred visits Rome, (c) Alfred encourages learning, (d) Alfred makes peace with Danes. . . . . . . . . . . .
4. (a) Edward, Confessor, rules England, (b) Romans invade Britain, (c) Harold, elected king by Witan, (d) William invades England. . . . . . . . . . . .

## QUESTIONS THAT MAKE YOU THINK

1. Explain (a) one difference and (b) one likeness between the Holy Roman Empire and the old Roman Empire.
2. "Charlemagne could not write. He was not interested in education." Do you agree? Give reasons.
3. Name three people who invaded England.
4. Why were the Norsemen feared by the French?
5. Give a good reason for calling Alfred, "the Great."
6. Point out one likeness between Charlemagne and Alfred.
7. Explain two achievements of Alfred.
8. Why was a section of England called "Danelagh"?
9. Explain two results of the Norman conquest.

10. "Was William, the Conqueror, a great man?" Explain your answer.

## QUESTIONS THAT TEST YOUR CHARACTER

1. Which was greatest: Charlemagne, Alfred, or Canute? Give two good reasons for your choice.
2. Explain two ways in which you should imitate Alfred, the Great.
3. Name two good qualities of Charlemagne.
4. Why did Charlemagne, William, and Alfred fight so much?
5. Compare the qualities of Charlemagne with those of St. Patrick.

## ACTIVITIES

1. Write a tombstone for Charlemagne. On it outline his achievements.
2. Draw a sketch of pupils in the Palace School.
3. Dramatize the crowning of Charlemagne.
4. Imagine yourself Alfred, the Great. Keep a diary, describing your trouble with the Danes.
5. Dress dolls like Charlemagne and William the Conqueror.
6. Draw a "minute movies" series of pictures on "The Life of Alfred, the Great."
7. Paste in your scrapbook pictures of Norsemen.
8. Make a model of a ship used by Norsemen.

## TOPICS FOR DISCUSSION

1. Charlemagne was a Frenchman.
2. The Norman conquest was a great evil for England.
3. King Alfred had more power than the king of England has today.
4. William had no right to the English throne.

## WORD LIST

| | |
|---|---|
| Treaty of Verdun | "Emperor of the Romans" |
| Treaty of Mersen | Holy Roman Empire |
| battle of Hastings | Danelagh |
| English navy | English literature |
| Norsemen | conquest |

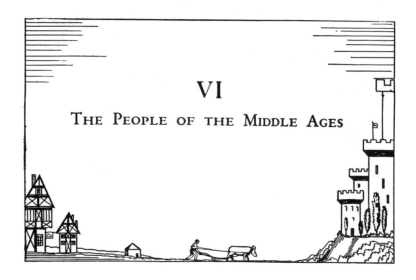

# VI
## THE PEOPLE OF THE MIDDLE AGES

### AIM

To understand why the people of the Middle Ages lived under the feudal form of society.

To realize that during the Middle Ages every man had his place.

DURING THE time when William the Conqueror was king of England and for more than three hundred years after his death, most of the people of Europe lived in the country, few in the towns. During that time, citizenship as we understand it, did not exist. In those days, almost all people—except those who embraced the religious life—belonged to the ruling class or to the working class. The ruling class consisted of land owners or *LORDS*, and land holders or *VASSALS*. Below this class were the *SERFS* who worked on the land. The system of society based on the ownership of land is called FEUDALISM. There was another small but important group, the craftsmen, who lived in the towns.

# VI

## Part 1: LORDS AND SERFS

Feudalism was not deliberately planned by any one. It came into existence because of the disorder of the times when central government had broken down and when it no longer could keep order or do those things which a government should be able to do. Each man therefore had to depend upon himself or else to look to some strong neighbor for help and protection.

THE FEUDAL SYSTEM. Feudalism divided the people into a ruling class and a working class. At the top were the feudal lords or land owners, usually called *lords*. Less important members of this class were the *vassals*. They were those who held land because some feudal lord had bestowed it upon them in return for a promise of military service or some other service. The *serfs* were those who worked on the land as laborers. It is important to remember that the feudal system was not just the same at all times and in all countries. The powers of a feudal lord in England differed from those of a feudal lord in France. The authority which a feudal lord enjoyed in one century his descendants might not possess at a later date.

THE FEUDAL LORD. If you were to visit what we call France during the tenth or eleventh centuries, you would find the country divided into a number of large estates called *fiefs*. Each fief was ruled by a noble. In England such estates were called *manors*. The noble ruling over such an estate or fief

**Lord and Vassal**

In this instance a great prince is rendering homage as vassal to his king. This prince has vassals of his own.

was called a feudal lord. How he got his large piece of territory would take a long time to tell. It might have happened that one of his ancestors received the land from his king; or he might have won it from a rival feudal lord in battle. Again, it often happened that some small independent land owner felt that he could not protect his property, so he gave his land to his more powerful neighbor, who, in return, granted him the use of the land and promised him protection. The feudal lord was, therefore, a land owner, but he was more than this. Many of the acts performed by this feudal lord were those we ordinarily expect a ruler to perform. The fact is that the feudal lord was not merely a landlord, he was also a ruler. Indeed he was really "the government" in the land he owned or controlled.

THE VASSAL. The one receiving land from a feudal lord is called a vassal. When the lord granted land to a vassal, the vassal received merely the use of the land, the lord still retained the title of owner. But notice that after the death of a vassal the land did not return to the feudal lord who was its legal owner; the use of the land passed to the sons of the vassal and in time the ownership of land became hereditary. Another peculiar thing about the position of the vassal is this, the vassal himself might be the lord of a vassal; thus Robert who was a vassal of feudal lord William, might in turn be a feudal lord to vassal Richard. The ceremony which took place when a man became a vassal shows the relationship between lord and vassal. The ceremony was called homage.

HOMAGE. The ceremony of homage was often impressive. The new vassal came into the presence of the lord, who was seated on a low throne in the great hall of his castle. Kneeling, and with head bowed, the vassal clasped the hands of his lord and promised to be his man. The lord then gave the vassal the kiss of peace and declared himself ready to defend the vassal even at the risk of his life. As a sign of the agreement the lord sometimes gave his new vassal a clod of earth or a green twig.

THE OBLIGATIONS OF THE VASSALS. The vassals were bound to render to the lord various services. The services promised varied considerably, but usually the vassal bound himself to fulfill promises such as these: (1) To serve in the army of the feudal lord about forty days during each year; (2) to give a sum of money when the eldest son of the lord was made a knight and upon the occasion of the first marriage of the lord's daughter; (3) should the lord be taken prisoner, the vassal agreed to help to ransom him.

*Drawn expressly for "The Old World and America"*

## Nobles and Serfs

The lordly Knight risked his life in battle while the lowly serf lived in peace but very humbly.

THE SERFS. The majority of the people of the early Middle Ages were farm workers. In many cases they were not free laborers but serfs or workers who were bound to the soil. This meant that the serfs generally had to remain on the land where they were born. For the use of the land each serf was obliged to make a payment to his lord. This took the form of laboring upon that portion of the lord's estate which the lord reserved for his own use. In addition to this, each serf usually had to supply the lord with certain quantities of farm produce.

THE LIFE OF THE SERFS. The serfs lived in small houses which clustered about the house or castle of their lord forming a village. The homes of the serfs were miserable houses consisting of a single room. There was almost no furniture. The food which they ate was of the plainest. Coarse black bread was the principal article of diet. They drank milk—if they had cows; otherwise, home-brewed beer. The taste of sugar was unknown to them; honey was their sweet. Meat was eaten probably on great feasts only. It would be wrong, however, to think that the serfs were unhappy. They knew, better than we, now to enjoy simple pleasures. They seem to have understood, also, that the things of this world alone cannot make men nappy.

There were some men in the village who were better off than the serfs. Usually, each village had a miller who ground the grain into flour. Farm implements had to be made or mended and so in each village there was a smith with his forge. Of course, the priest was there too. All the people lived under the protection of the feudal castle.

## ORAL DRILL

1. What are fiefs called in England?          . . . . . . . . . .
2. What were those who worked on the land called? . . . . . . . . .
3. Who had to render service to the feudal lord?     . . . . . . . . . .
4. Was the serf the same as a slave?          . . . . . . . . . .
5. Could the serf travel as he pleased?          . . . . . . . . . .

## OBJECTIVE TESTS

TEST 1: Completion Test.
1. The system of society consisting of lords and vassals is called . . . . . . . . . . . . . . . . .
2. France in the tenth century was divided into large estates called . . . . . . . . . . . . . . . . .
3. The noble ruling over an estate was called a feudal . . . . . . . . . . . . . . . . . .
4. Those who held land from the noble were called . . . . . . . . . . . . . . . . .
5. The ceremony which took place between a noble and a vassal was called . . . . . . . . . . . . . . . .

6. Those workers who were bound to the soil were called
.................

7. Each village had a man to grind grain into flour. Such a man is called the ................

8. The poor farm workers drank milk and ................

9. The dwellings of these workers were grouped into a
.................

10. The vassal had to serve in the ............ of the lord about forty days each year.

TEST 2: Vocabulary Test.

Select the correct definition.

1. What is a serf?
   (a) colored servant of the middle ages.
   (b) a vassal of the king.
   (c) a worker, bound to the soil.
   (d) a conquered slave.

2. What was feudalism?
   (a) a system of society based on land holding.
   (b) a system of warfare and disorder.
   (c) a means of keeping the poor under control.
   (d) a way of practicing Christianity.

3. What is a vassal?
   (a) one who will fight for pay.
   (b) a farm laborer.
   (c) a criminal who is lent to a lord.
   (d) one who owes service to a lord.

TEST 3: Relationship Test.

Arrange the following in the order of power each possessed. Put the most powerful first: vassal, lord, serf, slave, freemen.

## QUESTIONS THAT MAKE YOU THINK

1. Why don't we have the feudal system in the U. S. today?
2. Describe the power of a feudal noble.
3. "A man might be both lord and vassal." Show why this statement is true.
4. Name two duties of a vassal.
5. "Under the feudal system the lord had no duties." Show why this is false.

6. (a) What does the word "homage" mean today? (b) Use it in a sense. (c) Give the meaning it had in the Middle Ages.
7. Compare the rights of a lord with those of a vassal.
8. "The vassal had rights and duties." Explain.
9. Compare your home with that of a serf.
10. "Even a serf had some rights." Give an example of his rights.

## QUESTIONS THAT TEST YOUR CHARACTER

1. Describe a "bad" noble of the Middle Ages.
2. Name five qualities of a good noble.
3. "Religion helped the lord and vassal." Show that this is true.
4. "The serf was a human being." Why is it important for the lord to remember this?
5. Do you think the three great obligations of the vassals to their lord were just? Explain your answer.

## ACTIVITIES

1. Draw a pyramid to describe the feudal system. On the top draw a picture of the lord. Draw other pictures in different parts of the pyramid.
2. Draw a "minute-movies" series of pictures on "Feudal Days."
3. Tell the class about a story, or motion picture dealing with feudal times.
4. On a large cardboard outline "Feudal Times" and "Modern Times." In short phrases, show how they are different.
5. Dramatize: homage in feudal times.
6. Paste in your scrapbook pictures of lords and serfs.

## TOPICS FOR DISCUSSION

1. Feudalism was a bad system.
2. The serf was unhappy under feudalism.
3. The feudal lord was cruel.
4. Feudalism met the needs of the early Middle Ages.
5. Homage was a stupid ceremony.

## WORD LIST

| | | | |
|---|---|---|---|
| feudalism | estate | manor | homage |
| lord | vassal | village | service |
| fief | serf | hereditary | Middle Ages |

# VI

## *Part 2:* CASTLES AND KNIGHTS

During the Middle Ages, many a hilltop provided a base upon which a fort had been built. The fort was also a home in which dwelt a fighting man. Because this fighting man probably had taken the oath of knighthood he therefore lived according to a code called "chivalry." The castle and the knight belonged to the Middle Ages as truly as the auto mechanic and the skyscraper belong to our age.

THE CASTLE. The feudal lord lived in a great stone house or castle. It was a home and fort combined. The part of the castle which served as a fort was called the donjon or keep. As the chief purpose of the castle was to provide a means of defense against an enemy, the castle was built on the top of a hill. If no rocky height was available, the castle was erected in a marshy place. In this case, it was surrounded by a ditch or moat which was filled with water. The castle was well protected for it was like an island. To enter or to leave the castle, one had to cross a drawbridge. When not needed, this was drawn up close to the castle walls.

THE CASTLE A PLACE OF SAFETY. During an attack, the people in the castle were quite safe from the enemy. The castle usually could not be captured easily except by starving the garrison. This could be done if the enemy could besiege the castle long enough, for rarely was there a large food supply on hand. During the attack there would be many to feed because all the

© *Ewing Galloway*

## A Great Feudal Castle
The town nestles at the feet of the stronghold in the hill.

people of the nearby village went into the castle when warfare commenced.

THE ATTACK ON THE CASTLE. To attack a castle required great courage. Except for the difficulty of storing sufficient food, those defending the castle had the advantage. In almost perfect safety, the defenders could shoot arrows at the attacking party. It was, therefore, a great accomplishment for the attacking party to get near the castle. When they did come close their position was not enviable. Then the garrison hurled great stones down upon them. Sometimes the defenders poured oil or molten lead on the attacking force from those narrow slit-like openings you notice in the castle towers. Woe to the soldier who was below when this happened! 

Sometimes those who attacked the castle were aided by war

engines. These might be movable towers which could be brought up to the very walls of the castle. Battering rams were also used; the purpose of these was to make a breach in the walls of the castle through which the attacking force could rush.

THE CASTLE AS A HOME. The castle made a better fort than home. The most ordinary conveniences we have in our homes such as artificial light, running water and good heating were unknown to the castle dwellers. The place where the lord lived resembled a huge stone barn. The plan of the residence was simple. It consisted of a great hall with several smaller rooms opening into it. The rooms usually were connected with each other. There were no passageways, so that to get from one part of the residence to the other, you had to pass through the rooms between. There could be no privacy. When home, the lord and his family spent most of their time in the great hall. The walls were perfectly bare except for an occasional tapestry. There was little furniture and this was usually uncomfortable.

THE CASTLE HALL. The castle hall where the lord spent so much of his time was a large room. At one end of the hall upon a raised platform was the table where the lord and the family ate. The lord had a big chair for himself. He looked very important when seated in this chair. The lord was really a king in his own section of the country. The people about him respected and feared him much more than they feared and respected the real king. The lord was wise, therefore, in making himself appear impressive when in the castle hall. The hall was heated and lighted also by a great fire which burned in an open hearth in the center of the room. Food was usually cooked at this fireplace. Meat was roasted by being turned on great spits and then brought to the table by servants.

CASTLE AMUSEMENTS. The nobles were frequently at war. When at home they spent much of their time playing

*Courtesy Metropolitan Museum of Art, New York*

**The Castle Hall**

Here the lord and his guests ate, drank, and made merry.

games. Chess was a great favorite. The people of the castle were often entertained by strolling minstrels who got their board for their songs. In Southern France the minstrels were called troubadours. But listening to minstrels was little amusement surely. It must have been very dull for the ladies. They had very few books to read and these, of course, were not printed books. There were no musical instruments worth mentioning. The piano with the wealth of music written for it did not come until centuries later.

KNIGHTHOOD. To belong to a class of men called knights or to achieve knighthood was the ambition of almost every boy whose father was a feudal lord. Knights were soldiers who undertook to be especially brave, but they had other ambitions. Knights believed they must perform certain good acts. They were bound by a code called chivalry. The word, chivalry, comes from the French word for horse and it was adopted probably because the knights went about so much on horseback. Knight and horse were clothed in armor; the knight wore a suit of light steel or a coat of small chains called mail. At first, any young man could become a knight. Later, knighthood was open only to the sons of noblemen.

THE KNIGHT'S CODE. The young man who wished to become a knight usually made certain promises. He swore:

    To fear God and to maintain the Christian religion
    To serve the king faithfully and with valor
    To protect the weak and defenseless
    To refrain from giving offense
    To honor women
    To speak the truth
    To keep the FAITH.

Much, therefore, was expected of the young knight; "handsome in body, gallant, gentle, and modest, not given to talking."

THE PAGE. Just about the time our boys go to school the boy of the Middle Ages, if eligible, began to prepare for knighthood. He began as a page. For seven years he served in the castle of some great lord. He learned what was expected of a knight. The page took lessons in using some of the knightly weapons. His manners were not neglected; he was told to keep his hands and nails clean; the ladies at the castle taught him how to act as a gentleman. When the page reached his fourteenth birthday he might be promoted to be a squire.

THE SQUIRE. As a squire the boy learned more about the duties of a knight. Sometimes he accompanied his lord to war. He did not join in the fighting; he merely acted as an attendant to his knight. Above all he was taught to obey. "It is proper that the young man learn to obey before he governs, otherwise he will not appreciate the nobility of his rank when he becomes a knight." Having reached the age of twenty-one, the squire was ready to become a knight.

THE YOUNG KNIGHT. There was a beautiful ceremony attached to becoming a knight. It varied somewhat in different parts of Europe but the main features w e r e everywhere the same. S i n c e the Church had much to do with the ideals of chivalry, the ceremony was a religious one. If possible the ceremony took place on one of the great feasts of the Church, Christmas, Easter, the Ascension of Our Lord, or the feast of Saint John the Baptist. The candidate prepared for knighthood by a number of preliminary acts. A lock of his hair was cut as a mark

*Courtesy of B. F. Williamson*

**The Accolade**

Knighthood was conferred by a blow with the flat of the sword.

of surrender of his services to God. He bathed as a sign of the purity that was expected of a knight. Rest upon a hard couch was often part of the preparation; this was to remind the young man that he must look for his rest not in this world but in Paradise. The squire sometimes clothed himself in robes of different colors, white for innocence, red for the blood he must be willing to shed for his lord, and the black mantle, a reminder of death:

"Death and earth where you will rest
Whence you came and whither you return
This is what you must keep before your eyes."

The young squire prepared for knighthood by prayer. Toward evening of the day before the young man was to be made a knight, a procession was formed in the castle. In the procession were all those who were to take part in the ceremony of the morrow, together with the friends of the candidate. The knight's armor was carried in the procession which moved from the castle hall to the chapel. Arriving at the chapel, the armor was deposited on the altar. Then all save the young man withdrew. He was left alone in the church guarding his armor. He spent the night in prayer.

THE CONFERRING OF KNIGHTHOOD. In the morning the young man made his promises. After Mass the ceremony of knighthood was completed. The lord having charge of the ceremony struck the candidate across the shoulders with the flat side of a sword pronouncing the words, "In the name of God, of St. Michael and of St. George, I dub thee knight; be brave, bold and loyal." Then the knight donned his armor. Mounting his horse he gave an exhibition of his skill as a rider. At last he was ready to go forth to follow his noble calling and uphold the ideals of his order.

KNIGHTLY AMUSEMENTS. The knights had their amusements. They were especially fond of the tournament. This was a sham battle between two groups of knights. Often the knights from one castle would contend against the knights from another castle. Usually no great harm was done because they fought with blunted weapons. Sometimes two knights would have a little battle called a joust. Even the amusements of the knights called for skill and daring.

THE YOUNG KNIGHT'S VIGIL

*From a Fifteenth Century Manuscript at Brussels*

## Knightly Amusements

Tilting at a manikin. If the shield is not struck in the center the horseman receives a smart blow from the heavy whip.

KNIGHTLY IDEALS. The poet Tennyson describes the conduct of a knight very beautifully. You will find the description in the "Idyls of the King." In this poem King Arthur speaking of his knights says he made them take this oath:

"I made them lay their hands in mine and swear
To reverence the King, as if he were
Their conscience, and their conscience as their King,
To break the heathen and uphold the Christ,
To ride abroad redressing human wrongs,
To speak no slander, no, nor listen to it,
To honor his own words as if his God's
To lead sweet lives in purest chastity."

## OBJECTIVE TESTS

Test 1: Completion Test.

1. The part of the castle which served as a fort was called the ................

2. To enter the castle one had to walk over a ................

3. Another word for the great stone house in which the noble lived was a ................

4. The castle's walls were bare except for some pieces of ................

5. Wandering singers who visited castles were called ................

6. Soldiers who tried to be especially brave and good were called ................

7. To make a hole in the walls of the castle attacking parties used a ................

8. To train for knighthood the boy first had to begin as a ............... in the lord's castle.

9. After seven years of such service, the boy accompanied his master to war. He was called a ................

10. Sometimes two knights would have a little battle called a ................

Test 2: Meaning of Words.

1. What were the "Idyls of the King"?
   (a) dreams of King Arthur
   (b) a poem by Tennyson
   (c) a number of pagan gods
   (d) lazy habits of a king                    ............

2. What was a tournament?
   (a) a grand race
   (b) a prize-fight
   (c) a sham battle
   (d) a duel                                   ............

3. What was the donjon?
   (a) a dark cellar used as a prison
   (b) a drink for the lord
   (c) a doll for the lord's children
   (d) a part of the castle                     ............

4. What is chivalry?
   (a) conduct worthy of a knight
   (b) good horsemanship
   (c) a group of horses
   (d) dubbing a knight          . . . . . . . . . . . .

## ORAL DRILL

1. What was the home of the feudal lord called?
2. Where was it usually located?
3. Besides being a home, what other purpose did the dwelling of the feudal lord serve?
4. Which function of the dwelling was the more important?
5. On his own land what power did the feudal lord possess?
6. What was an important occupation of the feudal lord?
7. What amusement did the feudal lord enjoy most?
8. Why did the knight sometimes don a black robe?
9. What was the final preparation for knighthood?
10. Where was the lord's dinner cooked? Where did he eat it?

## QUESTIONS THAT MAKE YOU THINK

1. Why are there not many castles built today?
2. State two purposes for a castle in the Middle Ages.
3. Why was it difficult to capture a castle?
4. Compare methods of warfare in the Middle Ages with those of today.
5. Describe the ceremony of becoming a knight.
6. Show how knighthood has influenced the manners of today.
7. Compare modern and medieval entertainment.
8. Outline the training for knighthood.
9. Define each: donjon, castle, knight.
10. (a) Name two advantages of living in a medieval castle. (b) Name two disadvantages.

## QUESTIONS THAT TEST YOUR CHARACTER

1. Describe your idea of a modern gentleman.
2. Describe the medieval knight.
3. State three of the promises a young knight had to make.
4. Show how you can improve yourself by following the knight's code.

5. "The knight had good manners." Give examples of good manners in: (a) Middle Ages, (b) today.

---

## ACTIVITIES

---

1. Make a drawing comparing the dress of a knight with the uniform of an American soldier today.
2. Dramatize: the conferring of knighthood.
3. Suppose you were a knight. Write a few pages in your diary, telling your adventures.
4. From soap or clay build a model of a castle.
5. Tell the class of a motion picture about knights which you saw.
6. Dramatize: a medieval feast.
7. On a large cardboard show how knighthood gave us ideas about modern manners. Place the cardboard on the bulletin board.
8. Tell the class Mark Twain's story about "The Connecticut Yankee in King Arthur's Court."
9. Paste in your scrapbook pictures about knights and castles.
10. Write a short story "A Knight Comes to Life in the Twentieth Century."

---

## TOPICS FOR DISCUSSION

---

1. The knight was a perfect gentleman.
2. The castle was a healthful place to live.
3. The knight was a religious person.
4. People today are more polite than people in the Middle Ages.

---

## WORD LIST

---

| | | |
|---|---|---|
| castle | tournament | chivalry |
| squire | war engine | dub |
| page | donjon | joust |
| chess | knight | tapestry |
| keep | | garrison |

# VI

## *Part 3:* TOWNSPEOPLE AND CRAFTSMEN

Sometimes a knight could climb to the topmost tower of his castle and from that height see in the distance the walls of a town. Within those walls were hundreds of people busy at their daily tasks; some were merchants, others craftsmen. Their homes were two or three storied dwellings with high gabled roofs. Narrow winding streets and crooked lanes gave access to different parts of the town. Rising midst the homes of the people—its lofty spires uplifted in blessing—stood the principal church of the town.

ORIGIN OF THE TOWNS. Towns and small cities were scattered throughout Europe. Some of the towns were very ancient; they had been in existence during Roman times. These old towns were usually located along the trade routes which followed the rivers and made use of mountain passes. The increase in trade caused the old towns to grow larger and brought new ones into existence. Some of the newer towns had been villages on the estate of some feudal lord or they belonged to a monastery.

THE PEOPLE OF THE TOWN. The people who lived in the town made their living as traders, merchants, or craftsmen. Usually they were subjects of a feudal lord and although they did not work on his farm for him, they did, however, have to pay him taxes which were often heavy. To protect themselves the people built a wall about their town. Usually they **could** do this only with the permission of their feudal lord.

© *Ewing Galloway*

## A Medieval Town

This is a present day view of the original buildings in a medieval city. In those days buildings were built to last.

TOWN CHARTERS. The feudal lords sometimes made heavy and unjust demands upon the people of the town. Whenever they could, therefore, the people of the town strove to get a charter from the lord. A charter was a written agreement between lord and people. By the terms of these charters, the lords usually agreed to grant their people a certain degree of self-government. The people acquired the right of electing their own mayor and magistrates and aldermen. The amount of taxes the lord could get from the townsfolk was often stated in the charters. Sometimes the people openly rebelled. More often, however, they got charters by purchase.

THE UNITY OF THE TOWNSPEOPLE. The people of the towns usually lived together as good neighbors. "All the men of the commune (town) shall help each other with all their might" is a regulation which describes how important the people of one town looked upon good fellowship. When the number of workers in the town grew enough, the workers in each trade formed workingmen's organizations called gilds. Thus the butchers had a gild composed of those who were in that branch of the meat business; those who were stone cutters formed a gild of their craft; so also did those who were cloth weavers. In time there were as many gilds as there were occupations. Some were craft gilds, that is gilds whose members worked at a trade requiring a special skill such as the goldsmiths, or the shoemakers, or the wood carvers, or the sword makers. The merchants also had their gilds. The fact that most of the men in the town belonged to a particular gild helped to give the people of the town regard for one another and to make them proud of their town.

THE CRAFT GILD. Almost everything we use nowadays comes from the factory. In the Middle Ages there were no factories. In those days if you wanted a suit of clothes you went to the street where the weavers lived. Their homes probably were located on a street so narrow, indeed, that the man upstairs could lean out the window and almost shake hands with his neighbor across the street. Having found your weaver, you were shown samples of cloth. The kind you selected was woven for you. Then you took the newly woven cloth to the tailor. He made it into a suit. Should you need a sword you must see the armorer. Only the shoemaker could supply you with shoes. There were no department stores in the medieval towns. As a rule each man was his own manufacturer, storekeeper, and salesman.

THE GILD'S HIGH STANDARD. Each thing was made by hand by those who were masters of their craft. In making the article the craftsmen were bound by strict rules, for the gild system governed both the manufacture and sale of articles in

© *Ewing Galloway*

**Medieval Gild Halls at Antwerp, Belgium**

In the row are the Gild Halls of the Archers, the Coopers, the Carpenters, and the Clothiers.

the Middle Ages. Night work was prohibited, "for no man can work as neatly by night as by day." The craftsman who belonged to a gild agreed to obey various rules regarding the making of his product as well as the price charged. As a result, the quality of the work was high and usually the price was fair, for the Church insisted on a just price. There was the keenest kind of competition among the gildsmen, each striving his hardest to make the best article for the right price.

THE GILD SYSTEM. To be a member of any craft gild, one had to go through a course of training. When a boy was old enough he presented himself to a master craftsman as an apprentice. Only masters who were patient and good could train apprentices. If accepted the lad lived with this man whom he called his master. He worked hard making himself useful,

*Drawn expressly for "The Old World and America"*

## The Masterpiece

The craftsman puts the final touches on the piece that is to gain him admittance into the gild.

trying meanwhile to learn something about the trade. For his work he received his board but no pay. After he passed the period of apprenticeship, he became a journeyman. He could work by the day but he was still under his master. If the journeyman did his work well he was graduated as a master workman. To become a master the young artisan had to prove his skill by passing an examination. The examination took the form of making some article which those of a particular craft ought to be able to make. Thus, you can picture an eager young apprentice who has been taught to be a silversmith arriving at the meeting place or gild hall of the silversmiths. The young artisan carries carefully a candlestick which he himself has made. This he presents to the masters of the gild for their approval; it is his *MASTERPIECE.* If the masters are satisfied the young craftsman is declared a master and he may go into business for himself.

THE CHURCH AND THE GILDS. The Church played an important part in the operation of the gild system. Every gild pledged its members to do certain civic and religious acts. Some of the gilds prepared plays, called Mystery Plays, to teach the people the history of Our Lord's life. The importance of virtue was shown by another sort of theatrical production called a Morality Play. The great plays of William Shakespeare might not have been written if the gilds had not trained the people to take an interest in drama.

The gilds trained their members to perform acts of charity. All gilds looked after their sick members. If a gildman died his family was taken care of. The gild saw to it that prayers were said and Masses were offered for the departed brother. Besides this each gild performed particular acts of piety. It is most edifying to read how one gild provided the candles to be used in the procession on the feast of Corpus Christi, and another promised to see that all poor strangers who died were given decent burial. The spirit of the gilds is set forth beautifully in this grace before meals which was said by the Dublin merchants:

> "Christ that bread broke,
> Bless our bread and our all
> And all that we have, and shall have
> And feed us with Himself. Amen."

## OBJECTIVE TESTS

TEST 1: Completion Test.
1. A written agreement between the lord and the people was called a ................
2. ............ were workingmen's organizations.
3. Besides the merchant gild there was the ............ gild.
4. Before one could become a craftsman, he had to start as a ................

5. After a period of training, the young worker became a
   . . . . . . . . . . . . . . . . .

6. Before the skilled worker was considered a master, he had to
   prove his skill by making an article called a . . . . . . . . . . . .

7. A play which showed the importance of certain virtues was
   called a . . . . . . . . . . . . . play.

8. Plays dealing with Our Lord's life were called . . . . . . . . . . . . .
   plays.

9. The amount of taxes the lord could get from the townspeople
   was often stated in the . . . . . . . . . . . . . . . . .

TEST 2: Relationship Test.
   Arrange the following in the order of importance:
                    journeyman
                    apprentice
                    master workman

TEST 3: Matching Test.
   1. Mystery Play              (a) Importance of virtue
   2. Town Charter              (b) High Standard
   3. Gild System               (c) Our Lord's Life
   4. Morality Play             (d) Self-government

## QUESTIONS THAT TEST YOUR CHARACTER

1. Name two effects the Church had on town life.
2. Explain how the gild encouraged honesty.
3. State two advantages of the use of the apprenticeship.
4. Was it unfair not to pay wages to the apprentice? Give a
   reason.

## QUESTIONS THAT MAKE YOU THINK

1. Give two reasons for the location of towns in the Middle Ages.
2. What is the difference between a village and a town?
3. Describe a townsman in the Middle Ages.
4. Compare him with a modern townsman. Take your own town
   as an example.
5. (a) State two meanings for the word "craft." Use the dic-
   tionary. (b) What meaning is the one intended by this
   textbook?
6. State two kinds of gilds.
7. Tell how a gild is different from a labor's union.
8. Were the gilds good organizations? Give two reasons for your
   opinion.

9. "The gild had a high standard." Explain the meaning of this statement.
10. Compare a modern and a medieval street.

---

## ACTIVITIES

---

1. Make a sketch of a medieval town seen from a distance. Include the cathedral spire in your sketch, also the town wall, and so forth.
2. On a large cardboard make two columns: In one column, describe the gild in short sentences. Number each. In the second column, point out features of a labor union of today.
3. On a large scroll of paper, make a town charter.
4. Dramatize: the worker and his masterpiece.
5. Write a short Morality Play. Stage it in the assembly period.
6. Paste in your scrapbook pictures of town life in the Middle Ages.

---

## TOPICS FOR DISCUSSION

---

1. The gild was better than the labor union.
2. We should revive gilds' day.
3. Medieval town life was better than the modern city life.
4. The gild was democratic.

---

## WORD LIST

---

| | | | | |
|---|---|---|---|---|
| gild | village | commune | apprentice | masterpiece |
| master | town | charter | gild system | journeyman |

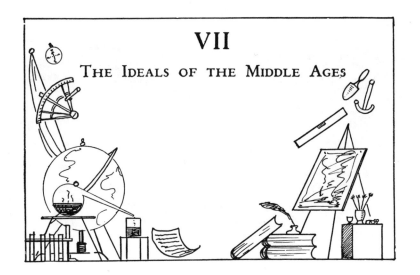

# VII

## THE IDEALS OF THE MIDDLE AGES

### AIM

To understand that the American government is based upon the ideal of order which flourished during the Middle Ages.

To realize that much of our learning, art, as well as ideals of fine conduct, come from Medieval times and that the basis of our civilization is Catholic Civilization.

PERHAPS THE chief reason we study about the Middle Ages is that from this period we get ideals of important matters. The people who lived in the Middle Ages had high ideals about holiness, about human rights, about learning, about art. You will observe that the ideals of the Middle Ages covered all the important things in life. We owe a debt to the people of the Middle Ages, therefore, because they had such high notions about everything important. Many of these ideals are with us today and the world is better for them.

# VII

## *Part 1:* ORDER

The city of Washington, D. C., is the capital of the United States. Here are found the buildings where the business of our government is carried on. The House of Representatives and the United States Senate are located in the Capitol. These two bodies make up that branch of our government which is called the law making or legislative branch. The United States Supreme Court meets in its own beautiful building. The Supreme Court is part of another branch of our government called the judicial branch. It is important for us to remember that the kind of government we have in this country is based upon ideas in which the people of the Middle Ages believed.

THE SUPREMACY OF LAW. The priests of the Middle Ages when they preached to the people, taught them the same lessons that our priests teach today. The necessity of obedience was often explained. The duty of obedience included obedience to the Laws of God, obedience to the laws of the Church, and obedience to the laws of the State. Since the Church taught that everyone must obey the laws of the State it was important that rulers and kings be compelled always to make good laws. In the making of good laws for the people two things helped. The teachings of the Church were a guide to good law-making. Then again the formation of committees selected by the people with power to make laws for them was another way of obtaining good laws. Both of these ideas have helped us in the United

States. We believe that the laws must be obeyed by everyone. On the walls of the Department of Justice Building in Washington there is carved this saying: "No free government can survive that is not based on the supremacy of the law." We, therefore, believe in the supremacy of the law. We also believe in representative government.

THE CHURCH AND LIBERTY. The Church strove constantly to get more liberty for the ordinary man. Popes, bishops and monks were interested in human liberty. They showed this in different ways. The Church tried to abolish slavery for slavery is the denial of human liberty. The Church tried to put a stop to war. War usually destroys freedom since most men do not fight from choice. Three customs aided peace. These were the *Peace of God,* the *Truce of God* and *Sanctuary.* The Church by the *Peace of God* threatened excommunication for anyone who would injure through war persons in the religious state, scholars, merchants, pilgrims, women, peasants; even the cattle, farm implements and the land and church buildings were protected. The *Truce of God* reduced the number of fighting days by forbidding private warfare on Sundays and holy days. It extended the number of peace days, until fighting was forbidden on three quarters of the days of each year. *Sanctuary* protected the lives and persons of those who had taken refuge in a church or even outside the church, or at a wayside cross. The Church also tried to set limits upon the power of kings. There were kings who would have interfered even with the religion of their subjects. The Church told those kings that there was a limit to their power. The bravery of one Churchman, Archbishop Thomas à Becket, in rebuking a despotic king cost him his life.

ST. THOMAS OF CANTERBURY. Thomas à Becket was a handsome and talented young man whose father, a London merchant, was able to give him a splendid education and to supply him with other advantages. Thomas made such good

use of his education that many people wanted to employ him. He held positions of importance in the world but the Church needed him. Thomas was called to the highest church office in England. He was made Archbishop of Canterbury. Soon the Archbishop found himself in a dispute with King Henry II. Henry had interfered with the rights of the Church which means that the king had interfered with human liberty. Henry II in a fit of rage cried out, "Who will rid me of this troublesome priest?" Perhaps he really did not mean what he said but some of his knights who heard it decided to attack the Archbishop.

*Courtesy B. F. Williamson*

**St. Thomas of Canterbury**
Because Becket defended the rights of the church, he lost his life.

THE MARTYRDOM OF SAINT THOMAS. The knights sought out Saint Thomas and they found him at evening before the altar in the cathedral at Canterbury. These knights murdered the Archbishop. When the news reached the people they were horrified. Archbishop Thomas was soon regarded as a Saint and thousands including the King visited his tomb which became a place of pilgrimage. St. Thomas died in defense of the Church and in the name of liberty.

## THE GREAT CHARTER

KING JOHN OF ENGLAND. The fact that the law is supreme and that even the king must obey the law was made clear in England during the reign of King John. King John lived about a hundred years after the time of William the Conqueror or King William I. John was the son of King Henry II. From the very beginning of his career he gave little promise of being a good king. In the first place, John was a bad Catholic. He neglected his religious duties shamelessly. On the very day he was crowned, he did not go to Communion.

"LACKLAND." John's older brother, Richard the Lion Hearted, who succeeded their father, Henry II, died leaving no heir. John was made king. Yet at one time no one ever thought John would be king for he was the youngest of the sons of King Henry II. Indeed John's chances of getting any territory to rule seemed so slight that his brothers called him "Lackland." Now, all the brothers were dead, and John was the king. Early in his reign, which began in 1199, King John lost a large part of the English possessions in France. The English rulers, since the time of William the Conqueror, had held large pieces of French territory. War broke out between the English monarch and his French subjects. As a result the English lost valuable territory in France.

THE GREAT CHARTER (1215). King John interfered so outrageously with the Church that Pope Innocent III was forced to excommunicate him. That is, John was cut off from the Church. This was a terrible scandal to the English. The thought that their king was so wicked as to merit such punishment filled them with great horror. But King John did not seem to care about their disapproval. He also quarreled with the barons. Finally, the barons banded together under the leadership of Archbishop Stephen Langton to make John act as a king should. To prove his good faith John was forced to put the King's seal a document called the Great Charter. Often it is called by its Latin name, Magna Carta, which means great charter. By the terms of this document the people secured for themselves some liberties which for a long time they had believed they should possess. (See frontispiece.)

THE PROVISIONS OF MAGNA CARTA. Magna Carta contains sixty-three provisions. The most important ones may be summed up as follows:—(1) The Church is to be free from interference. (2) The king cannot tax the people without their consent. (3) Every man accused of crime has the right to trial by jury. Justice is not to be sold, denied or delayed.

THE VALUE OF MAGNA CARTA. The value of Magna Carta comes from the fact that it is a contract between the ruler and the people. The ruler agrees to do what is right by respecting the rights of his subjects. The agreement affects all classes from the highest to the lowest. Thus a poor man is guaranteed justice in matters of personal rights. For example, a poor man could not be convicted of a crime without a trial, just because he was poor. The Charter is often called the foundation of English liberty.

THE GROWTH OF ENGLISH LIBERTY. Magna Carta was an important step forward in the progress of English liberty. During the same century, the Thirteenth, the people succeeded in obtaining from the king additional rights and privileges. This occurred during the reign of King Henry III, who succeeded John and who was somewhat like him. At first, people did not realize the kind of king Henry III would prove to be for when he was made king he was too young actually to rule. But when he grew old enough to take charge of the

*Drawn expressly for "The Old World and America"*

### De Montfort Calling the First Parliament

These men were determined to check the power of the king. They demanded and got a voice in the government.

government he refused to obey the terms of Magna Carta although he had taken an oath to be bound by them.

THE BEGINNINGS OF PARLIAMENT. The king had a body of advisers composed of the prominent men of England, nobles, bishops and abbots. This Great Council began to be called Parliament, a word of French origin which means to speak. The members of this body and other prominent men in England began to fear that King Henry III would turn out to be like his father, King John, a bad ruler. Led by Simon de Montfort the barons made war upon King Henry III. The King was defeated and taken prisoner. While De Montfort held the King prisoner a Parliament was called. This body differed from previous Parliaments because some representatives of the towns were summoned to the meeting as well as the important nobles, the bishops and the abbots. This parliament, which met in 1265, is sometimes called "The First Parliament."

THE MODEL PARLIAMENT 1295. In 1295 a better plan was devised for calling Parliament so that the gathering that met in that year is sometimes called the Model Parliament. Probably as a result of the Model Parliament the custom developed of having two houses in Parliament. The upper was called the House of Lords, the lower house became known as the House of Commons.

THE MOTHER OF PARLIAMENTS. England was not the first or the only country in Europe to have representative government. Throughout Europe, in Spain and Portugal, in Poland, France, and Hungary, and even in Iceland, there were parliaments or gatherings of the representatives of the people. The English Parliament is perhaps the most famous of parliaments and the English body deserves to be called the "Mother of Parliaments." At any rate the founders of our own government got some useful ideas for the Congress of the United States from the English Parliament.

---

## OBJECTIVE TESTS

---

TEST 1: Completion Test.
  1. "No free government can survive that is not based on the supremacy of the . . . . . . . . . . ." is a statement carved on the walls of the Department of Justice Building in Washington, D. C.
  2. The Great Charter was signed by King . . . . . . . . . . . . . . . .
  3. "Lackland" was a nickname given to . . . . . . . . . . . . . . . .
  4. Five noble thoughts about the important things of life are called . . . . . . . . . . . . . . . .
  5. The Church taught obedience to the Laws of God, to the laws of the Church, and the laws of the . . . . . . . . . . . . . . . .
  6. The Pope cut off King John from the Church. This means John was . . . . . . . . . . . . . . . .
  7. The English Parliament is called the . . . . . . . . . . . . of Parliaments, because of its great influence.
  8. The barons under the leadership of Archbishop . . . . . . . . . . . forced John to sign the Great Charter.

9. The ................ was the first great step in the progress
   of English liberty.
10. ............... was the most important diocese in England.

TEST 2: Matching Test.
   Copy Column B. Write the correct number from Column A
which matches each.

| Column A | | Column B |
|---|---|---|
| 1. Langton | ( ) | refused to obey Great Charter |
| 2. de Montfort | ( ) | improved Parliament |
| 3. John | ( ) | Norman conquest |
| 4. William | ( ) | Lackland |
| 5. Henry III | ( ) | Canterbury |

TEST 3: Order of Events.
   Arrange each in the order of time:
   (    )  Richard dies
   (    )  Norman conquest
   (    )  Great Charter
   (    )  revolt under de Montfort
   (    )  city of Washington, D. C. is founded

## ORAL DRILL

1. What document made it clear that even the
   king of England must obey the law?          ............
2. What was John called in his youth?          ............
3. Who succeeded Richard Lionhearted?          ............
4. Where in Europe did England lose territory
   during the reign of King John?              ............
5. What is the law making body in England
   called?                                     ............
6. What nobleman usually receives the credit
   for calling the first Parliament?           ............
7. Which Pope excommunicated King John?        ............
8. What do the words *Magna Carta* mean?       ............

## QUESTIONS THAT MAKE YOU THINK

1. What is representative government?
2. Name two ways in which the United States is based upon
   ideals of the Middle Ages.
3. (a) Point out one likeness between Congress and Parliament.
   (b) Point out one difference.

4. Was Stephen Langton a great man? Give one good reason for your answer.
5. State three provisions of the Great Charter.
6. Why should Americans know the great Charter?
7. Give three steps in the growth of English liberty.
8. "The Middle Ages helped develop democracy." Explain this statement.
9. Define "ideal." Give two examples of ideals today.
10. Name two ideals given by the Middle Ages.

## QUESTIONS THAT TEST YOUR CHARACTER

1. State three bad traits of King John.
2. State one good trait (a) of Stephen Langton, (b) of Simon de Montfort, (c) of Richard, the Lion-Hearted.
3. Why should we obey the laws of the school? Mention two of these laws.
4. Mention two laws of the government. Why should we obey them?
5. Was the Great Charter fair to the king? Give one good reason for your answer.

## ACTIVITIES

1. Dramatize: the Great Charter is accepted by King John.
2. On a large scroll, imitate the Great Charter. On it write its chief provisions.
3. From soap make a model of the English Parliament.
4. Suppose you were Simon de Montfort. Tell of your war with the king.
5. Make a series of "Strange Facts of History" cartoons, based on English liberty.
6. Make a "peep-box" showing the signing of the Great Charter.
7. Dress a doll like Stephen Langton, Simon de Montfort, King John.
8. Paste in your scrapbook pictures and clippings about English democracy.

## TOPICS FOR DISCUSSION

1. England is a democracy.
2. Without the Great Charter England would never have become a great nation.
3. King John was the weakest of English kings.
4. The Catholic Church is a friend of democracy.

## WORD LIST

noble thoughts
representative government
obedience
ideal
barons
Parliament

liberty
democracy
law
trial by jury
diocese
Great Charter

# VII

## Part 2: LEARNING

Learning in the Middle Ages was a matter of the greatest importance. Since the priests and monks were the best educated men of the time they took charge of education. Students not only received information but they were also taught to think. The system of education extended from the schools to the Universities.

THE SERVICE OF THE MONKS. The education which the people of Europe received during the Middle Ages was the result of the zeal of monks. The most famous of the monastic teachers were the Benedictine monks, but there were others also. Education which the monks gave to the people was complete for they taught the people how to pray, how to work, and how to study. When the monks came to a new part of the country, they selected a suitable place and there built a monastery. This was a church, a house, a school, and a farm combined. The monks were expert farmers. They taught the people who lived near the monastery the best methods of farming. That section of the country where the monastery was located was always prosperous looking. The land was cleared, swamps were drained, orchards were planted, and the whole countryside made happy.

THE MONKS AS HISTORIANS. The monks kept records of all that happened in the country. Their records are the chief source of information that we have of those days. They did

**Monks Copying Manuscripts**
Compare this toilsome way of producing a book with the speed and perfection of the printing presses of today.

another service for later ages. The monks copied and preserved the writings of the learned men of Greece and Rome. We would know nothing, probably, of the writings of the ancient world except for the monks.

THE MONKS AS COPYISTS. Printing had not yet been invented, consequently there was only one way that a book could be reproduced; that was by copying. You would find it a big task to write out by hand this little book. The monks copied by hand books much larger than this one. Nor were they satisfied with a plain copy. Each letter was done most carefully. Often the monks ornamented or illuminated the borders of the pages with beautiful designs. A whole lifetime could be spent copying a single book. Today these illuminated volumes are priceless. The museums which have them consider themselves fortunate indeed.

*Courtesy Metropolitan Museum of Art*

## A Monastery Chapel

The Monks believed that one had to be good to do good.

THE INFLUENCE OF THE MONKS. The Monks were engaged in every work that would make the people happier and better. The first hospitals were organized by the monks. The monastery door was never closed against a stranger. The poor man was always welcome.

THE MONKS AS TEACHERS. The monks were busily engaged in teaching. Monastic schools were of two sorts; one school was for young men who wished to become monks; the other school was kept for boys in the world. Some of the subjects which are taught today in our schools were not taught in those days. But the pupils received a good education which was sufficient for their needs. Besides the schools which the monks maintained there were in some places schools in charge of the parish priests. These schools might be called parish schools.

MEDIEVAL HIGH SCHOOLS. During the Middle Ages a kind of higher school existed for advanced instruction. Schools of this sort were usually located at the cathedral or in some important monastery. For many years these higher schools were the only ones where a boy could get instruction in the higher branches of learning. At a later time, that is, during the Thirteenth Century, many of the great universities of the Middle Ages were founded.

GREAT MEDIEVAL UNIVERSITIES. The love of learning increased to such an extent that universities were organized. Many of those founded in the Middle Ages are still in existence. One of these is the famous University of Paris where students went to learn theology. Another, Bologna, was famous for its law courses both in church or canon law and in civil law. The universities of Bologna and Paris each claim the title of "Mother of the Universities of Europe." The great University of Oxford in England, about which we often hear, was founded in the year 1150. A century later it is said to have had twenty thousand students. The University of Cambridge in England was also famous.

THE ORIGIN OF THE UNIVERSITIES. The universities of the Middle Ages came into existence at different times and for different reasons. Sometimes a large number of students would come together to hear a famous teacher. Other good teachers might journey to the same place. Before long students and teachers in such great numbers would come to that place that a university would be created. Perhaps some wealthy man or powerful prince would help the young university with a gift of land or money. Sometimes a university would be composed of a number of colleges. Oxford is an example of this kind of university. The names of the colleges tell us much about the faith of these early university men. One college at Oxford was called "All Souls College"; another college "Corpus Christi" was named for the Blessed Sacrament.

---

## ORAL DRILL

---

1. Name a famous University in France.
2. Who published books in the Middle Ages?
3. How were books produced in those days?
4. What does "illuminated" mean?
5. For what is Oxford famous?
6. Who were in charge of high schools in the Middle Ages?
7. Who organized the hospitals in the Middle Ages?
8. In the Middle Ages where were the schools of Agriculture to be found?

---

## OBJECTIVE TESTS

---

TEST 1: Matching Test.

Copy Column B on a piece of paper. Next to each item write the correct number from Column A.

| Column A. | | Column B |
|---|---|---|
| 1. Oxford | ( ) | papacy |
| 2. Rome | ( ) | famous monastery |
| 3. Paris | ( ) | study of law |
| 4. Monte Cassino | ( ) | study of theology |
| 5. Bologna | ( ) | "Corpus Christi College" |

TEST 2: Completion Test.

1. The most famous of the monastic teachers were the
   . . . . . . . . . . . . . . . . .
2. The monks lived in a . . . . . . . . . . . . . . . .
3. The monks taught the neighboring people the best methods of . . . . . . . . . . . . . . . .
4. The . . . . . . . . . . . copied the learned writings of ancient times.
5. . . . . . . . . . . . . University was the first great university in England.
6. Most of the great medieval universities were founded during the . . . . . . . . . . . . . . . century.
7. The University of . . . . . . . . . . . . . . . was famous for its law courses.

8. The University of ............... was famous for its courses in theology.
9. Sometimes a ............... would be composed of a number of colleges.
10. The University of Paris claimed the title of ...............

## QUESTIONS THAT MAKE YOU THINK

1. "Learning in the Middle Ages was a matter of importance." Show that this is true.
2. "The monks improved the neighborhood of each monastery." Explain this statement.
3. Define "university." Name (a) a great American university. (b) A great European university.
4. Name two orders of monks: How did they get their names
5. State one contribution of the monks to history.
6. State one contribution of the monks to art.
7. Why were books very expensive in the Middle Ages?
8. "The medieval monastery was also a hotel." Explain.
9. Summarize the contributions of the monks to civilization.
10. Why was education in the hands of the priests and monks during the Middle Ages?

## QUESTIONS THAT TEST YOUR CHARACTER

1. Name five qualities necessary to become a good monk.
2. "The monks were charitable." (a) Explain. (b) State one way how you can be more charitable.
3. "The monks were patient." (a) Explain. (b) State one way in which you can be more patient.
4. "The monks were great students as well as teachers." (a) State two ways in which you can become a better student.

## ACTIVITIES

1. From soap make a model of a monastery.
2. Draw a picture of a medieval university.
3. Make a poster describing a class in a medieval school.
4. Prepare a conversation between the abbot of a monastery and a young man who wants to become a monk.
5. Make a poster showing the monk as a copyist.

6. Have a pageant on "Contributions of the Church to Learning."
7. Imagine yourself a monk. Tell of your daily schedule.
8. On a large map, locate the chief universities of the Middle Ages.
9. Dress a doll like: (a) a medieval teacher, (b) a medieval student.
10. Paste in your scrapbook pictures of universities and of monasteries.

## TOPICS FOR DISCUSSION

1. The Church preserved learning during the Middle Ages.
2. The monks were great artists.
3. People were ignorant during the Middle Ages.
4. There was no liberty of thought in the medieval universities.

## WORD LIST

| | |
|---|---|
| monks | canon law |
| copyist | theology |
| historian | hospital |
| cathedral school | university |

# VII

## *Part 3:* BEAUTY

Many facts show that the people of the Middle Ages had high ideals. For example they built beautiful cathedrals. Cathedrals represent faith. Faith is the most important thing in life. The cathedrals are great acts of faith in stone. The fine ideals of the people who lived in the Middle Ages are clearly seen in the fact that some people were so holy that they were saints. A holy life is the supreme expression of beauty.

THE CATHEDRALS AS HISTORY. The story of the building of the great cathedrals of the Middle Ages helps us to understand the history of the Church. After the time of Our Lord, his followers were persecuted. Often they could not practice their religion openly. Then in the year 313 the Roman Emperor Constantine allowed the Christians to practice their religion freely. They were now permitted to build churches. In building their first church they copied the old Roman law courts or basilicas. Later they built a church in a better way. This was called Romanesque architecture.

THE ROMANESQUE ARCHITECTURE. The old basilica type of building was not found suitable. The roof, usually, was made of wood and therefore a prey to fire. Besides, a wooden roof would not last. So the monks, who were the builders in those days, began to build churches with stone roofs. They employed the round vaults that the Romans had used. But the monks were not mere copyists. They improved upon Roman methods in several essential ways. The new form of church architecture, which the monks helped to develop, is called Romanesque architecture. Dignity, strength, solidity were qualities of those churches. But there were drawbacks too. Romanesque churches have certain shortcomings. Windows must be few and small, for window spaces weaken the walls. Strong walls are needed to support the heavy vaulted roof of this style. Nor can churches built in Romanesque style be of great height. Consequently, Romanesque churches were often dark. The Catholic religion, which is the religion of joy, required something better.

THE GOTHIC CATHEDRAL. Gothic architecture was the result of this longing for something that would express more perfectly the faith of the people of the Middle Ages. The Gothic cathedral is the most perfect house of God made by human hands. Its spires reach towards the heavens; its arches rise yearningly to the Lord. About the cathedral are splendidly carved statues which teach men the truths of their religion. For the cathedral was really the poor man's Bible. Those who could not read could see in the carvings about the cathedral the story of the great characters of the Old Testament, Abraham and Isaac, David, Solomon, and the prophets. They could also study the history of Our Lord's life. Frequently the statue of Christ was placed in front of the principal doorway. He was there to welcome the people to His house for He had said, "I am the door." Mary, about whom it was written: "They found the child with His Mother," was there also for this was the house for Her Son.

Go into the Cathedral. You are rendered speechless by the sheer glory of it. The soft light streams through the jewel-like windows. The columns rise beyond the rainbow lights until they

## BASILICA

The first church buildings were basilicas. They were oblong in shape with two rows of columns and wooden roof. There were very few windows.

## ROMANESQUE

An improvement over the Basilica. The roof was arched and could be built of stone but the walls were very thick and the windows were small.

## GOTHIC

This most beautiful style of architecture with its pointed arches, gave grace to the church. Heavy columns were replaced with graceful pillars. The Gothic church really has no walls. The wall space is filled with jewel-like windows and its stone ceiling is supported from the outside by flying buttresses.

are lost in the shadows beneath the arches of the vaulted roof. Gaze down the long dim aisle to see the reason for the cathedral, the altar, God's dwelling place.

THE "CATHOLIC STYLE." Where are these great cathedrals? They may be found in any of a hundred places in Europe, in York in England, or Burgos in Spain, Cologne in Germany, Rheims in France, or Prague in what is now Czechoslovakia. Among these buildings there would be the widest possible variations in structure, ornamentation, height, vaulting, spire, and sculpture yet they would all alike be beautiful. A great American architect says that these glorious buildings were erected in the "Catholic Style."

BEAUTY AND HOLINESS. The most beautiful thing in this world is a good life. The Saints, who are friends of God, are examples to all men of the value of a beautiful life. Many great Saints lived during the Middle Ages. Some have an important influence upon our lives today. Saint Dominic and Saint Francis of Assisi have followers today who preach the word of God and who teach millions in church and in schools. Both these leaders did something of greatest value for their fellow men. They planned to have their followers live in cities and in towns in the midst of people and to teach by word and to show by example how to live. This method differed from that of the Benedictine and other monks whose monasteries usually were located out in the country. The followers of Saint Francis of Assisi and Saint Dominic were charged with the duty of being in the world but not of it.

SAINT DOMINIC AND THE DOMINICANS. A young Spaniard named Dominic resolved to give his life to the service of God. This was not an extraordinary thing for a Spaniard to do, for Spain has always had many splendid religious both men and women. But Dominic was a man of exceptional talent

**St. Dominic.** This great but humble founder of the Dominican Order traveled barefoot over the country preaching and teaching in highways and towns.

**St. Thomas.** The boy who was known as the "dumb ox" became the greatest of writers, the "Angelic Doctor."

and unusual holiness. He soon attracted followers. Realizing that the people had great need of lessons in their religion because teachers of false docrtines were deceiving many, Dominic organized his followers into an Order. The order was called the Order of Preachers and the Pope approved of it in 1216. Dominic performed another important service for the Church by founding an order for women. Every Catholic owes a special debt to St. Dominic because he helped to spread devotion to the Mother of God through the Rosary. This has continued to be a great work of the Dominican Order.

ST. THOMAS AQUINAS. The Dominican order gave to the Church St. Thomas Aquinas, one of the greatest scholars of all time. In honor of his great learning he is called the "Angelic

Doctor." This "Prince of the Christian Schools" was a great educator. His splendid books are read by many more scholars today than during his own lifetime. Every Catholic university and seminary uses his writings constantly. It is interesting to note that when St. Thomas was young, many of his friends thought he was very slow to learn. Although he did not get high marks in his lessons, he always passed. Not being the first in his class, some spoke of him disrespectfully as the "dumb ox." But while St. Thomas may have been slow, he was sure. Soon Thomas was the first scholar in his class. Not long after, he was the first scholar in Europe. This should convince us that talents are worth only what use we make of them.

ST. FRANCIS OF ASSISI. Assisi is the name of a hill town in Italy where St. Francis was born. The father of Francis was quite well-to-do, so Francis had many things—but not everything. Happiness he did not have. One day he learned why. Listening to the words of the gospel where Our Lord speaks about being absolutely poor, Francis began to realize that these words applied to him. He determined to live in utter poverty, just as Our Lord had lived. St. Francis knew he would find happiness by living in poverty for by so doing he would be fulfilling God's will.

THE FRANCISCANS. St. Francis began to practice perfect poverty. Then he preached it. Although he set the example of the hardest possible way of living, many men wanted to follow him. They, like St. Francis, wished to imitate the poverty of Our Saviour. The many men who came to him St. Francis organized into an Order which the Pope approved in 1223. St. Clare, who saw the splendid things done by the followers of Francis, or Franciscans, determined with God's help to start an Order for women. Like the Order of the men, that for women has the special work of caring for the poor.

*From the mural painting by Aubin Havier*

## St. Francis Preaches to the Birds

Why do we call this great saint "everybody's St. Francis"?

THE THIRD ORDERS. Besides these Orders for men and women who lived apart from the world, the Third Order for people in the world was founded by St. Francis and St. Dominic. Kings, statesmen, artists, musicians, scholars, the greatest and the humblest, have been glad to have been numbered among those who sought to follow more closely the rule of Christ. This fact played an important part in making the people better. Men and women of all classes, the rich and the poor, the learned and the ignorant, the skilled craftsman and the worker in the fields tried to imitate the life of Our Lord because of the example of the "little poor man of Assisi," and of the great Dominic. These saints were, therefore, great social reformers.

EVERYBODY'S SAINT FRANCIS. The beautiful life of St. Francis led people to love him; he was "Everybody's St. Francis." He denied himself everything that he might devote his whole being to the service of God by serving God's children. Everything that God made Francis loved. The great warming sun, the soft breeze at evening, the music of the birds, all reminded him so clearly of our Heavenly Father that he always called the things of God's creation his brothers and sisters.

THE CHURCH IN THE MIDDLE AGES. It would be impossible to appreciate all that the Church wished to do for men during this time. She cared for the bodies of her children. When they fell ill she nursed them in her hospitals; when hungry, she fed them; homeless, she provided shelter. For men's minds she had her schools and universities. For men's souls she had her cathedrals, her saints, her doctrine which is Christ's.

---

## OBJECTIVE TESTS

---

TEST 1: Completion Test.
1. The early Christians in building their first church copied the old Roman law courts, or ................
2. The ............... architecture had small window space.
3. The ............ cathedral has tall graceful spire.
4. ............ was the greatest scholar of the Middle Ages.
5. ............ organized an order pledged to take care of the poor and to live in poverty.

TEST 2: Matching Test.
Copy Column B on a piece of paper. Next to each item write the correct number from Column A.

| Column A | | Column B |
|---|---|---|
| 1. St. Clare | ( ) | lover of nature |
| 2. St. Thomas Aquinas | ( ) | rosary |
| 3. St. Francis of Assisi | ( ) | Angelic Doctor |
| 4. St. Dominic | ( ) | Monte Cassino |
| 5. St. Benedict | ( ) | order of nuns |

Test 3: Description Test.

Select the adjective that best describes each.

1. St. Thomas Aquinas: lazy, learned, poor, handsome. . . . . . . . . . . . . .
2. St. Dominic: strong, talented, impatient, jealous . . . . . . . . . . . . .
3. Gothic: clumsy, dark, graceful, large. . . . . . . . . . . . .
4. Romanesque: slender, massive, delicate, tall. . . . . . . . . . . . .

---

## ORAL DRILL

---

1. What buildings are called "Acts of Faith in Stone"?
2. What style of architecture makes use of flying buttresses?
3. Why were the windows of the medieval Cathedral called jewel-like?
4. What style of architecture preceded the Gothic?
5. Which style is famous for its carvings?
6. Why is the Gothic Cathedral called the "poor man's bible"?
7. Who was the "little poor man of Assisi"?
8. Who was called the "Dumb Ox"?
9. Mention one thing for which Saint Clare is famous?
10. Who is the "Angelic Doctor"?

---

## QUESTIONS THAT TEST YOUR CHARACTER

---

1. Show how the story of the "dumb ox" should give us all courage.
2. Tell how the life of St. Francis of Assisi should teach us to be better human beings.
3. Name two good qualities of St. Thomas Aquinas.
4. Show how the story of St. Clare should make us better Christians.

---

## QUESTIONS THAT MAKE YOU THINK

---

1. (a) What do you mean by "an act of faith carved in stone"? (b) Is this a good description? Explain.
2. Show the difference between the Romanesque and the Gothic church.

3. "The cathedral was the poor man's Bible." Explain the meaning of this statement.
4. Describe a Gothic cathedral.
5. Why were the stained glass windows important?
6. Explain these titles: "Angelic Doctor," "Prince of the Christian Schools."
7. Show the connection between the Third Order and the Franciscans.
8. "The Gothic cathedral was a place of beauty." Show why this statement is true.
9. "The cathedrals may teach us history." Explain.
10. (a) Look up the definition of cathedral. (b) Is every church a cathedral? Give reason for your answer.

## ACTIVITIES

1. From wood or soap construct a model of a Gothic cathedral.
2. Tell the class of the beautiful windows in some church you visited.
3. On a large cardboard, draw pictures showing the Romanesque and Gothic styles.
4. Ask your pastor what kind of architecture your parish church represents. Tell the class of the interior of your church.
5. Dramatize: St. Francis of Assisi Preaches Poverty.
6. On a map show the great cathedral cities of Europe.
7. Draw sketches of St. Francis, St. Dominic, St. Thomas Aquinas.
8. Paste in your scrapbook pictures of cathedrals and of the great medieval saints.

## TOPICS FOR DEBATE

1. St. Thomas was the greatest thinker of the Church.
2. The cathedral was a waste of money.
3. The Gothic cathedral is more beautiful than the Romanesque.

## WORD LIST

| | | | |
|---|---|---|---|
| basilica | Third Order | spires | poverty |
| Gothic | Dominicans | arches | Franciscans |
| Romanesque | | vaulted roof | |

# VIII

## AGE OF NEW INTERESTS

### AIM

To show how the Crusades helped trade between the
East and West.

To realize that noble ideals and noble deeds must go
together.

Two adventures which occurred in the Middle Ages added
greatly to the knowledge of geography and helped trade.
The *Crusades* in which tens of thousands took part changed the
habits of the people of Europe and prepared for the *Age of Discovery*. The journeys to the East of *merchants and missionaries* also hastened the discovery of America.

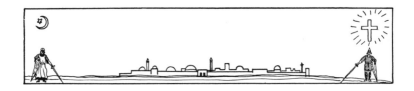

# VIII

## *Part 1:* CRUSADES AND CRUSADERS

One excellent way to learn is to travel. For about two hundred years, during the Middle Ages, men from all parts of Europe were traveling to Palestine where Our Lord was born. These men of Europe were not traveling merely for the pleasure of visiting new places but for a high purpose. They wished to get control of Palestine. This enterprise is called the Crusades. The lives of the people of Europe were affected in many important respects by the Crusades.

THE HOLY LAND IN MEDIEVAL TIMES. Mohammed and his successors, we learned, got and kept possession of the Holy Land. This was a sad state of affairs. The Christains in Europe hated to think that the places made sacred by Our Lord's Passion and Death were in the possession of unbelievers. However, in the beginning, the Mohammedans did not seriously harm the Christians who came to Palestine from all over Europe. When the Mohammedan Turks got control of the Holy Land the pilgrims began to suffer.

The Mohammedan Turks, an Asiatic people, got control of the Holy Land in 1076. From this time on, the Christians often had to suffer severe hardships when in the country held by the Turks. The Christians sometimes were robbed; some were captured and sold into slavery, and some were even murdered. There were many Christians who felt that the time had come to rescue the holy places from the infidel Turks.

*Courtesy New York Public Library*

## "God Wills It"

The stirring words of Pope Urban are repeated by a thousand voices. The age of the Crusades has started.

THE SERMON OF POPE URBAN II. About this time there was a Pope named Urban. Pope Urban II went to Clermont, a town in France, where a council was held. This was in the year 1095. Pope Urban II preached a most eloquent sermon before the gathering. He described the terrible sufferings of the Christians who made pilgrimages to the Holy Land. He told of the disrespect shown to the holy places by the infidel Turks. Then he called upon the men of Europe to rescue the Holy Land from the power of the unbeliever. The Pope's words struck deep into the hearts of the listeners. "God wills it" they cried, and these words became the motto of all those who were willing to help rescue the Holy Land from the Turks.

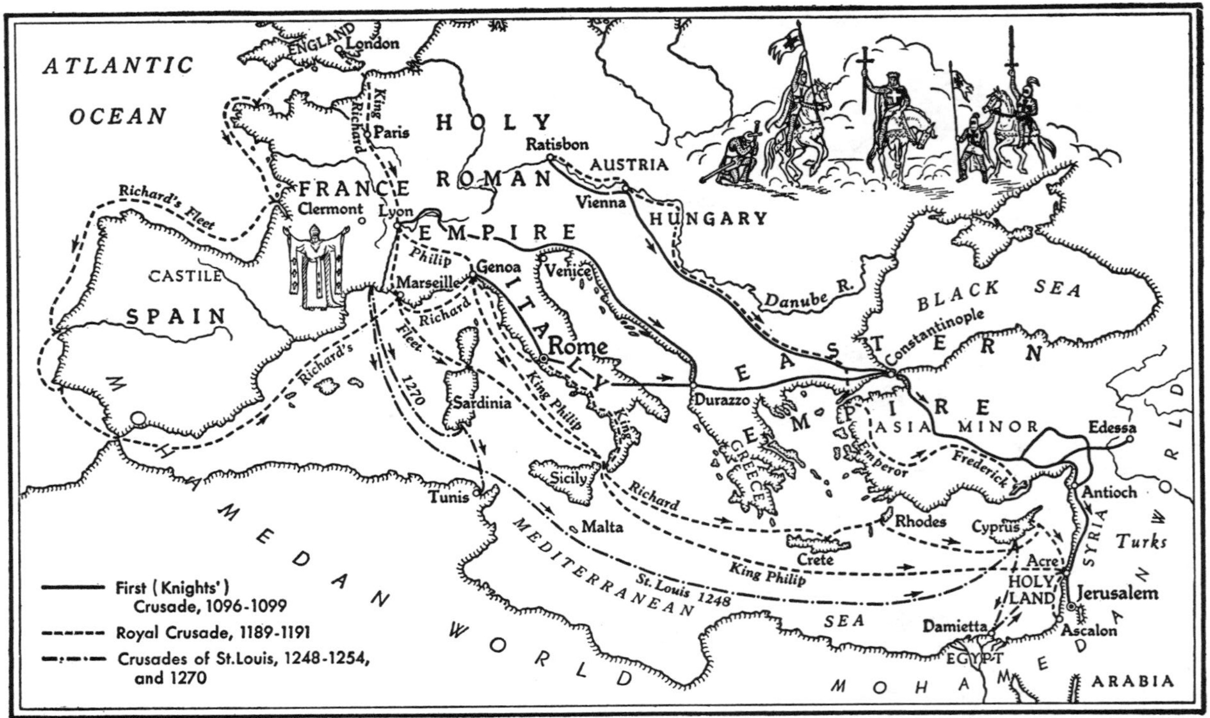

The Crusaders

Drawn expressly for "The Old World and America"

Legend:
- First (Knights') Crusade, 1096-1099
- Royal Crusade, 1189-1191
- Crusades of St.Louis, 1248-1254, and 1270

218

A CRUSADE. Such an undertaking was called a crusade. The word comes from the Latin word for cross. The soldiers who went on these expeditions (there were several) usually wore red crosses attached to their coats of mail or they marked their shields with crosses as a reminder of their noble purpose. When we speak of the crusades we mean the various expeditions that were launched against the power of the Mohammedans in the Holy Land.

In a short time all Europe was talking about the sermon of Pope Urban II. Speakers went about Europe urging the men to go on a crusade. Soon a mighty wave of enthusiasm was sweeping over Europe.

PETER AND WALTER. In a short time two large bands of men—they could hardly be called two armies—were marching towards Palestine. Peter the Hermit was in charge of one group and a knight called Walter the Penniless was at the head of the other. These groups were not well fitted to accomplish what they undertook. At length this wretched army reached Asia Minor. Here most of the men were killed or captured by the Turks. Very few of those who started ever saw Jerusalem. Walter himself was killed. Peter the Hermit and a few followers remained to join the army of the First Crusade which at this time had not yet left Europe.

THE FIRST CRUSADE. The first real crusade is often called the Knights' Crusade because it was under the leadership of famous knights. Godfrey of Bouillon was recognized as the leader. He was, in fact, the most prominent leader in the crusade. We can imagine the feelings of the crusaders when at last they beheld the Holy City for which they had sacrificed so much. Some kissed the ground; many wept for joy. Jerusalem, however, was not easily taken. The crusaders laid siege to it and captured the city only after overcoming the most stubborn

*Drawn expressly for "The Old World and America"*

### The Crusaders' First View of Jerusalem

The Crusaders, raising their swords as crosses, salute the Holy City. What does this picture tell you about the motives of the Crusaders?

resistance on the part of the Turks. Godfrey himself was the first to leap from the siege tower upon the walls of Jerusalem. After the city had been captured, the Crusaders, sad to say, but probably to make sure of holding the city, killed many of the inhabitants. Many of the Crusaders seemed to have forgotten the sacredness of human life.

THE KINGDOM OF JERUSALEM. The kingdom of Jerusalem was established with Godfrey as king. When the ceremony of coronation was about to take place Godfrey pushed aside the crown. He said he could not wear a royal crown in the place where his Lord Jesus had worn the crown of thorns.

Thus it was that in the year 1099, Jerusalem, after having

been held by the Mohammedans almost since the time of Mohammed, was taken by Christians. It was not long, however, before the Mohammedans began to win back territory. In 1147, the Mohammedans captured the city of Edessa. The fall of Edessa was a great blow to the Christians.

SALADIN AND THE SARACENS. The Saracens were Mohammedans who were noted for their hatred of the Christians. Some time after the fall of Edessa, a Mohammedan warrior named Saladin placed himself in charge of an army of Saracens. Under Saladin's able leadership the Saracens began to conquer the territory near Jerusalem. At length the city itself was taken, in 1187. When this news reached Europe, people were thunderstruck. A new Crusade was immediately organized to regain Jerusalem.

THE ROYAL CRUSADE. The new Crusade was under the direction of three monarchs. There was the Emperor Frederick Barbarossa—which means Frederick of the red beard; France was represented by her king, Philip; while England sent her ruler, Richard the Lion-Hearted. Each of these rulers was at the head of a division. Everything at first seemed to point to success, but soon misfortune overtook the enterprise. The first trouble to come upon the Crusade was the death of Frederick. Now Philip and Richard were in charge. Unfortunately these men could not get along together. Philip even threatened to take his army back to France. At last, he did this.

Richard next gravely insulted the young Austrian Duke, Leopold. Richard so far forgot himself that he slapped the duke across the face with his mail-covered hand. The duke could not tolerate such treatment so he too withdrew his force.

RICHARD IN SOLE COMMAND. Richard was now sole commander of the Crusade. However, he could not conquer the Saracens alone nor could he capture Jerusalem. Nevertheless,

**The Insult**
The hot-headed Richard makes an enemy of an ally.

**The "Royal" Crusade**
Richard of England, Philip of France, Frederick of Germany.

Richard did succeed in making a satisfactory agreement with the enemy. By its terms, the Christians were to be allowed to pass freely to and from the Holy Land.

THE END OF THE CRUSADES. A number of attempts were made to take away the Holy Land from the control of the Mohammedans. These attempts did not succeed. Even the children of Europe tried. Under a French boy named Stephen thousands of children set out for the Holy Land. This group reached the port of Marseilles where they were put on ships to be sold to Mohammedan slave dealers. A German lad, Nicholas, led another group. These children reached Rome where they met the Pope. He spoke kindly to them and told them it was their duty to return home to their parents. So they trudged back but many died on the way.

The last Crusades were led by Saint Louis IX, the King of

France. Saint Louis was able to obtain freedom for thousands of Christians who were held captive in Africa by the Mohammedans. St. Louis himself died in the East while on a crusade.

## OBJECTIVE TESTS

TEST 1: Completion Test.
1. The Crusades were started after a famous sermon by .......
2. The Christian pilgrims were robbed in the Holy Land by the ..........................
3. The first real Crusade is called the ............. Crusade.
4. ..................... was the leader of the first Crusade.
5. The Crusaders established the kingdom of ............. in the East.
6. ................... was the great leader of the Saracens.
7. The ........................ were nomads from Arabia.
8. The Royal Crusade was led by Philip, Richard and .......
9. .,............... was the hot-headed Crusader who quarreled with his officers.
10. The Crusade led by Stephen and Nicholas is called the ........................ Crusade.

TEST 2: Character Test.
1. Richard: modest, gentle, quarrelsome, rich.
2. Urban: peaceful, eloquent, smart, holy.
3. Godfrey: modest, loud, cruel, serious.
4. Saladin: mean, treacherous, able, bad.
5. Peter: wealthy, quiet, jealous, religious.

## ORAL DRILL

1. In what country was our Lord born?
2. What were the Crusades?
3. What was the purpose of the Crusades?
4. What symbol did the Crusaders wear?
5. What was the motto of the Crusaders?
6. Which Pope preached the First Crusade?
7. Name two Kings who were Crusaders.
8. Name two boys who were Crusaders.
9. Why was one Crusade called the "Royal Crusade"?
10. Name one famous Mohammedan warrior.

## QUESTIONS THAT MAKE YOU THINK

1. What is meant today when a man is called a "Crusader"? Explain.
2. State two causes of the Crusades.
3. Define "Crusade."
4. Why are Peter and Walter said to be like each other in some respects?
5. What is meant by the Knights' Crusade?
6. Name one victory and one defeat for the Crusaders.
7. Why was not the second Crusade a success?
8. Tell the story of the Children's Crusade.
9. Give two results of the Crusades.
10. Were the Crusades a religious movement? Give a reason for your answer.

## QUESTIONS THAT TEST YOUR CHARACTER

1. Give two good and two bad traits of Richard.
2. Explain the lesson of the Children's Crusade.
3. Were Peter and Walter great men? Explain.
4. Give three good traits of Godfrey of Bouillon.
5. Tell how the story of the Crusades should make you a better person.

## TOPICS FOR DISCUSSION

1. The Crusades were a failure.
2. The Crusaders were brutal warriors.
3. Saladin was a greater man than Richard.
4. Peter was foolish in starting his Crusade.

## ACTIVITIES

1. Make a set of posters about the First and Second Crusades.
2. Dramatize: Godfrey is crowned king of Jerusalem.
3. Deliver a short speech in imitation of Pope Urban's sermon.

4. Suppose you were Richard. Write in your diary about your troubles in the Holy Land.
5. Dress a doll like a Crusader.
6. Suppose you were in the Children's Crusade. Write a letter telling your mother in England about your adventures.
7. Make a sketch illustrating the story behind "God wills it."
8. Make a pictorial map of the Holy Land. Draw little sketches about the Crusades.
9. Read a novel about the Crusades. Tell the story to the class.
10. Paste in your scrapbook pictures and sketches about the Crusades.

## WORD LIST

| | | |
|---|---|---|
| Crusades | Children's Crusade | Knights' Crusade |
| Holy Land | siege | pilgrims |
| Pope Urban | Royal Crusade | |

# VIII

## *Part 2:* SILKS AND SPICES

The Crusaders had fought to get lasting control of the Holy Land. This they did not succeed in doing. However, it would be a great mistake to believe that the Crusades were a failure. The Crusades checked somewhat the power of the Mohammedan Turks even though the Turks in 1453 succeeded in capturing Constantinople which they still control. Had the Mohammedans not been checked they might have overrun much of Europe.

Besides checking the power of the Turks, the Crusades greatly helped trade. Silks and spices and other products of the East were brought to Europe. The trade in silks and spices became exceedingly important. Indeed the search for a new trade route led to the discovery of America.

NEW FOODS FOR EUROPE. The Crusaders on their travels to the East learned to eat foods which were new and strange to them. When they returned to their homes in Europe they kept their new customs. Sugar began to replace honey as a sweet. The lemon, the melon and spinach came to the tables of Europe as a result of the Crusades. Asparagus also was now cultivated. Spices, pepper, perfumes, and various drugs were well known in the East. The Crusaders, when returning to Europe brought these articles with them.

NEW CLOTHES FOR EUROPE. Not only did the Crusaders introduce foods new to Europe, they also brought back new cloths and fabrics. Yards of silks, velvets, brocades, damask, and cotton were obtained in the East and forwarded to Europe. Dyes of many hues, especially purples and blues, were bought by Italian merchants and shipped to the towns of Europe. Precious stones, pearls, jewels, also were imported. Also came fine oriental rugs and carpets almost as beautiful in color as the jewels whose colors the Eastern rug makers may have sought to copy.

TRADE WITH THE EAST. The Crusaders, when they returned home, had wonderful tales to tell of all the beautiful products of the East. Often they carried samples of these articles with them. Then the people of Europe began to want the articles of the East, silks, spices, perfumes, drugs and gems. To supply these articles the Italian merchants sent ships to the East. Great trading cities grew up in Italy. Venice became very prosperous. Genoa, Pisa, Amalfi, Palermo, also shared in the prosperity of Eastern trade as did Barcelona in Spain and Marseilles in France.

IDEAS FROM THE EAST. Some of the Mohammedans were very cultured people. The Old Roman Empire in the East was now largely under their control. The Mohammedans learned from the people living in the eastern part of the old Roman Empire many of their splendid ideas and skills. Thus they knew something about Roman and Greek architecture. They also had learned some of the teachings of the Greek philosophers. The Crusaders in turn learned some of these things from the Mohammedan Arabs. A very practical gift of the Arabs to the people of Europe was their system of numbers which is the one we use today. Thus we write: 1, 2, 3, 4, 5, instead of I, II, III, IV, V. In addition, the Arab mathematicians had developed the study of algebra.

## A Camel Train

Long caravans of camels carried goods from the far East and the Indies across the deserts of Asia to the ships of the Italian traders.

THE CRUSADES AND THE TOWNS. The Crusades did much to aid the building of the towns. The great development in trade between East and West naturally brought about an increase in the size and influence of the towns. The towns were the places where the eastern articles found the best market. The Crusades also helped the growth of liberty in the towns. The feudal lord who wanted to take part in a Crusade had to have money. The money he usually had to obtain in the town which was located on his land—but at a price. The price was often a charter granting some measure of self-government to the people of the town. As the power of the lords lessened, the authority of the king increased. At the close of this period the king is the actual ruler in the land. The lords are no longer independent. The condition of the people was greatly improved.

Courtesy New York Public Library

**Making Silk in China**

Silks and spices and perfumes brought to Europe by the Crusaders had a direct effect upon the discovery of America.

THE CRUSADES AND LIBERTY. Besides the greater freedom brought to the townsfolk and villages through the diminished power of the feudal lords, a new spirit of liberty had been born. In the Crusades, men from different walks of life fought side by side. The distinctions between high and low, rich and ordinary folk, could not be kept up so easily among the Crusaders. The dangers of disease had to be faced by all. Pestilence was no respecter of persons nor were the swords of the enemy. Men who went through such experiences—and these were shared by generation after generation for nearly two hundred years—were bound to learn something of the spirit of democracy.

THE CRUSADES AND AMERICA. There is a direct connection between the desire for travel, together with the growth of trade brought about by the Crusades, and the discovery of America. To carry troops and supplies by water to Palestine, hundreds of ships had to be constructed that otherwise might not have been built. In this way a merchant marine was created. In the years after the Crusades it was busily engaged in carrying eastern goods to western markets. Later it became necessary to look for a new water route to the East, partly because Constantinople had fallen into the hands of the unfriendly Mohammedans. The search for a new route led Columbus to sail westward where he discovered the new world.

## ORAL DRILL

1. From what language does the word *crusade* come?
2. What was used for sweetening in Europe after the Crusades?
3. Why did Venice become a trading city?
4. What was the source of Mohammedan culture, art and learning?
5. Name three cities in Europe that were helped by the Crusades?

## OBJECTIVE TESTS

TEST 1: Selecting the Odd Item.

Write down the item in each statement which is not true:

1. The Crusaders brought back (a) potato, (b) sugar, (c) lemon, (d) melon.
2. (a) Spices, (b) pepper, (c) drugs, (d) wheat were brought back from the East.
3. (a) Silks, (b) wool, (c) cotton, (d) velvets were sold to Europe by Eastern merchants.
4. Europeans imported (a) coal, (b) dyes, (c) jewels, (d) spices from Asia.
5. The cities of (a) Paris, (b) Pisa, (c) Venice and (d) Genoa shared in the Eastern trade.

6. The Mohammedans understood (a) mathematics, (b) Christianity, (c) Greek architecture, (d) Greek philosophy.
7. The Crusades helped the growth of (a) lawlessness, (b) towns, (c) king's power, (d) trade.
8. Leaders of the Crusades were (a) Charlemagne, (b) Richard, (c) Walter the Penniless, (d) Frederick Barbarossa.
9. The Crusades helped (a) shipbuilding, (b) Italian cities, (c) pilgrims, (d) power of lords.
10. (a) Genoa, (b) Barcelona, (c) Pisa, (d) Palermo is not an Italian city.

TEST 2: Historical Vocabulary.

1. What is damask?
   a) a fine type of steel
   b) a medieval garment
   c) a kind of textile
   d) a carpet

2. What is a charter?
   a) an agreement granting some privileges
   b) a medieval parchment
   c) a guide for merchants
   d) a carpet

3. What is a pestilence?
   a) a rat
   b) a difficult time
   c) a plague
   d) a war

4. What is a crusade in the modern sense?
   a) a series of battles
   b) a campaign for reform
   c) a foreign journey

TEST 3: Order of Time.

Arrange in the order of time:
        Columbus discovers America
        Turks take Constantinople
        Crusades revive trade with East
        "God wills it"
        Death of Frederick Barbarossa

---

## QUESTIONS THAT MAKE YOU THINK

---

1. "The Crusades revived trade." Explain.
2. Mention three foods of today which were introduced by the Crusaders.
3. Show how the Italian cities were helped by the Crusades.
4. Explain the effect of the Crusades upon the power of the king.

5. Why did towns grow during the period after the Crusades?
6. "A new spirit of liberty was born." Prove this statement.
7. The feudal lords lost a great deal of their power as a result of the Crusades.

## QUESTIONS THAT TEST YOUR CHARACTER

1. "The Crusades encouraged the spirit of liberty." Why is liberty a precious right?
2. Give two examples of your liberty.
3. Why must our liberty sometimes be limited for our own good?
4. "The Crusades showed that people may learn a great deal from their enemies." Explain why this statement is true.

## ACTIVITIES

1. Bring to class three foods introduced to Europe by the Crusaders.
2. Make a large map showing the trade routes used by the Italian merchants.
3. Draw a sketch showing the European debt to the East.
4. Use a large scroll of paper. On it compose a medieval charter granted to a French town.
5. Draw a "minute movies" sketch, showing that the Crusades drew men from all walks of life.
6. In your scrapbook paste drawings and pictures illustrating medieval trade and merchants.

## TOPICS FOR DISCUSSION

1. The Mohammedans were more cultured than the medieval Christians.
2. The Crusades were a commercial revolution.
3. The Crusades increased patriotism.
4. The Italian cities were helped by the Crusades, more than the French towns.

## WORD LIST

| | | | |
|---|---|---|---|
| fabrics | spices | textiles | charter |
| damask | brocades | liberty | merchant marine |

# VIII

*Part 3:* MISSIONARIES AND TRAVELERS

After the Crusades, two classes of men helped to add to the knowledge of geography. These were the missionaries and the travelers. The people of Europe before the time of the Crusades, as a rule, did not know much about the world. Indeed they knew very little even about the land where they lived. Those who lived in the country rarely left the farm where they were born. Some of the merchants and the craftsmen of the towns traveled. In this way they learned about the people who lived in distant places. But these people were exceptions. Because of the Crusades, the knowledge of geography became more widespread. Missionaries and travelers also added to the knowledge of geography.

THE FRANCISCAN MISSIONARIES. Our friend St. Francis of Assisi had always wanted to be a missionary. He was anxious to go to the East to convert the Mohammedans. Circumstances prevented him personally from doing all he had hoped to do in this way but some of his followers were able to make missionary journeys to the East. Franciscan missionaries reached China. Two of the missionaries are especially famous. John of Carpini was sent by the Pope to visit the ruler of China, who was called the Great Khan. Another John, John of Corvino, visited India as a missionary and later went to China, where he was appointed Archbishop by the Pope. The Franciscans greatly added to the knowledge of Asia and its products. The introduction of the silkworm into Europe was due to a missionary who carried

*Courtesy New York Public Library*

## Marco Polo at the Court of the Great Khan

Kublai Khan greets Marco, who is shown at the left with a sword in his hand.

the eggs of a silkworm in his cane. However, it was from the Polo family of Venice that most of the information came concerning Asia.

THE POLO FAMILY. Towards the close of the thirteenth century, there lived in Venice two brothers named Polo. Anxious for adventure, they decided to take a trip to China to see the land of silks and spices. The journey was made and after seeing some of the country, they returned home. But the Polos soon tired of Venice. The desire to return to the East was too strong to be resisted, so packing their belongings, they set out again for the land of riches. One of their brothers took his young son, called Marco, on the trip.

AT THE COURT OF THE GREAT KHAN. After three years of traveling they came at last to Cathay, or China, where they sought out the ruler of the country whose name was Kublai Khan. He was very glad to see them. The ruler liked young Marco particularly. The brothers were given important tasks to perform. For their services, they were paid in sapphires and rubies. After a time they began to resemble the people about them. They had long since put aside their European dress and had given up their western manners. Yet in spite of the honors and riches heaped upon them, they could not quite forget their friends in Venice. After twenty years away from home, they still remembered those whom they had left behind. The Polos asked the Khan to let them return home. The great Khan was very unhappy when he heard their request. At first he was unwilling to let them go. At length, however, he gave the Polos permission to return.

THE RETURN TO VENICE. After many exciting adventures, the brothers with Marco, who was now grown to manhood, reached Venice in safety. The appearance of all three was very much changed. When they called on their relatives and old friends, no one recognized them. People would not believe their stories. To prove the truth of their reports the brothers prepared a splendid feast. They invited all their friends and kinsfolk. After the feast, the brothers brought out their old coats. They had worn these on the trip back from Cathay and, of course, the coats were very shabby.

MARCO POLO'S SURPRISE BANQUET. We may believe that the neighbors thought it very queer to invite people to see three old coats. Very likely they began to whisper impolitely. Then Marco, taking a pair of shears, ripped out the lining of his travel-stained coat. A shower of sapphires, rubies, and diamonds fell on the floor. The neighbors could hardly believe their eyes. The news was spread abroad very quickly. Indeed

*Drawn expressly for The Old World and America.*

## The Return of the Polos to Venice

Notice the queer clothes they are wearing and the Chinese dog Marco is leading. The old neighbors of the Polos' seem to be astonished at the sight.

for the next hundred years there were some people who talked and dreamed of the great adventure of the Polos.

MARCO POLO'S BOOK. Marco wrote a book about his travels. It happened that in a war between the rival cities of Genoa and Venice, Marco was captured. He was put into prison. While in prison he prepared the book describing his travels. There is one important fact mentioned in this old book, a fact which the Franciscan missionaries to China had also reported: Polo's book told of the existence of a sea which touched Asia on the east. Thus in the very city of Columbus's birth a book was written describing the seas which Columbus hoped to cross on his way to Cathay. Columbus believed that the earth is round. By sailing west, he expected to reach the sea which Polo said bounded China on the east.

## ORAL DRILL

1. What was the title of the ruler of China in the Middle Ages?
2. When did the people of Europe have more complete knowledge of Geography (a) before the Crusades? or (b) after the Crusades?
3. Which priests added to the knowledge of Geography?
4. Name the distant country visited by the Polo family.
5. Who was the Archbishop of China in the Middle Ages?
6. Give the name of a famous Franciscan missionary to China in the Middle Ages.
7. Where was the home of the Polo family in Europe?
8. Which one of the Polos was an author?
9. What sort of a book did produce?
10. Mention one important fact told in Polo's book.

## OBJECTIVE TESTS

TEST 1: Historical Vocabulary.

1. What is a missionary?
    a) a traveler
    b) one who visits foreign lands
    c) one who brings news
    d) one who carries a religion to a foreign land
2. What is Cathay?
    a) an island
    b) a continent
    c) a country
    d) an ocean

3. What is meant by Mohammedans?
    a) followers of a certain religion
    b) Turks
    c) Arabs
    d) Africans
4. What is a banquet?
    a) a great feast
    b) a famous speech
    c) part of a bank
    d) a French game

TEST 2: Completion Test.

1. St. Francis wanted to convert the . . . . . . . . . . . . . . . .
2. Cathay is a name for . . . . . . . . . . . . . . . . . . . . . . . .

3. The name of the Khan who greeted the Polo family was
   ....................... Khan.
4. John of Corvino visited the countries of ................
   and ...............................
5. While in .............. Marco Polo wrote of his travels.

## QUESTIONS THAT TEST YOUR CHARACTER

1. "The Franciscan missionaries had courage." Prove this.
2. Name one other good quality which these missionaries possessed.
3. What three qualities of Marco Polo should you imitate?
4. Was Kublai Khan a great man? Explain your answer.

## ACTIVITIES

1. Dress dolls like Franciscan missionaries to China.
2. Suppose you were John of Carpini. Write a week's record in your diary. Tell of your impressions of the East.
3. Dramatize: Marco Polo leaves Kublai Khan.
4. Draw a picture showing the Oriental dress of the Polos.
5. Dramatize: Marco's Surprise Banquet.
6. Tell of an imaginary visit to the court of Kublai Khan.
7. Write a record of an imaginary conversation between a Franciscan missionary and the Great Khan.

## TOPICS FOR DISCUSSION

1. The Franciscan missionaries were heroes of history.
2. The Great Khan was more powerful than Charlemagne.
3. Marco Polo was a good Catholic.
4. Marco's travels helped Columbus discover America.

## WORD LIST

| | | |
|---|---|---|
| missionary | Kublai Khan | sapphires |
| Great Khan | banquet | Cathay |

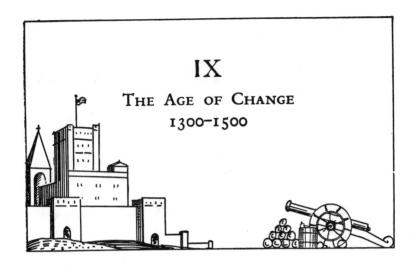

# IX

## THE AGE OF CHANGE
### 1300–1500

### AIM

To understand that great changes in history take a long, long time to happen.

To learn why the period from 1300-1500 should be called the Beginning of Modern Times.

THE year of the discovery of America was 1492. This most important happening was one in a long series of events going back 150 years and more before that time. New ideas had been brought to Europe by the Crusaders. During that time there had been a great increase in trade between city and city and between Europe and Asia. Meanwhile the feudal form of society was changing. The power of the nobles was becoming weaker while the power of the king was increasing. Wars were bought; the effect of these wars was felt for a long long time. Many new and important inventions appeared. There were new loyalties or a new sort of patriotism; people were thinking about new matters; new inventions and devices were changing, to some extent, people's lives.

# IX

## *Part 1:* NEW LOYALTIES

The Hundred Years' War was a long struggle between the people of England and the people of France. This contest is called the Hundred Years' War because it lasted over a century. Fighting did not continue all the time; there were long periods of peace, but the war which began in 1346, some say 1338, did not end until 1453. Rivalry between the new nations England and France was the underlying cause of the war. There had grown among the people a feeling that they belonged to a nation instead of to a feudal estate. Thus patriotism, love of one's own country resulted. This is what is meant by a *new loyalty.*

THE HUNDRED YEARS' WAR. The Hundred Years' War was fought between England and France. It was the result of a new spirit of patriotism which showed itself in rivalry in commerce, or business. The Flemish people, subjects of the French King, used a great quantity of wool, because cloth manufacture was practically their only occupation. The wool they procured from England. English wool was of the best quality. The French King, Philip VI, did not want the Flemish people to trade with the English and so tried to force them to give up the use of English wool in favor of French wool. The weavers would not hear of such a thing. They sent a committee to the king of England, Edward III, asking him to help them against the French king. Edward was delighted to have an excuse to fight the French king.

## THE ENGLISH KING A FEUDAL LORD IN FRANCE.

The difficulty over the wool trade was not the only cause of ill feeling between England and France. A more serious one was the position of the King of England as a feudal lord in France. This condition was a result of the Norman Conquest (1066), and it caused much ill feeling. All the great nobles in one large section of France were vassals of the English king. They had to do homage to the king of England for their land. The French king did not like this arrangement. He could hardly be in control of his own country while such a system was in effect. Various means were tried by the French to rid themselves of English control. The French even helped the Scots to fight England.

## CLAIMS OF THE ENGLISH KING TO THE FRENCH CROWN.

The King of England thought he had a right to the French throne. He announced his intention of making good his claims by carrying an army over to France. Some of the French were very angry when they heard about the English king's claim. They thought it insolent because it was against the old laws of France. The English people at the same time were beginning to dislike the French. Fights between English and French sailors were taking place in the English Channel. Matters were reaching a breaking point very rapidly. War seemed to be certain. It came at last when the English invaded France. The first important battle of the war was a victory for the English. It is known as the battle of Crécy, from the place where the battle was fought.

## THE GREAT BATTLE OF CRÉCY.

The battle of Crécy was one of the most famous in history. The credit for the victory belongs largely to the son of the English king. Like his father, he also was named Edward but he is usually called the "Black Prince" because he wore a suit of black armor.

**The Battle of Crécy**

Can you tell the difference between the cross-bows of those fighting for France and the long-bows of the English?

THE PREPARATIONS FOR THE FRAY. The English troops, after crossing the Channel to France, marched some days before meeting the French army. The French had every advantage. Opposed to the small English force was the great French army three times as large as its rival. The English had only a few knights, while the French army was made up largely of splendidly equipped knights. In addition to these, the French had hired some Italian cross-bowmen from Genoa. Just as the battle was about to commence the skies suddenly became black. Flash after flash of lightning brightened for an instant the dark earth. Soon the rain began; the rain came down in tor-

*Courtesy B. F. Williamson*

## King John of France Surrenders to the Black Prince

Notice that the English lions and the French lilies are draped on the armor of the Black Prince. This shows that he claimed both the thrones.

rents. Then quite as suddenly as it had commenced the storm ceased. The battle then began in earnest.

THE ENGLISH VICTORY. The French advanced in utter confusion. Their horses, frightened by the storm and beyond control, pranced and shied. Into this confused mass, the English sent a storm of well-aimed arrows. The English had kept their bows in cases which protected them against the rain. The English archers were doing deadly work now. The Genoese with their clumsy cross-bows attempted to join the battle. Their cross-bows which had been thoroughly wet by the rain were useless. When night came on, the field, covered with the French dead, was completely in the possession of the English.

The following year the important seaport of Calais was taken by the English. A truce then was signed. Soon both sides had a bigger misfortune to think about than the war. The Black Death is the name given to this calamity.

THE BLACK DEATH, 1348. The Black Death was a terrible disease that afflicted many people in Europe, from 1348 and for some years afterward. The disease was disastrous for many reasons. Those who had the disease suffered intensely and generally died from it, often within a few hours after being taken sick. It is said that this dreadful disease took one out of four among the people of the countries where it was most severe. So many died of the disease that the bodies of the dead could not be buried. The Church suffered terribly for many of her fine priests, in the course of duty, caught the disease and died. In England, where the disease was especially severe, very few priests escaped. Farming and manufacturing could hardly be carried on because men could not be found to do the work. It was many years before Europe recovered even partially from the effects of the Black Death.

THE RENEWAL OF THE HUNDRED YEARS' WAR. To tell the whole story of the Hundred Years' War would take a long time. For the most part the war was an unfortunate one for France. Besides the defeat at Crécy the French were beaten in an important battle at Poitiers. Again at Agincourt, in 1415, the French suffered a terrible defeat. Other calamities followed. The city of Orleans was besieged by the English. Indeed matters had reached a point where the French had to agree that upon the death of their king, the English ruler should be the monarch of France. France as a separate country, would be no more. That this disaster did not come to pass was due to a brave young woman, Joan of Arc.

JOAN OF ARC. In a little French town lived a gentle, saintly girl named Joan. Joan had heard of the terrible condition of her country and longed to do something to help. Joan began to

**The Voices**
The Maid of Orleans hears the voices of her saints.

**The Battle**
The Maid has become the victorious leader.

pray earnestly for France. After praying Joan heard marvelously beautiful voices speaking a message to her. The message came from St. Michael, St. Catherine, and St. Margaret who told her to free France. The voices kept repeating the command. Poor Joan was terribly worried. She answered the voices saying, "I am only a poor girl; I do not know how to ride or fight." The heavenly message was delivered again and again, and finally the voices added, "It is God who commands it." Joan now knew that she must seek out the king. At first the king refused to see her. Finally, however, the king agreed to give Joan an army with which to fight the English.

THE SAVING OF ORLEANS. Joan set out on her mission. Clad in shining white armor, mounted on a great white charger, this girl of seventeen was determined to save her country. She

**Coronation**

Joan stands by as Charles is crowned King of France.

**Death**

A saint gives up her life after saving her country.

raised the siege of Orleans and drove the English from that part of the country, a task far too difficult for the best French generals. Everywhere the maid was victorious. The English dreaded to meet her. Soon she had under French control a large part of the territory formerly held by the English. Then she begged the French King, Charles, to go to Rheims to be crowned. This city had seen the coronation of many French kings and Joan of Arc wanted her king to be crowned there.

A KING IN FRANCE AND THE DEATH OF A SAINT. The coronation took place in the grand old cathedral. Joan stood next to the king, holding in her hand the white war banner. Joan knew that her work was over, so she begged to be allowed to go home. But the king would not hear of it. He felt that she could win further victories for the French. Charles may have dreamed of a France free of English control, but this was not to be at that time. Joan was taken prisoner by those who should have supported her. She was turned over to the English. The maid was put into prison where she suffered terribly. For a while she was kept in an iron cage. Chains were placed about her arms and neck. This punishment lasted for a year. Then she was brought to trial. After a most unfair trial Joan was condemned to death by burning at the stake. The execution took place May 30, 1431. Joan was tied to the stake and the fire was lighted. As the flames mounted she called upon the name of Jesus. Joan of Arc is a splendid ideal for American girls for Joan did a man's work, yet remained a woman and became a saint.

THE END OF THE HUNDRED YEARS' WAR. The war dragged on after the death of St. Joan. In killing her the English did not put a stop to French victories. St. Joan had not died in vain. Little by little, the English were driven from French soil. Finally, only Calais remained in English possession. The war ended in 1453.

NEW LOYALTIES. The Hundred Years' War made Englishmen believe that they must be patriotic. They must love England and their king. Frenchmen too became more patriotic. They began to feel a stronger attachment to their king and country. In Spain the feelings of patriotism for rulers and nation were growing stronger. National feeling was probably not as strong in countries like Germany and Italy, which were divided into little kingdoms or city-states. However, generally speaking, the people of Europe felt a new, a stronger kind of attachment or patriotism for their country because this was the *Age of New Loyalties.*

## ORAL DRILL

1. How long did the Hundred Years War last?
2. Where did the Flemish people live?
3. Why should some of the French nobles feel obliged to fight on the side of the English?
4. Who won the battle of Crecy? When was it fought?
5. Why was the English leader called the "Black Prince"?
6. What was the Black Death?
7. Who betrayed St. Joan of Arc?
8. Where did the coronation of the French king take place?

## OBJECTIVE TESTS

TEST 1: Order of Time.
Arrange the following in the order of time:

Death of St. Joan     (   )     Death of Columbus     (   )
Norman Conquest       (   )     Discovery of America   (   )

TEST 2: Selecting the Correct Item.
Select the correct item in each sentence:

1. The Hundred Years' War was fought between England and: (a) Flanders, (b) France, (c) Spain, (d) Belgium.
2. The Flemish people were subjects of: (a) France, (b) England, (c) Burgundy, (d) Spain.
3. The battle of Crécy showed the strength of: (a) longbow, (b) cavalry, (c) Scots, (d) Italians.
4. A thunderstorm helped decide the battle of: (a) Crécy, (b) Agincourt, (c) Calais, (d) Poitiers.
5. The Black Death was especially severe in: (a) France, (b) Ireland, (c) England, (d) Italy.
6. French kings were crowned at: (a) Paris, (b) Marseilles, (c) Rheims, (d) Flanders.
7. The countries of: (a) England and Scotland, (b) France and Switzerland, (c) Germany and Italy, (d) Belgium and Netherlands were divided into little kingdoms and City-states.
8. The Hundred Years' War ended in: (a) 1453, (b) 1492, (c) 1400, (d) 1300.

9. The French encouraged attacks on England by: (a) Scots, (b) Flemish, (c) Irish, (d) Swedes.

TEST 3: Matching Test.

| Column A | | Column B |
|---|---|---|
| 1. Edward III | ( ) | French king |
| 2. Crécy | ( ) | military leader |
| 3. Calais | ( ) | claimed French throne |
| 4. Rheims | ( ) | city saved by St. Joan |
| 5. Black Prince | ( ) | killed many in Europe |
| 6. Black Death | ( ) | French city owned by English |
| 7. Orleans | ( ) | victory for footmen |
| 8. Agincourt | ( ) | French beaten in 1415 |

## QUESTIONS THAT TEST YOUR CHARACTER

1. Do you admire St. Joan? Give two reasons for your answer.
2. Point out two ways in which St. Joan is: (a) like you, (b) not like you in character.
3. "The life of St. Joan is a story of faith." Prove this statement.
4. Compare St. Joan and the Black Prince with regard to their good qualities.

## ACTIVITIES

1. Make a series of "Minute Movies" picturing the story of St. Joan of Arc.
2. Draw a sketch of the Black Prince.
3. Dramatize: St. Joan at Rheims.
4. Suppose you were a soldier under St. Joan. Tell of your experiences.
5. Suppose you were an eyewitness of the Battle of Crécy. Describe the battle in a letter to your Mother or Father.
6. Dress a doll like St. Joan of Arc.
7. Write two lines in rhyme about St. Joan of Arc.
8. Make a model from clay, soap or wood of the cathedral of Rheims.
9. Use a scroll of paper. Draw up a declaration of war by the English king.

10. Paste in your scrapbook pictures and clippings about medieval warfare.

---

## QUESTIONS THAT MAKE YOU THINK

---

1. Why is the Hundred Years' War called a time of "new loyalties"?
2. Name two causes of the Hundred Years' War.
3. "The English king was a feudal lord in France." Explain the statement.
4. Why was the battle of Crécy important?
5. Account for the name "Black Prince."
6. Show how a thunderstorm helped the English at Crécy.
7. What is meant by the Black Death?
8. Give two results of the Black Death.
9. Explain one result of the Hundred Years' War.

---

## TOPICS FOR DISCUSSION

---

1. The French should have won the battle of Crécy.
2. The Black Death was worse than the Hundred Years' War.
3. The Hundred Years' War shows the evil of war.

---

## WORD LIST

---

| | | |
|---|---|---|
| patriotism | cross-bow | Black Prince |
| feudal lord | Black Death | long-bow |
| weaver | | |

# IX

## *Part 2:* NEW INTEREST IN OLD IDEAS

After the Crusades certain ideas were uppermost in the minds of many people in Europe. They began to think more about the king and their native land. Many also began to have more regard for money and the things of this world. Men's minds began to be occupied by new interest in old ideas in other matters. For example, they began to admire the accomplishments of the Greeks and Romans who lived in ancient times. More people therefore began to read books written by the Greeks and Romans. They erected buildings according to Roman plans and methods. Some people went so far as to imitate the lives of the Greeks and Romans. This period is called the Renaissance. The word means rebirth. The Renaissance means a rebirth of interest in the old ideas of the Greeks and Romans.

THE ROMAN EMPIRE IN THE EAST. There was a famous city in ancient times called Byzantium which was located on the Bosporus. Caravan owners and traders from many parts of Asia came to Byzantium where they met merchants from Greece and Italy. Byzantium became the most important city in the eastern portion of the Old Roman Empire. This section of the Roman Empire is called the Greek portion because Greek was the language most commonly spoken there. The people living in this section usually were called Greeks. When Constantine became the Roman Emperor he decided to move his capital to the East. He therefore selected the city of

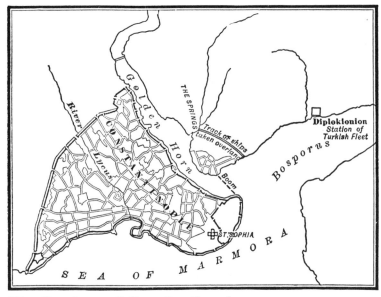

## The Capture of Constantinople

The Greek emperor gave his life defending his city. The Turks finally captured it by dragging their ships overland from the Bosporus to the Golden Horn.

Byzantium as his capital but he changed its name to Constantinople, naming the city for himself. The city of Rome declined while the importance of Constantinople increased.

CONSTANTINOPLE, HOME OF CULTURE. Constantine soon changed Constantinople from a city of brick to a city of marble. The city was famous for its beauty. Marbles of many colors from distant places were brought to Constantinople to adorn the churches, palaces, and other buildings. Pictures made of thousands of small tiles or pieces of glass called mosaics adorned the interior of these buildings. Constantinople was an important trading city. It was a beautiful city, and it was a center of learning. Constantinople was famous for its schools and libraries.

THE FALL OF CONSTANTINOPLE, 1453. Mohammed and the Generals that followed him captured large portions of the Eastern Roman Empire, but they did not capture Constantinople itself. Therefore, the great Eastern part of the Roman Empire Constantine had ruled over was now no longer under control of his successors. Finally, in 1453 Constantinople fell.

GREEK SCHOLARS AND THE RENAISSANCE. For some years before 1453 when Constantinople was captured by the Mohammedans, Greek scholars and teachers had been in the habit of visiting the cities of northern Italy. Many of them decided to live in Italy where they were made to feel at home. The Crusaders, of course, had made the people of Europe acquainted with the wonders of Constantinople. The people of Europe, however, really began to know about Constantinople and its libraries and schools only when the Greek scholars began to visit Europe and to live there.

Meanwhile the Greek scholars began to come to Italy in larger numbers for it seemed to many of them that the time was not far distant when the Mohammedans would capture the city of Constantinople. Some of these Greek teachers were given positions in the University of Florence where they taught Greek literature. These Greek scholars taught the people who lived in the cities of northern Italy a great deal about the ancient Greeks and Romans. This renewed interest in the writings and the art of the ancient Greeks and Romans became so great that the word *Renaissance*, which means rebirth, is used to describe it. The interest in the accomplishments of the ancient Romans spread from Italy to other countries of Europe.

THE RENAISSANCE AND ART. At first people studied the fine writings of the old Romans and those of the Greeks when they could obtain them. Next they began to admire

*Courtesy B. F. Williamson*

## St. Peter's in Rome

Perhaps the finest edifice ever built by man.

greatly what they had done in art. Interest did not stop at this point. Some even thought the lives of the old Romans worthy of imitation. Here they made a great mistake, for as we learned before, the lives of the pagans were often unholy. But the Renaissance had this good result, it helped somewhat the development of the arts of painting and architecture.

GREAT ITALIAN ARTISTS. During the time of the Renaissance (1300-1500) there lived in Italy, three men whose work has been the admiration of the world since their time. Their names are Leonardo da Vinci, Raphael, and Michelangelo. Leonardo da Vinci was born in 1452, the year before the Fall of Constantinople. He is remembered for his lovely paintings. His picture of the Last Supper is known the world over. Raphael, born in the year 1483, was also a famous painter. He

**THE MADONNA "DEL GRAN DUCA" BY RAPHAEL**

One of the great pictures of the world, painted on wood when the artist was twenty-four years old.

*Drawn expressly for "The Old World and America"*

## Michaelangelo Painting in St. Peter's

This fresco which Michaelangelo had to paint while lying on his back took four years to complete.

painted some very beautiful pictures of our Blessed Mother. Michelangelo was not only a painter, but a poet, an architect, and a sculptor as well. He was born near Florence in 1475, spending most of his long life painting pictures and carving statues that we still admire.

These great artists had learned their art from those who lived before their time. For example, the artist Giotto made many experiments with colors which were of value to the artists who lived after him. Fra Angelico, painted beautiful pictures of our Lord, of the Angels (for which he is especially famous), and of the Saints. His paintings served as models for other artists. It would be quite impossible to describe the work of even a few of the great painters of this time for there were so many. This is also true of the sculptors. Some sculptors carved their statues out of marble: Donatello, for example. Others cast their statues in bronze, like Cellini, and still other artists, the della Robbia, made statues of baked clay. But their work had one thing in common; it was really beautiful.

THE AGE OF NEW WRITERS. In the many new important cities of Italy new writers appeared. They differed from the writers of earlier times because often they did not write in Latin but in the language spoken by the ordinary people of their own country. Many wrote about new subjects. Dante is perhaps the greatest of the Italian poets. Petrarch is also famous. He has been called the first modern man. Petrarch seems to have been more interested in this world than in the next. Meanwhile in other parts of Europe writers were producing interesting books. Erasmus, a monk from Rotterdam wrote a number of volumes which educated men read eagerly. Saint Thomas More in England also wrote books of importance.

## ORAL DRILL

1. How did Constantinople get its name?
2. What is Constantinople called today?
3. Who captured Constantinople in 1453?
4. In what language did Dante write?
5. In what language did Petrarch write?
6. Which city is connected with Erasmus?
7. Where did Sir Thomas More live?
8. Who painted pictures of Angels?
9. Name an artist who cast statues in bronze.

## OBJECTIVE TESTS

TEST 1: Completion Test.
1. .................. was the learned man from Rotterdam.
2. ........................ is the greatest of Italian poets.
3. ........................... is noted for the Last Supper.
4. The Renaissance revived the study of Roman and .........
   learning.
5. Byzantium was the ancient name for ...................
6. Petrarch was called the ...............................

7. Pictures made of small tiles or pieces of glass are called . . . . .
8. . . . . . . . . . . . . . . . . . . . . founded the city of Constantinople.
9. The della Robbia made statues of baked . . . . . . . . . . . . . . . . .
10. . . . . . . . . . . . . . . . . is noted for his paintings of the Blessed
   Mother.

TEST 2: Matching Test.

| Column A | | Column B |
|---|---|---|
| 1. Petrarch | ( ) | first modern man |
| 2. Dante | ( ) | Divine Comedy |
| 3. St. Thomas More | ( ) | English scholar |
| 4. Erasmus | ( ) | Dutch scholar |
| 5. Michelangelo | ( ) | a combination of sculptor, painter, architect |
| 6. Mosaics | ( ) | pictures in tile or glass |
| 7. Fra Angelico | ( ) | paintings of Angels |
| 8. Leonardo Da Vinci | ( ) | Last Supper |
| 9. Raphael | ( ) | Blessed Mother |
| 10. Donatello | ( ) | carved statues from marble |

TEST 3: Order of Time.
   Arrange the following in the order of time.
   ( ) Reign of Constantine
   ( ) Crusades
   ( ) Fall of Constantinople
   ( ) Greek scholars go to Italy
   ( ) Discovery of America

## QUESTIONS THAT MAKE YOU THINK

1. "Constantinople was the home of culture." Explain.
2. What was the Renaissance?
3. "Michelangelo was a versatile man." Find out what this means.
4. Name two great sculptors of the Renaissance.
5. (a) Make a list of five great scholars of the Renaissance. (b) Tell why each is important.

## QUESTIONS THAT TEST YOUR CHARACTER

1. Name one great scholar of the Renaissance. In what way may you profit from his life?

2. Whom do you admire more, St. Francis of Assisi or Petrarch? Give your reasons.
3. Why is it a mistake to imitate the lives of the Romans in all things?
4. Name one good and one bad feature of the Renaissance.

## ACTIVITIES

1. Get pictures of Gothic sculpture and Renaissance sculpture. Which do you prefer? Why?
2. Bring to class a copy of one of the great Renaissance paintings.
3. Dramatize: St. Thomas More visiting Erasmus.
4. Make a series of "Minute Movies" entitled "Great Men of the Renaissance."
5. Write an imaginary letter to a friend in which you tell of a visit to Constantinople before 1453.
6. Write an imaginary conversation between Dante and Petrarch.
7. Paste in your scrapbook pictures and clippings about the Renaissance.

## TOPICS FOR DISCUSSION

1. The Renaissance was a pagan movement.
2. The fall of Constantinople had an effect on American history.
3. Religion played a great part in the Renaissance.
4. The Renaissance changed all Europe.

## WORD LIST

| | | | |
|---|---|---|---|
| culture | route | poet | architect |
| mosque | painter | sculptor | Renaissance |

# IX

## *Part 3:* NEW INVENTIONS

During the Renaissance many new inventions and devices appeared. These changed ways of living or they made travel safer or the exchange of ideas easier. For example, gunpowder not only changed warfare, but it also rendered castles somewhat useless. Other and more important changes in the lives of the people occurred because of new inventions.

THE USE OF GUNPOWDER. The use of gunpowder and the discovery of a new way of casting iron cannon, changed methods of warfare. After the use of gunpowder became common the knight on his prancing horse was not so important. His fine armor could be pierced easily by a bullet. His castle was no longer a safe place from which he could defy an enemy or even his king, for cannon and gunpowder could make the castle useless as a stronghold. A few well-aimed cannon balls could destroy the castle walls. Gunpowder really helped the king to be master in his own country, for the king usually had the money to buy ammunition in large quantities.

THE COMPASS. The compass was a most valuable device. The Chinese had used it for centuries but it became common on European ships only after about the year 1200. The compass at that time was very crude. It consisted of a magnetic needle mounted on a piece of straw or cork floating in water. Before the compass came into use the captain of the vessel had

*Drawn expressly for "The Old World and America"*

**Compass**                    **Gunpowder**

    Which of these inventions do you think benefited mankind more? Give reasons for your answer.

to keep within sight of land whenever possible. If he wished to make a trip out into the ocean, he had to depend upon the sun and the stars to know in which direction he was steering. But suppose storm clouds hid the stars? Then the captain was in a most unfortunate position. With a compass on his ship, the captain could steer with confidence although he could see neither land nor stars. The compass would help him know exactly in what direction he was going. Columbus could hardly have made his voyages without the aid of the compass. So this instrument is of very great benefit to man.

THE INVENTION OF PRINTING. You remember that frequently a monk would spend years in copying a single book. Books therefore were scarce. They were expensive too. It was not until printing was invented that books became at all plentiful and cheap. The process of printing books by means of

**The First Printing Press**

Gutenberg, the first master printer, reads a proof from his press with the new movable type.

movable type was the result of some experiment. The first step was the making of many picture books from a single set of plates.

A NEW METHOD OF MAKING PICTURE BOOKS. An unknown inventor thought of this simple means of making many picture books easily and cheaply. He took a block of wood and on it he carved the desired picture. The few words of explanation under the picture he carved at the bottom of the block. He repeated this process on as many blocks as there were to be pages. Then having put ink on his cartoons, he pressed the paper upon them. Behold the result! A fine picture book, and not merely a single book, but from the one set of cartoons any number of books might be made.

THE STORY BOOK. Picture books are not story books. Soon, however, story books were made. It is said that John Gutenberg was the first to make story books by the use of movable type. In place of carving out pictures, Gutenberg carved out letters. The letters he could make into words, the words into sentences. The sentences could be put together in page form. When the lines on the page were just as the printer wished them to appear, he locked his carved letters in a form. On the letters ink was spread. Then the ink-coated letters were pressed upon a sheet of paper just as it had been done in the making of the picture book. Instead of a picture, a story was the result. After the book had been printed the type could be used for printing other books. Simple as it was, printing was one of the most important inventions ever made by man. In a short time, every town in Europe had a printing press. Marco Polo's book—a sort of travel book and geography with notions about the sea beyond China—was one of the books printed by the early printers.

## ORAL DRILL

1. What invention made castles somewhat useless as forts?
2. About what time did the European mariners begin to use the compass?
3. What is the purpose of the compass?
4. For what is John Gutenberg famous?
5. Name one advantage of moveable type.

## OBJECTIVE TESTS

TEST 1: Completion Test.
1. Castles were rendered useless by the invention of . . . . . . . . . .
2. Learning was spread by the invention of . . . . . . . . . . . . . . . .
3. . . . . . . . . . . . . . . . is famous for the development of printing.
4. The compass was used in ancient times by the . . . . . . . . . . . . . people.
5. . . . . . . . . . . . . . . . could not have made his voyages without the compass.

TEST 2 : Matching Test.

| Column A | | Column B |
|---|---|---|
| 1. Navigation | ( ) | Gutenberg |
| 2. Learning | ( ) | gunpowder |
| 3. Warfare | ( ) | compass |
| 4. Crécy | ( ) | Dante |
| 5. Literature | ( ) | cross-bow |

TEST 3 : Order of Time (Review).

Arrange the following in order of time.

Fall of Constantinople
Hundred Years' War starts
Feudalism
Marco Polo visits China
Discovery of America

---

## QUESTIONS THAT MAKE YOU THINK

1. Explain two effects of the invention of gunpowder.
2. Why was the invention of gunpowder an aid to the king?
3. "Gunpowder meant the end of feudalism." Explain.
4. (a) What is the compass? (b) Why is it valuable?
5. Explain the effect of the invention of the compass upon navigation.
6. "Could Columbus have discovered America without a compass?" Explain your answer.
7. Why was printing a revolutionary invention?
8. What is the difference between printing and penmanship?
9. Explain the steps in the growth of printing.
10. Name two effects of the invention of printing.

---

## QUESTIONS THAT TEST YOUR CHARACTER

1. "An inventor must have perseverance." Explain.
2. Name two inventions which were a benefit to mankind.
3. Name two inventions which have proved harmful to the human race.
4. "Necessity is the mother of invention." What lesson may we learn from this statement?

## ACTIVITIES

1. Make a model of a compass.
2. Draw a picture of a compass. Include printed explanation of each part.
3. Dramatize: Gunpowder is used against a strong castle for the first time.
4. On a large cardboard trace the steps in the use of gunpowder. Include the latest methods of modern warfare.
5. Visit a modern printing press at work. Write a report of your visit for the local newspaper.
6. Draw a series of "Minute Movies" showing the growth of printing.
7. Make a collection of as many different kinds of printing as you can find. Display these on the bulletin board.
8. Paste in your scrapbook pictures of inventors and inventions.

## TOPICS FOR DISCUSSION

1. Without printing public education is impossible.
2. Printing gives rise to learning.
3. Gunpowder has brought more evil than good.
4. The compass is the sailor's most valuable instrument.
5. Modern ocean travel would exist without the compass.

## WORD LIST

| | |
|---|---|
| compass | gunpowder |
| printing | feudal warfare |
| press | navigation |

# X

## THE AGE OF DISCOVERY

### AIM

To become acquainted with the lives of the great discoverers.

To study the great accomplishments of the Discoverers and Explorers who opened up the New World to the people of Europe.

IN LESS than fifty years the people of Europe learned many important facts about the earth. These facts they had not previously known. Thus within a half century the people of Europe learned about the size of the earth, the extent of the oceans, and the existence of great continents.

# X

## *Part 1:* FORERUNNERS OF COLUMBUS

The discovery of the continents of North America and South America was due to many causes. For many years mariners had been learning better methods of sailing their ships. Seamen had learned to use the compass on the ocean and out of sight of land. Better maps were being made which sailors were learning to read with greater skill. The ships themselves were larger and sturdier. Sailors were becoming bolder and more eager for adventure. Some believed that by learning more about the earth and the people who lived in distant places they could help the spread of the Catholic Church, for then, as now, there was a keen interest in foreign missions. Many of the mariners who lived in the time of Christopher Columbus believed that great wealth would come to the seaman who could discover a new water route to India and China.

---

## THE SEARCH FOR NEW TRADE ROUTES

---

TRADE AND TRADE ROUTES. A most important result of the Crusades was the great increase of trade between East and West. About the time Columbus was born, people in Europe were eager to buy goods from India and China. European merchants were anxious to obtain the silks and the spices, the precious jewels and the perfumes that came from the East. However it was difficult for the merchants to get the silks and spices for their European customers. In the first place the goods

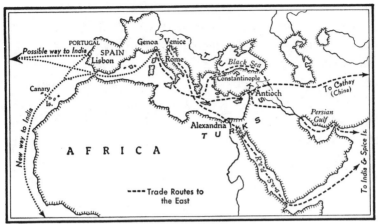

*Drawn expressly for "The Old World and America"*

## Trade Routes

This map shows the old routes to the East and the new ones to the south and west.

had to be carried a great distance. Then again the only fairly convenient trade routes to the East ran through territory that was largely under Turkish control.

THE TURKS AND THE EUROPEAN TRADERS. The Turks sometimes made trading dangerous for European traders. Turkish pirates sometimes captured the trading ships of the European merchants and after stealing the cargo, set the crew adrift.

The Turks could do as they pleased in the eastern Mediterranean, for their power there was supreme. For many reasons it was desirable for the European traders to find a new trade route. As a land route was practically out of the question, a water route had to be found. Where should the mariners hope to find one?

POSSIBLE TRADE ROUTES. There were two possible and untried routes to the East. Some thought India could be reached by sailing south along the coast of Africa. This is called the southern route. Today you know that a captain could have sailed his ship around Africa; your map tells you that. But the mariner of 1450 did not have the good maps that you can study. No one then had any clear idea of the size of Africa or whether one could actually sail around it, though some Italians believed that Africa was a continent. On the other hand, there were a few people who pictured the unknown part of Africa as the dwelling place of hideous monsters. There was said to be a sea of boiling water about this land. The mariner who dared venture too far south would certainly be lost!

A ROUTE BY WAY OF THE WEST. Besides the possibility of reaching India by a southern route, some thought that India might be reached by sailing west. But no one knew for certain. The sea to the west, according to some stories going about, was even worse than the boiling sea that washed the southern shores of Africa. No one dreamed that America was to the west, although it had been visited by Europeans, the Northmen.

THE VISIT OF THE NORTHMEN TO AMERICA. We can be quite certain that the Northmen or Norsemen visited America. It seems that about the year 1000 some of the bolder among them had crossed the Atlantic. Their first long trips out into the Atlantic had brought them to Iceland, where in the year 867, they planted a colony. Greenland was settled by them a few years later. Finally about the year 1000, the Norsemen visited North America.

LEIF ERICSON. Leif Ericson was a Norseman who was living in Greenland with other Norse colonists. While on a visit to his old home in Europe, Leif Ericson became a Catholic and on his return to Greenland brought missionaries with him.

© *Culver Service*

## The Norsemen at Greenland

These hardy sailors left Greenland and succeeded in reaching the coast of North America.

Later, about the year 1000, this daring Norseman, with a number of companions, left Greenland and sailed west until he reached the coast of Labrador. Thence he sailed south to a country he called Vinland because many grape vines grew there. Leif Ericson probably landed somewhere on the coast of New England. There he cut down some trees and sailed back with a load of timber.

THE RETURN TO VINLAND. In Greenland no one seems to have been very much excited over the discovery. A few years later the brother of Leif Ericson returned to Vinland but remained only a short time. This was probably the last trip of the Norsemen to America. Few people in Europe knew anything about the discovery.

## THE PORTUGUESE NAVIGATORS

PRINCE HENRY THE NAVIGATOR. In Portugal there lived a young Prince named Henry whose father was the king of Portugal. Henry, therefore, belonged to the first family in the land. When he was a young man, he went to North Africa to fight the Moors. While on this expedition, he picked up a great deal of information about the East. He pictured to himself the wealth which awaited the country that could send ships to carry it back in safety. For the present, the young prince had to think only of fighting the Moors. Meanwhile he planned a campaign of his own, one which had little to do with the Moors in Morocco. Some day he hoped to carry out this campaign. What was it?

PRINCE HENRY'S CAMPAIGN. Prince Henry's campaign had to do with the conquest of the sea. He began this campaign just as soon as he returned to Portugal. Although urged to take up a military career Prince Henry refused. Leaving his friends at court Prince Henry built a house on a high point that looked out on the sea. There he planned a way to discover a water route to the East by sailing south around Africa. Portugal would become a wealthy country if the Portuguese had such a trade route. In addition to this advantage, Prince Henry saw the possibility of helping the foreign missions. He knew that the people of the East were ignorant of Christ. Prince Henry hoped to have missionaries visit these peoples to convert them to Christianity.

THE NEED OF TRAINED NAVIGATORS. The plan to reach India by sailing around Africa seems simple. But it was not really so simple to carry out. As you have seen, no one knew what the size of Africa was, although it seems that several

*Drawn expressly for "The Old World and America"*

## Prince Henry's School

Prince Henry left as little as possible to chance. His thorough preparation finally led to success.

Europeans had visited the interior of Africa. In those days most of the geographers said that the Indian Ocean was a closed sea—an immense inland lake. Prince Henry felt that in order to reach India his men would have to be trained in geography and astronomy. Just to know how to sail a ship would not do. It was part of his plan to found a school for mariners. By studying about maps and the use of scientific instruments, sailors would learn to sail their ships with accuracy. To this end he started his famous school.

PRINCE HENRY'S SCHOOL. Prince Henry turned his home into a school. He himself spent much of his time high up in the tower where he could gaze out upon the sea, or look up to the stars. Here he had his precious maps and charts. The rooms of the house were made into classrooms. The mariners were taught to read maps and to make maps. After he had trained a number of sailors, whom, he thought, had sufficient knowledge, he sent them out to explore the west coast of Africa.

THE VOYAGES TO THE SOUTH. In spite of Prince Henry's maps and encouraging advice, the sailors who began to explore the west coast of Africa were timid. They sailed along the coast, always careful to keep in sight of land. Finally, some more daring than the rest, got as far south as the Gulf of Guinea— the place where the coast of Africa turns sharply eastward. When the news of this success was reported to Prince Henry, he was greatly pleased. He was sure that his idea was correct, namely, that Africa was a continent ending in a cape. Before this could be proved, Prince Henry died. His death occurred in the year 1463.

THE MEMORABLE VOYAGE OF DIAZ. Prince Henry had started men thinking. Of course, some believed that he was mistaken, but many had confidence in his views. Bartholomew Diaz was such a man. In August, 1486, Diaz set sail from Portugal. His general direction was south. Not so long after the beginning of his voyage, a strong wind arose which blew him out of his course and out of the sight of land. For days the prow of his little ship cut through the waves. On and on she went before the strong wind. After a time the wind died down. Diaz turned his ship east, expecting at any moment to see land. But no land was sighted. This was strange indeed.

THE COURSE OF DIAZ. At first Diaz had sailed due south before the wind. Although he was actually out of sight of land, he was sure that land was not far away. Now he had turned east but no land appeared. What was he to do? Diaz then turned north. At last land appeared. He sailed on until he reached the Indian Ocean. Here his crew refused to sail farther. They thought they were lost. What actually had happened was this:

Diaz had rounded the southern point of Africa without knowing what he had really done.

THE "CAPE OF GOOD HOPE." The return voyage was a difficult one. Diaz decided to keep close to land in order that he might make a map of Africa. He wanted to know something about the cape around which he had just sailed. Soon he had a very trying experience because of this same cape. It is a bad place for ships on account of the great storms that arise there. Diaz was caught in one of these storms. His vessel almost was wrecked. Diaz called this point the "Cape of Storms." He so named it in the report of the voyage which he made to the King of Portugal. The King did not like the name. "Call it the Cape of Good Hope," he said. The King believed, and rightly, that Diaz had made a great discovery.

Some years after the journey of Diaz, another mariner, Vasco da Gama, by rounding this cape and continuing north along the east coast and through the Indian Ocean reached the land of silks and spices.

DA GAMA'S VOYAGE. Vasco da Gama set sail from Lisbon during the summer of 1497. The route Da Gama followed was much like that of Diaz. Da Gama stopped at a number of places along the African coast where he did some trading with the natives wherever he found them willing to do business on his terms. In exchange for ivory, which was worth its weight in gold, the Africans were willing to take metal balls and glass beads.

THE ROUNDING OF THE CAPE OF GOOD HOPE. When Da Gama reached the southern cape, he found out why Diaz, eleven years earlier, wanted to call it the "Cape of Storms." The storms he met there were the fiercest he had ever encountered. The cape was navigated only after several attempts to round it had met with failure. This obstacle overcome, the

*Drawn expressly for "The Old World and America"*

**Vasco da Gama and the Merchants of India**

The Portuguese are seen bargaining for silks, rugs, spices, and other valuable products. This marked the beginning of Portuguese influence in India.

trip was continued. Calicut, a town on the west coast of India, was reached in May, 1498. Da Gama filled the hold of his ship with a cargo of enormous value.

VASCO DA GAMA'S SUCCESS. After months of sailing, Vasco da Gama steered into Lisbon harbor. He was given a royal welcome. When the longshoremen came aboard Vasco Da Gama's ship to help unload, they could hardly work so great was their astonishment at the treasures he had brought back. There were caskets of jewels, rich spices sewed up in bags of silk, and bales of damask robes, the like of which had rarely been seen. These were some of the treasures which were lifted out of the dark hold of the ship. Portugal had won the race for the way to the riches of the East.

THE VALUE OF THE ROUTE FOR PORTUGAL. The Portuguese, now, were alone in possession of a practical route to the East. It was a route that had many advantages. In the first place it was an all water route. An all water route was cheaper than a route that was in part overland. It was fairly safe. Before the discovery of this route, all trade with the East passed through the Mediterranean. The enormous wealth of the Italian cities, especially Venice and Genoa, came from this source. The success of the Christian Portuguese made the Mohammedans bitter. They had controlled the trade with India and China for many centuries. In a fierce naval battle (Diu, 1509), the Portuguese were victorious. This victory meant that the rich trade of the East would now be controlled by the Christian merchants of Europe.

THE NEW TRADING CENTER. The trading center of Europe during the Middle Ages had been located along the Mediterranean. By the new discoveries, the trading center of Europe was removed from the Mediterranean to its present location, along the Atlantic. This is an important fact which had great influence upon later history.

---

## OBJECTIVE TESTS

---

TEST 1: Completion Test.
1. ................. was called the Navigator.
2. The Cape of Good Hope was reached for the first time by the Portuguese navigator ..........................
3. A great school for training navigators was ............... school.
4. .................... was the first man to reach India by sailing around Africa.
5. The father of Prince Henry was the King of .............
6. In the year 867 the Norsemen settled in ................
7. Leif Ericson was a leader of the .....................
8. Ericson reached a country south of Labrador which he called ......................................

9. The Gulf of Guinea is the place where the coast of . . . . . . . turns sharply eastward.
10. The tip of Africa is called . . . . . . . . . . . . . . . . . . . . . . . . . . . . . .

TEST 2: Arrange each of the following in the order of time.

Rounding Cape of Good Hope for first time
Portuguese reach India by new route
Columbus discovers America
Norsemen reach Vinland
Turks take Constantinople
Crusaders take Jerusalem

TEST 3: Matching Test.

| Column A | | Column B |
|---|---|---|
| 1. Calicut | ( ) | famous school of navigation |
| 2. Lisbon | ( ) | rounds Cape of Good Hope |
| 3. Prince Henry | ( ) | reaches India |
| 4. Diaz | ( ) | town in Hindustan |
| 5. Da Gama | ( ) | capital of Portugal |

## ORAL DRILL

1. What effect did the Crusades have upon trade between Europe and the East?
2. Where were Turkish pirates chiefly active?
3. Which part of Europe did the Turks control?
4. In what respect were the maps of 1450 deficient?
5. What people visited America after the year 1000?
6. What was the name of the leader of these sea rovers?
7. Why was Prince Henry called an educator?
8. What special title is given to Prince Henry?
9. What mariner first rounded the Cape of Good Hope?
10. What mariner first reached India?

## QUESTIONS THAT MAKE YOU THINK

1. What is a trade route?
2. What do Leif Ericson and Prince Henry the navigator have in common?
3. Why were the Norsemen such successful sailors?
4. Explain the contribution of Prince Henry the Navigator.
5. Why were the Portuguese eager to find a new route to the east?

6. Explain the effect of Da Gama's work upon the trade of Venice and Genoa.
7. Why do we speak of the "memorable voyage of Diaz" in 1486.
8. Explain the value to Europe of the route to the Indies.

## QUESTIONS THAT TEST YOUR CHARACTER

1. "Vasco da Gama had courage." Explain.
2. (a) Name two Portuguese navigators whom we should admire. (b) Tell why we should admire each.
3. "Prince Henry teaches us the need for careful study." Explain.
4. "The voyage of Vasco da Gama was Prince Henry's reward." Explain.

## ACTIVITIES

1. Make a large map showing Da Gama's famous voyage.
2. Make a drawing, comparing maps before and after Da Gama's voyage.
3. As a member of Da Gama's crew, write in your diary the story of the voyage.
4. Dramatize: Da Gama reports to the King of Portugal.
5. Dress dolls like Leif Ericson, and his followers.
6. Give a short talk on: The Norsemen in the New World.
7. Paste in your scrapbook pictures and sketches of explorers.

## TOPICS FOR DISCUSSION

1. The Norsemen discovered America.
2. Prince Henry is more important than Leif Ericson.
3. Vasco da Gama's voyage helped the world as a whole.
4. Da Gama ruined the trade of the Italian cities.

## WORD LIST

| | | |
|---|---|---|
| astrolabe | navigator | astronomy |
| mariner | inland lake | trading center |

# X

## Part 2: THE DISCOVERY OF THE NEW WORLD

The Spaniards were not very glad to hear that their rivals, the Portuguese, had succeeded in sailing around the southern point of Africa. They feared that Portugal would beat them in the race for control of the trade with the East. As a result they were willing to listen to the plan of a great navigator, Christopher Columbus, who hoped to discover some new lands, not by sailing south but by sailing west. Results of extraordinary importance followed upon the discovery of the New World by Christopher Columbus.

## CHRISTOPHER COLUMBUS

CHRISTOPHER COLUMBUS. The birthplace of Christopher Columbus is not known for certain, but it seems very likely that Genoa in Italy was the town where he was born. We do not know his birthday but if you remember that it probably occurred about the year 1453, you will have a date that is near enough to the true one. The year 1453, you recall, saw the fall of Constantinople, an event that may have had something to do with hastening the discovery of America.

THE EARLY LIFE OF COLUMBUS. Those who think that Genoa was the birthplace of Columbus say that Christopher's father was a wool-worker there. Like many boys of his time, Christopher learned his father's trade, but from all accounts he did not like it. Very likely Columbus was more interested in ships than in learning to be a wool carder. There is a story that he attended the University of Pavia. It seems certain that Columbus was fond of mathematics; he also liked geography. Map making seems to have been his hobby. By and by, when he became a sailor, Christopher Columbus had an opportunity to draw maps of what he saw.

THE PROSPECTS OF COLUMBUS. In Genoa the prospects of succeeding as a sailor were none too good. There had been a time when Genoa was a prosperous seaport. In those days Genoa controlled most of the trade with Constantinople. Later her rival Venice took away a great deal of this valuable trade. The fall of Constantinople to the Turks further injured the prosperity of Genoa.

By the time Columbus was a man, Genoa no longer was a city of opportunity. Her big shops were not busy; her commerce had almost ceased. A bright young sailor like Columbus would have little opportunity to advance himself in the service of Genoa's merchants and sea captains. Columbus decided to try elsewhere. Portugal offered the best chances, so there he went. A brother of his, Bartholomew, also went to Portugal. Bartholomew Columbus saw Diaz when he returned from his voyage to the Cape of Good Hope. Christopher Columbus therefore believed that in the Portuguese service he might get a chance to try out a long and carefully planned scheme. The scheme seems to have been the discovery of lands in the western sea which were rich in pearls and spices.

THE THEORY OF COLUMBUS. Christopher Columbus's idea was not entirely his own. There was a famous map maker, named Toscanelli, who had studied all the books of geography then in existence. With information from all sources, Toscanelli drew a map. The map showed Japan and China, directly

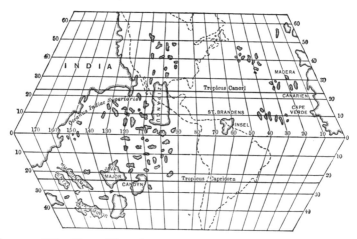

**Toscanelli's Map Showing the Indies Across the Atlantic From Europe**

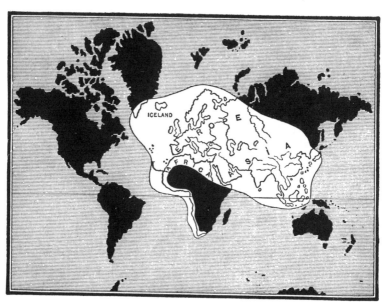

**Known World at the Time of Columbus**

west of Spain. Toscanelli did not know that a whole continent, America, lay between Spain and Asia. His plàn was simple: sail west, Toscanelli advised, and you will reach those fertile countries which abound in spices and precious stones. Perhaps Columbus consulted with Toscanelli, although this is doubted by some. At any rate, whether Columbus depended upon the ideas of Toscanelli or upon those of another geographer named Martin Behaim, or upon his own ideas, Columbus had to have money, men, and ships.

COLUMBUS AND THE KING OF PORTUGAL. Columbus sought ships and money from the King of Portugal. Now at that time Portugal was deeply interested in finding a route to India. But the Portuguese were more intent upon following out Prince Henry's plans, that is, seeking a route to India by sailing around Africa. The Portuguese king promised to help Columbus at some future time. This was not definite enough. Columbus soon saw that the king's promise was not sincere. He left Portugal, hoping to get aid in Spain.

COLUMBUS IN SPAIN. The reception Columbus received in Spain was not very encouraging. The king told Columbus he must wait. Spain was busy just then trying to conquer the Mohammèdan Moors who still had a stronghold at Granada in southern Spain. Granada was taken in 1492. The Moors thus lost their last great stronghold in Spain. When the capture of Granada seemed certain, Spanish rulers felt free to turn their attention to other matters.

FERDINAND AND ISABELLA. Columbus was again invited to explain his plans to King Ferdinand and his wife, Queen Isabella. They listened eagerly to what he had to say. Their adviser, Father Perez, who was a friend of Columbus, was firmly convinced that the plan was sound. Father Perez was

*Heaton, National Capitol, Washington*

## Columbus Recalled to Spain

Just when he had given up hope Columbus was recalled by a messenger from the Spanish court.

the guardian of the monastery of La Rabida where Columbus's little boy went to school. The queen was thoroughly convinced that Columbus had a practical plan for finding islands and a continent in the ocean to the west. The advisers of the king thought differently. They made all sorts of objections to the plan. Besides Columbus had made demands for honors and a share of the profits which seemed unfair to those at the Spanish court. Aid was refused. Columbus evidently decided to go to some other country, probably to France, to get help. He had not gone far from the court of Ferdinand and Isabella when a messenger on horseback overtook him. Columbus, they promised, could have his ships and the honors and rewards which he claimed should also be given to him.

THE TASK BEFORE COLUMBUS. Columbus was attempting an amazing undertaking. By sailing west, he confidently expected to find new islands and a continent. He had no idea

From *Adventures in the Wilderness, being Volume I, The Pageant of America*
© *Yale University Press*

### The Departure from Palos

Columbus is seen taking leave of his friend, Father Perez. This good priest had persuaded Queen Isabella to help in this greatest of adventures.

how far he had to sail. The map he had to go by had been drawn largely by guesswork. His instruments for navigation, the compass and the astrolabe, were very crude. Accurate sailing was almost impossible. To make this voyage Columbus was given three tiny ships. They were the *Santa Maria* (Holy Mary), the *Pinta* and the *Nina*. The *Santa Maria,* the largest vessel, was the flag-ship. The *Nina* and the *Pinta* were smaller and may have been without covered decks. All were uncomfortable and, perhaps, not seaworthy. Only men of extraordinary courage were willing to sail on them.

THE FAITH OF COLUMBUS. In face of these and other enormous difficulties, Columbus was willing to try to reach a country whose exact location he did not know. His strong faith perhaps more than any other motive led Columbus to undertake this journey. He saw in the success of his voyage a chance to gain for himself some of the wealth of this world. He saw also an opportunity to help others by taking to them the most precious of treasures, the knowledge of Christ. He felt as though he were going on a crusade. Indeed it was one of his hopes one day to lead a crusade that should restore the Holy Sepulcher to the Christians.

THE FIRST VOYAGE. Columbus and his sailors prepared for the voyage properly by going to Mass and Communion. Early in the morning of August 3rd the little fleet hoisted sail. The wind filled the sails, each painted with a great cross, and the most important voyage in history began. The hundred and twenty men who made up the crew never dreamed of the far-reaching results that were to follow.

A halt was made at the Canary Isles long enough to repair the rudder of the *Pinta*. Columbus had occasion to do some plain talking to the sailors. They were becoming less confident about the trip. Some of them wanted to go home. After hearing the Admiral talk, the sailors agreed to continue the voyage without grumbling. But the sailors soon forgot their promise. They continued to grumble and some of them may even have formed a plan to throw Columbus overboard.

FIRST SIGNS OF LAND. Whether the sailors actually planned to mutiny is a question. At any rate matters were certainly getting to a serious pass. For many, many days now they had been without sight of land. Columbus must have been gravely worried over the outcome. One day as he was pacing his tiny deck gazing anxiously every little while for some good sign, a flock of birds appeared. Soon the broken branch of a bush floated by the ship. The men cheered this sight. Columbus called to his men. He promised a handsome vest to the first

*Drawn expressly for the Old World and America. From Joaquin Miller's poem, "Columbus."*

## SAIL ON

"Brave Admiral say but one good word
What shall we do when hope is gone?"

The words leapt like a leaping sword:
"Sail on! sail on! sail on! and on!"

*From Adventures in the Wilderness, being Volume I, The Pageant of America*
© *Yale University Press*

## The Landing of Columbus

Can you imagine what the poor Indians thought of these splendid beings and their great ships?

one who should sight land. The vest would be useful to the winner when he called upon the ruler of the land they were soon to see.

"LAND, LAND." There was intense excitement on the ships. The anxiety to win the prize kept them all alert. They were as yet out of sight of land. Night came but no one cared to go to sleep. As they approached land, the sailors were afraid to trust their sight lest they should be mistaken about the dark spot that appeared on the horizon. Suddenly, at two o'clock of the morning of October 12, 1492, the lookout signaled, Land! He could not be mistaken. There in the distance was a track of snowy foam made by the waves breaking upon the shores of the New World. America was discovered!

SAN SALVADOR. Before dawn Columbus prepared to visit the land he had discovered. Clad in his armor which was covered with the admiral's cloak of crimson, Columbus awaited the coming of daylight. At daybreak he stepped into a small boat to be rowed to land. Upon landing, Columbus knelt down to give thanks to God. His men imitated him. Columbus called the place San Salvador (Holy Saviour), and took possession of it in the name of the King and Queen of Spain. Then he unfurled the banners with their green crosses and the letters of the Spanish monarchs.

THE FIRST COLONY. Columbus began a tour of investigation. He visited many of the islands in the locality, including Cuba. He did not know what to think of the people he met. Columbus could not understand their language, nor could they understand his. They were different from any people he had ever seen. Thinking that he had found what he was searching for, India, he called the copper-skinned inhabitants Indians. The life and ways of the Indians puzzled Columbus very much. He had expected to find people who possessed great riches. He had been dreaming of golden palaces set with the most wonderful jewels. The Indians that Columbus saw did not live in golden palaces but in dirty huts. He also was hoping to find spices. There seemed to be none. Columbus was disappointed, but he drew great comfort from the thought that these people could easily be made Christians.

Columbus resolved to plant a colony on the island we call Hispaniola (Haiti). He decided that while the men of the colony were finding the gold, he would return to Spain to report the discovery.

THE RETURN AND WELCOME. The journey home was difficult from the start. Columbus had lost his own ship, the *Santa Maria,* which was the largest and best of the three. This

*Courtesy New York Public Library*

**Return of Columbus**

It is an hour of splendid triumph for the great Admiral.

loss left him with two inferior ships. A somewhat stormy voyage marked the return. At last the two vessels cast anchor in the harbor of Palos, March, 1493. Columbus was called to the king's court where he was received with great honor. Those who had laughed at his schemes now sought to show him the most extravagant signs of respect. A parade was organized in honor of the man who had found a new route to the land of gold and gems. After listening to his report, the king decided that a new voyage should be undertaken to bring back the riches of this newly discovered land, which all believed was part of India.

THE FIRST MISSIONARIES TO AMERICA. The Spanish people were interested in something besides gold and spices. They wanted to see the heathens converted to Christianity. For this purpose, a priest was sent as a member of Columbus's company. This time Columbus had a fleet of seventeen ships and a crew of willing sailors.

Columbus arrived in the New World on his second journey there in the month of November, 1493. He landed somewhat south of the point reached on the first voyage. Thence he sailed north to see how his colony had progressed—the one he had planted the previous year. But alas! he found not a single trace of it. Undoubtedly the Spaniards had been killed by the Indians. Columbus turned from the place with a heavy heart.

THE COLONY AT ISABELLA. A new colony was founded. It was called Isabella after the Queen. Columbus had with him about fifteen hundred men. From this number he hoped to get enough worth-while colonists. A town was laid out. After the building operations had made some progress, Columbus decided to take a voyage of exploration. Columbus explored a number of the islands in the vicinity and then began to think about returning to Spain. He was anxious to get back. His health had not been good during this expedition and at one time he was so seriously ill that he nearly died.

THE LAST VOYAGES. Although the second voyage to the New World had failed to discover lands where spices and gems were to be had, nevertheless a third voyage was planned. On this the third voyage (1498-1500), Columbus touched the coast of South America at the mouth of the Orinoco River. Meantime reports reached Spain that Columbus had been cruel to the natives. A ship was sent from Spain to investigate.

The official sent by Spain to look into the conduct of Columbus took the law into his own hands. Columbus was arrested, put in chains, and sent aboard ship to be returned to Spain. The unfortunate man never recovered from this disgraceful treatment. He never forgot the experience, although the king

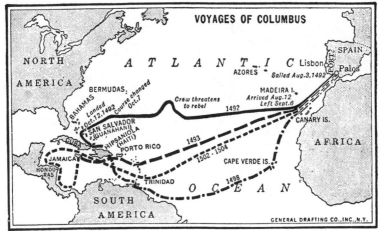

© *William H. Sadlier, Inc.*

## The Four Voyages of Columbus.

and queen took great pains to show their sympathy. They even sent him on a fourth voyage (1502) to the New World as a mark of their confidence in him. On this, the fourth voyage, he found the coast of Central America and the Isthmus of Darien.

THE END OF COLUMBUS. On the fourth voyage Columbus was attacked by a serious illness which left him in bad health. He returned to Spain to find that people had lost confidence in him. To many Columbus was a failure, for he never succeeded in getting gold, nor did he ever reach India by sailing west. But he had done a far greater thing. Christopher Columbus had discovered the New World.

---

### ORAL DRILL

---

1. What country won the race for the riches of the East?          . . . . . . . . . . . .

2. What did Columbus call the inhabitants of the lands he discovered?          . . . . . . . . . . . .

3. What is the name of the geographer whom
Columbus probably consulted?                ............

4. What direction did Columbus' ship take to
reach the East?                             ............

5. From what country did Columbus try to get
help before visiting Spain?                 ............

6. What stronghold did the Moors hold in Spain
until 1492?                                 ............

7. Who were the Spanish rulers who helped
Columbus?                                   ............

8. What priest helped Columbus?             ............

9. What land did Columbus first reach?      ............

10. What products did Columbus bring back
from the New World?                         ............

## OBJECTIVE TESTS

TEST 1: Completion Test.

1. Columbus discovered America on the ............ day of
............ 1492.

2. Columbus on his first voyage reached the island of
................

3. On the first voyage the ship ................ was lost.

4. The priest ............ advised Ferdinand and Isabella to
help Columbus.

5. The geographer ................ thought Japan and China
were directly west of Spain.

TEST 2: Order of Time.

Arrange the following in the order of time:

Fall of Constantinople
Columbus discovers America
Norsemen reach Vinland
Columbus reaches South America
Columbus reaches Central America
Vasco da Gama reaches India

TEST 3: Matching Test.

1. Granada       (   )  Holy Mary
2. Perez         (   )  advisor to Ferdinand
3. Palos         (   )  Holy Saviour
4. San Salvador  (   )  Moorish stronghold
5. Santa Maria   (   )  port from which Columbus sailed

## QUESTIONS THAT MAKE YOU THINK

1. Why have many cities claimed to be the birthplace of Columbus?
2. "The early life of Columbus prepared him for a life of navigation." Explain.
3. "Map making was Columbus' hobby." Why is this important?
4. "The fall of Constantinople injured the prosperity of Genoa." Explain this statement.
5. Show the relation between the work of Toscanelli and the work of Columbus.
6. Why did the king of Portugal fail to help Columbus?
7. Why was the fall of Granada a good thing for Columbus?
8. How did Father Perez help Columbus?
9. Why was Columbus put in chains?
10. Why was it Columbus was less popular than Vasco Da Gama?

## QUESTIONS THAT TEST YOUR CHARACTER

1. "Columbus was a real hero." Explain.
2. Name three good qualities which Columbus had.
3. "The life of Columbus shows the fickleness of the public." Explain why this is true.
4. "Was Columbus a good Catholic." Give a good reason for your answer.
5. "Columbus was a self-made man." Give two reasons for the truth or falsity of this statement.

## ACTIVITIES

1. Make models of the three ships of Columbus' first voyage.
2. Write an imaginary conversation between Columbus and the king of Portugal.
3. Dramatize: Columbus returns to Spain.
4. Suppose you were a member of Columbus' crew. Tell in your diary the story of the first voyage.
5. Dramatize: death of Columbus.
6. Deliver a Columbus Day speech on the achievement of Columbus.

7. Draw a series of Minute-Movies on the life of Columbus.
8. Write the name of C O L U M B U S. Let each letter of his name begin a word describing his character.
9. Dress dolls like: Columbus, Indians, Ferdinand and Isabella, Father Perez.
10. Paste in your scrapbook pictures of Columbus and other explorers of his time.

## TOPICS FOR DISCUSSION

1. Columbus did not discover America.
2. Columbus was greater than Vasco da Gama.
3. Columbus was a greedy man.
4. Columbus died in disgrace.

## WORD LIST

| | | | |
|---|---|---|---|
| hull | mapmaker | mutiny | Indians |
| woolcarder. | guardian | San Salvador | isthmus |

# X

## *Part 3:* THE FOLLOWERS OF COLUMBUS

You may be sure that the great feats of Columbus were a constant topic of conversation among the seafaring men. It is true, of course, that he did not bring back from the lands across the sea a cargo of gold and silks. His enemies in Spain never tired telling of Columbus's great failure. Some nicknamed him "the Admiral of the mosquito land." But the wiser and more broad-minded of the mariners in Europe knew that Columbus had done a great thing. For example, John Cabot, a sailor from Venice, made a voyage for King Henry VIII of England in 1497. Cabot discovered some part of North America. Meanwhile Spain's seamen continued to sail to the West.

THE DESIRE TO EXPLORE. One result of the voyage of Columbus was the renewed interest of the Portuguese in navigation. There was great anxiety on the part of the Portuguese to reach the East by the southern route. Spain and Portugal were both racing for the East. To avoid trouble it was suggested by the governments of both countries that a boundary line be made marking off the territory to which each country had claim.

THE LINE OF DEMARCATION. Accordingly, Pope Alexander VI declared that an imaginary line should be drawn running from north to south, dividing the world into two parts. It was called the "line of demarcation." Newly discovered lands east of this line were to belong to Portugal, those west of it to

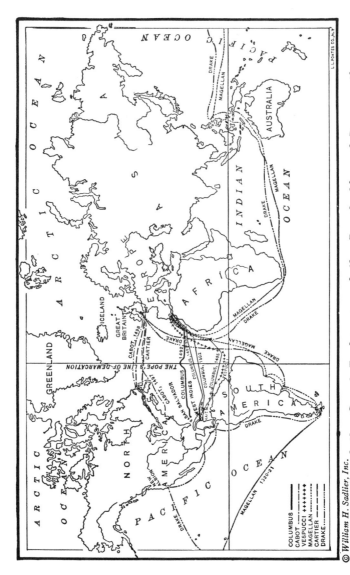

© *William H. Sadlier, Inc.*
**Voyages of the Great Explorers and the Pope's Line of Demarcation.**

Spain. The Spanish, or the Portuguese, as the case might be, would have the right to colonize the newly acquired lands. The missionaries of each country would have the responsibility of preaching Christianity to the heathens there. This boundary line was made a year after Columbus's first voyage. The following year, 1494, the line of demarcation was changed by the Treaty of Tordesillas. This change gave Portugal a claim to Brazil.

## PORTUGAL IN THE NEW WORLD

THE VOYAGE OF CABRAL. Portugal could claim Brazil since Brazil was located east of the line of demarcation as fixed by the treaty of Tordesillas. The claim was further strengthened by the discovery of a navigator named Cabral. Cabral had been commissioned by the king of Portugal to make a voyage around Africa to India. The wind seems to have carried Cabral's fleet off his course, at any rate the ships came within sight of the coast of Brazil which Cabral claimed for Portugal. Later the Portuguese settled in Brazil, and to this day Portuguese is the language spoken there. It is the only country in the western hemisphere south of the United States where Spanish is not the official language of the country. Portugal's influence on the New World is seen in another fact. The name of this continent comes from a Florentine in the service of Portugal.

THE NAME AMERICA. There was a Florentine business man who found himself in Portugal. His name was Americus Vespucius. He seems to have had a great desire for travel for he joined an expedition which was going to the New World. He made four voyages, perhaps more. He kept a long but not an entirely truthful account of his travels. Americus began to suspect that the land to the west which he and other mariners had visited was not a part of Asia, but really a continent. The existence of this continent had been hitherto unknown. The account of the travels of Americus Vespucius fell into the hands of a German, Martin Waldesmüller, who at this time was busy writing a new geography. Using Americus's description of the newly discovered lands as his guide Martin Waldesmüller drew a map of his idea of the western hemisphere naming the new continent America.

## THE FIRST TRIP ROUND THE WORLD

FERDINAND MAGELLAN. There was a Portuguese mariner named Ferdinand Magellan who was eager to imitate and to surpass, if possible, the exploits of Diaz and Da Gama. He took part in voyages around Africa to the Spice Islands which are located far east of India. Magellan did not like the route around Africa very much. In fact, Magellan preferred the course of Columbus, that is, reaching the east by sailing west. Magellan tried in vain to interest the king of Portugal in his project. Disgusted, he left his country and sought the aid of Spain. He succeeded, finally, in being placed in command of a small, poorly equipped fleet. With this he began his voyage.

THE VOYAGE AROUND SOUTH AMERICA. Magellan steered his fleet across the Atlantic. Then sailing south he skirted the east coast of South America looking carefully the while for a water passage which would lead to India. One time he thought he had found it. He sailed up what he supposed was such a passage only to find that he was sailing up a river that was not navigable some miles from its mouth. Retracing his course, Magellan got out to the Atlantic. After many adventures the fleet passed through the strait now called after him, but

*Courtesy New York Public Library*

**Magellan's Ships**

Of this small fleet only one ship returned safely home.

which he called the Channel of All Saints. Magellan steered out upon a mighty body of water. This was the same body of water that the Spanish explorer, Balboa, had discovered by crossing the Isthmus of Panama. Balboa had named it the South Sea. The sea was calm. Magellan, therefore, called it the Pacific Ocean because of its peaceful waters.

MAGELLAN AT THE PHILIPPINES. Although the sea was calm, the sailors suffered terribly. A dreadful disease broke out among them. They were without fresh water and the food supply was almost exhausted. Reduced to starvation, the unfortunate sailors ate their shoes and the leather from the ship's rigging.

Magellan continued to sail across the Pacific to the Philip-

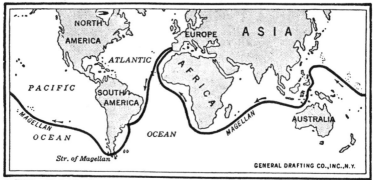

© *William H. Sadlier, Inc.*

## Magellan's Voyage

Map of the first circumnavigation or sailing around the world.

pine Islands. Here he took part in a tribal war in which he was killed. The few sailors who remained took the best ship of the fleet and set sail for Spain. September 6, 1521, nearly three years after their departure the few survivors returned to Spain. When the voyage began, Magellan had under his command a fleet of five vessels and perhaps two hundred and eighty men. At the close of the voyage, about twenty starving men on a leaky ship remained to tell the story.

LESSONS OF MAGELLAN'S VOYAGE. Magellan's voyage added greatly to the knowledge of geography and cleared up several problems. While educated people for some time had believed that the earth is round, there could now be no further question about it. The size of the earth was not accurately known. Magellan's voyage taught people the size of the earth. The voyage also showed that America was not an island but a large continent. Further information about the west coast of America was supplied by Juan Cabrillo.

CABRILLO, THE DISCOVERER OF THE CALIFORNIA COAST. Juan Cabrillo was a Portuguese by birth. Cabrillo, like Magellan, had entered the service of the Spanish king.

In the course of time he came to America stopping for a time in Mexico. While there he was given a chance to take a prominent part in an expedition which was to sail from the western coast of Mexico out across the Pacific. The expedition divided. Cabrillo in charge of two vessels steered his little fleet north. He cruised along the coast, going north probably as far as Oregon. He explored with some thoroughness the coast of California. His, therefore, is the honor of discovering this region, and his voyage added to the knowledge of the coast of America.

## ORAL DRILL

1. Give the reasons why Columbus wished to undertake so dangerous a voyage.
2. What was the purpose of the line of demarcation?
3. Who made the line of demarcation?
4. What is the name of the treaty which changed the line of demarcation?
5. Which city was the native city of Americus Vespucius?
6. What geographer named the New World?
7. Which country sent Magellan on his voyage around the World?
8. Did Magellan himself sail around the world? If not, how far did he sail?
9. Which ocean did Magellan name?
10. What mariner explored the coast of California?

## OBJECTIVE TESTS

TEST 1: Completion Test.
1. California was discovered by the explorer ...............
2. ............... was killed in the Philippines.
3. South Sea was another name for ................
4. The Channel of All Saints is now known as ...............
5. The name America was given in honor of ...............
6. As a result of the treaty of Tordesillas, Portugal could lay claim to ................
7. ............ is the only country in the western hemisphere where the language is Portuguese.

8. The Pope's boundary line was called ................ .
9. The explorer Cabral reached the country of .............
10. "Admiral of Mosquito Land" was a nickname given to
   ............... .

TEST 2: Selecting the Best Item.
  1. Cabral: Philippines, Guiana, Brazil, Italy.
  2. Pope Alexander VI: Tordesillas, Portuguese, San Salvador, Darien.
  3. Martin Waldesmüller: Columbia, Portugal, America, West Indies.
  4. Ferdinand Magellan: Philippines, West Indies, Cuba, Brazil.
  5. Vasco Da Gama: Guiana, Holland, Japan, India.

TEST 3: Order of Time.
  Arrange the following events in order of time:
       Line of demarcation
       voyage of Da Gama
       voyage of Diaz
       Magellan sails around South America

## QUESTIONS THAT MAKE YOU THINK

  1. Explain the meaning of the word "America."
  2. What is meant today by "drawing a line of demarcation"?
  3. Did Portugal have a right to claim Brazil? Give a reason.
  4. "Magellan's voyage taught the world a valuable lesson." What was this lesson?
  5. Why did the Spanish claim California?
  6. Explain the contribution of each: Cabral, Cabrillo, Magellan, Waldesmüller.
  7. Explain the nickname "admiral of mosquito land."

## QUESTIONS THAT TEST YOUR CHARACTER

  1. Why were Columbus's enemies jealous of him?
  2. Was the name "America" fair and just? Give a reason.
  3. Do you admire Americus Vespucius? Give a reason.
  4. Do you admire Magellan? Give a reason.
  5. Tell the class of the hardships of Magellan's voyage.

## ACTIVITIES

1. Make two cardboard discs, one larger than the other. By making holes in one, make a game to show the work of the followers of Columbus.
2. As a member of Magellan's crew, keep a diary of the trip. Read a week's story from the diary.
3. Make a copy of Waldesmüller's map of America. Display it on the bulletin board.
4. Make a model of Magellan's ship Victoria.
5. Draw a series of "Minute-Movies" on the "Followers of Columbus."
6. Make a little sketch showing the meaning of "line of demarcation."
7. Dramatize: Magellan's ship returns to Spain.
8. Make a speech welcoming Cabral on his return from Brazil.
9. Paste in your scrapbook pictures of the followers of Columbus.

## TOPICS FOR DISCUSSION

1. The New World should be called "Columbia."
2. Magellan's voyage was more important than Da Gama's.
3. Portugal had no right to Brazil.
4. Alexander VI had no right to make the line of demarcation.
5. Magellan was a great man.

## WORD LIST

| | |
|---|---|
| demarcation | strait |
| hemisphere | Pacific Ocean |
| continent | Channel of All Saints |
| America | Straits of Magellan |

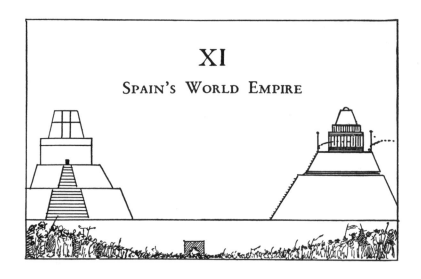

# XI

## SPAIN'S WORLD EMPIRE

### AIM

To appreciate the achievements of the Spanish explorers and missionaries.

To realize the variety and greatness of Spain's gifts to the New World.

SPAIN was not only the first country to explore the New World, she was also first to colonize it. Columbus himself had tried to plant a colony on his arrival in the New World after his second voyage. Although this was not a success, it was not long before Spain had a number of settlements that were the result of magnificent courage and amazing energy.

# XI

## *Part 1:* SPAIN'S FEARLESS EXPLORERS

The energetic Spaniards followed discovery by exploration. Before a quarter of a century after Columbus's first voyage, brave Spaniards were exploring the mainland. The exploits of Balboa, De Leon, Coronado, as well as the conquests of Cortés and Pizarro, added to Spain's power in the New World.

THE DISCOVERY OF THE PACIFIC OCEAN. A brave Spaniard Vasco Nuñez de Balboa came to America to make his fortune. In 1513 Balboa made a great discovery. He was exploring the country on the eastern side of what is now called the Isthmus of Panama in the hope of finding gold. One night an Indian chief came to his camp; he told of a country to the south that was rich in gold. Balboa and his two hundred men set out at once.

They pushed across the isthmus. Climbing to the top of a high hill, Balboa saw in the distance a mighty body of water. With his followers he rushed down the slope. Entering the water and waving his sword, in the name of the King of Spain he took possession of all the lands touched by this sea. He called it the South Sea. You have already heard of Magellan, who later gave it the name Pacific.

PONCE DE LEON. That same year, 1513, in which the Pacific Ocean was discovered, Juan Ponce de Leon discovered Florida.

He was one of the first colonists to settle in the New World and had been rewarded by being made the first governor of Puerto Rico. While there, he seems to have heard of the marvelous fountain of youth. Those who drank the waters of this fountain, according to the story of the Indians, would never grow old. Anxious to discover this magical fountain, De Leon set forth in a small ship. At Eastertime he discovered a low lying land which he thought was an island. Because it was Eastertime, he called this land Florida, which is the Spanish name for Easter. Ponce de Leon was mistaken in believing Florida an island, and he was disappointed in his search for the fountain of youth.

© *William H. Sadlier, Inc.*

**Balboa Enters the Pacific**

With sword and banner he formally claims the sea for Spain.

THE CONQUEST OF MEXICO. One day a party of Spaniards from Cuba landed on the coast of Mexico. There they met some of the inhabitants who were Indians. These Indians seemed to be somewhat more civilized than those the Spaniards had known. The gold ornaments that they wore showed that they had some skill in metal work.

Among other things, the exploring party learned that there were different large groups among the Indian inhabitants. The various tribes belonged to an association or confederacy. The ruler of the confederacy was called Montezuma. He was a member of the most important group of Indians called Aztecs.

The chief city of the Aztecs, Tenochtitlan, or Mexico, as we shall call it, was built on an island in a lake in the interior of Mexico.

HERNANDO CORTÉS. Hernando Cortés was the man given charge of the expedition to Mexico (1519). Cortès was commanded to act as a Christian leader in the service of a Catholic king. The natives were to be impressed by the Catholic Spaniards. Some preparations were made of a military character in case the Indians proved unfriendly. Cortès had sixteen horses for his soldiers and a number of brass cannon. The horses were the first to be brought to the New World. The Spaniards thought so much of the horses that their names were recorded.

*Courtesy B. F. Williamson*

**Hernando Cortés**

Perhaps no one ever conquered a greater empire with a smaller force than did Cortes.

THE MARCH TO MEXICO. The object of the expedition now was to reach the City of Mexico. The march to the capital proved to be no easy matter. The journey was made over rough country with the hot sun overhead. The natives were unfriendly and even hostile. There were several bloody encounters. However, a mere handful of pale-faced strangers were successful against a force of Indians many times as large. This had the effect of making the Aztecs decide not to oppose the Spaniards by force.

EMBASSIES FROM MONTEZUMA. Montezuma, the Indian chief, seems to have been frightened when he heard of the ability of the Spaniards as fighters. This alarm was further increased when told that the invaders had "pale-faces." There was a tradition among the Aztecs to the effect that one of their gods, the fair-skinned sky god, had been driven out of their country by the god of darkness. One day, however, he would return to rule the kingdom. There were some, Montezuma among the number, who believed that Cortés was the sky god who was coming back to be ruler in Mexico. Montezuma tried by presents and by stories of danger to turn Cortés from his evident purpose. Cortés, however, was determined to push on. At last he came near the city of the Aztecs.

MONTEZUMA AND CORTÉS. Seeing that Cortés was determined to enter the city, Montezuma decided to show him no unfriendliness. When Cortés neared the city he was met by a large delegation headed by Montezuma.

The Aztec ruler tried hard to make a brave display. He was carried on a seat which was supported on the shoulders of four chieftains. Over his head was a canopy made of gorgeous green feathers. Cortés gave no sign to show that he was greatly impressed. The slightest show of fear on his part would have been fatal. Within a brief time Cortés had things pretty much his own way. The crowning piece of audacity was the imprisonment of Montezuma in his own capital. The Aztecs believed their ruler Montezuma was a god, yet Cortés, apparently careless of consequences, captured him.

THE MOURNFUL NIGHT. Some time afterwards during the absence of Cortés the Spanish garrison did something which had made the Aztecs furiously angry. The Spaniards had

*Drawn expressly for "The Old World and America"*

## "The Mournful Night"

In the terrible fighting the armor of the Spaniards probably saved the survivors from complete destruction.

shown disrespect to the Mexican gods. The Aztecs, therefore, attacked the Spaniards.

Cortés began to realize that his position was desperate. He prepared his forces for retreat, hoping to leave the city under the cover of darkness. But the darkness did not cover him. Mexico, Aztec city, was built on an island in the lake. The island was connected with the mainland by a causeway. Hundreds of canoes paddled by Aztecs were lined up on both sides of the causeway across which the Spaniards must go on their way from the city. The Mexicans allowed the Spaniards to get fairly on the causeway. Then the attack began in deadly earnest. Cortés's force was almost cut to pieces. When at length, the remnant of the Spanish army reached a place of safety, a halt was made to allow the exhausted men to rest.

Cortés, thinking of his lost soldiers, could only weep. The Spaniards ever after spoke of the disaster as the "mournful night."

About a year later the Spaniards returned and captured the city which they held permanently. Later a new city of Mexico was built on the site of the Indian City.

A NEW LAND OF WEALTH. The Spaniards had been hearing stories about a distant land rich in treasure. Balboa, who discovered the Pacific Ocean or South Sea, as he called it, was really looking for this land of wealth. He had no great interest in discovering an ocean. However, his quest was a failure. At last came Francisco Pizarro, a man of extraordinary courage who succeeded in crossing the Andes Mountains. At length his party arrived in Peru, the country of the Inca Indians.

THE CAPTURE OF THE INCA. Pizarro now began to move with caution. He sent one of his bravest men, Ferdinand De Soto, with a small company to look over the ground. De Soto was gone for some time. He returned not only with the desired information but with an envoy from the ruler who was called the Inca. After some fighting and many adventures, Cuzco, the sacred city of Peru, was captured. There the Spaniards found stores of gold. Cuzco the chroniclers called the richest city in the world. But Pizarro reaped no reward for his labor. He was killed by his own men.

FERDINAND DE SOTO. One of Pizarro's trusted captains was Ferdinand De Soto. His experiences in the land of the Incas made him wish for further adventures. He had made a large fortune as the result of his campaigns in Peru. De Soto returned to Spain but he was not content to stay. He was appointed governor of Cuba by the king. The king also gave him a commission to explore the southern part of what is now the United States.

In the city of Havana, De Soto made his preparations.

*Drawn expressly for "The Old World and America"*

## De Soto Discovers the Mississippi

The great explorer gazes for the first time on the "Father of Waters" which afterwards became his burial place.

Everything pointed to the success of the expedition. Six hundred men and more were ready to take part. Some of these men had taken part in other expeditions. They were veteran explorers. Unfortunately there were others in the company who were not fit for so difficult an expedition. De Soto was joined by a number of gay nobles who acted as though they were going on an outing.

DE SOTO'S EXPEDITION. The equipment of the party was unusually good. They had a number of horses, and even a herd of swine. The party left Havana, sailing in the direction of Florida where a landing was made at Tampa Bay.

The march through Florida was one of extreme difficulty. To add to their troubles, the explorers were constantly attacked by Indians. The Spaniards traveled this way and that, across swamps and through thickets, until they were utterly exhausted. As the general direction was west, they came at length to a great river (1541). It was the "Father of Waters," the Mississippi. De Soto was the first white man to see this mighty stream. Boats were constructed to cross it. De Soto tried to continue the journey but was forced to return. The party had just reached the banks of the river again when their brave leader was stricken with a fever. His poor tired body was too weak to fight the disease which attacked him. The great leader died.

THE BURIAL OF DE SOTO. Knowing how much the Indians feared De Soto, his followers were most careful to conceal the fact of his death. His body was wrapped in a blanket which was weighted with sand. Then in the dead of night his friends stole out on the Mississippi and lowered the .body into its muddy waters. His followers, now much fewer in number, then made their way to the mouth of the river and finally reached home.

CORONADO'S EXPEDITION. There was a Spaniard named Francisco Vasquez de Coronado who led an expedition into the Southwest. In this region there were many Indian villages called pueblos. In one section, according to an Indian tale, there were seven marvelous cities. These were the "Seven Cities of Cibola." Here were to be found great stores of wealth. Coronado set forth with a band of 300 Spaniards and about 800 Mexican Indians. They traveled many miles. They saw the great plains where the buffalo roamed. They also discovered the beautiful Grand Canyon of the Colorado. They never found the wonderful Seven Cities; these did not exist

The failure of Coronado's expedition as well as De Soto's discouraged further exploration in this part of North America.

Spain's interest in the New World was confined thereafter to the countries south of our present border, with the exception of a settlement in Florida.

THE SPANISH CONQUERORS. Spain's explorers and soldiers had gained possession of a vast territory. This territory extended from the Rio Grande (River) in North America away down to the end of South America. The entire continent of South America, except Brazil, soon became the site of dozens of small Spanish settlements and several important cities. This was the situation before the English had succeeded in planting their first permanent settlement at Jamestown (1607). That Spain could accomplish so much in so short a time was due in large measure to the zeal and courage of the Spanish missionaries.

## ORAL DRILL

1. Who was the discoverer of the Pacific Ocean?
2. In what year was the Pacific Ocean discovered?
3. What were the native inhabitants of Mexico called?
4. What was the name of the native ruler of the inhabitants of Mexico?
5. Where does Florida get its name?
6. What is the name of the inhabitants of Peru whom the Spaniards conquered?
7. For what is Ferdinand De Soto famous?
8. Name a famous city of Peru visited by the Spaniards.
9. Who was the conqueror of Peru?
10. Where were the famous "Seven cities of Cibola" located?

## OBJECTIVE TESTS

TEST 1: Completion Test.
1. In 1513 . . . . . . . . . . . made a great discovery near Panama.
2. . . . . . . . . . . . . . . . . discovered Florida.
3. Cortés left the island of . . . . . . . . . . . . . for Mexico.
4. The ruler of the Indian confederacy in Mexico was . . . . . . . . . . . . . . . . . .

5. The Incas called ............. the richest city in the world.
6. ............... was killed by his own men in Peru.
7. ............... was buried in the Mississippi.
8. The Mississippi was called the ............ by the Indians.
9. All South America except ............. was settled by the Spaniards.
10. ............. sought the fountain of youth.

TEST 2: Matching Test.

1. De Soto            (    )    sacred city of Peru
2. Balboa             (    )    fountain of youth
3. Ponce de Leon      (    )    Father of Waters
4. Cortés             (    )    South Sea
5. Pizarro            (    )    conquered Aztecs
6. Coronado           (    )    ruler of Aztecs
7. Montezuma          (    )    western U. S.
8. Inca               (    )    capital of Aztecs
9. Cuzco              (    )    ruler of Peru
10. Tenochtitlan      (    )    conqueror of Peru

TEST 3: Order of Time.
Arrange the following in the order of time:

Discovery of San Salvador
Conquest of Mexico
Conquest of Peru
Vasco da Gama reaches India
Fall of Constantinople
Norsemen reach Vinland
Spaniards take Granada.

---

## QUESTIONS THAT MAKE YOU THINK

1. What is meant by the fountain of youth?
2. "The Aztecs belonged to a confederacy." What does that mean?
3. Why was Cortés interested in Mexico?
4. Show that the Spaniards had regard for their horses.
5. Give one reason why Montezuma wanted to be a friend of the Spaniards.
6. What is meant by the "mournful Night?"
7. Was Cortés wise in taking Montezuma prisoner?

8. Give two reasons why Pizarro was interested in Peru.
9. Explain two important results of the work of Cortés.

## QUESTIONS THAT TEST YOUR CHARACTER

1. Point out two bad traits in the character of Cortés.
2. Point out two good traits in the character of Cortés.
3. Was Ponce de Leon superstitious? Explain your answer.
4. De Soto has been called one of the bravest of the explorers. Give a reason for agreeing or disagreeing.
5. Describe the character of Montezuma.

## ACTIVITIES

1. Draw a sketch: Cortés Burns His Ships.
2. Make a series of "Minute Movies": The Spanish Conquerors in the New World.
3. Suppose you were a soldier in Cortés's army. Keep a diary of your invasion of Mexico.
4. Dramatize: Cortés and Montezuma.
5. Make a chart comparing the work of the Spanish explorers.
6. Dramatize: Balboa's Great Discovery.
7. Make a large map for the bulletin board. On it draw pictures showing the work of the explorers.
8. From clay make a model of the palace of Montezuma.
9. Paste in your scrapbook pictures of Spanish explorers.

## TOPICS FOR DISCUSSION

1. Cortés was a cruel man.
2. De Soto was the greatest of the Spanish explorers.
3. The Aztecs were highly civilized.
4. The conquest of Mexico was an evil for Spain.
5. The Pacific is the largest ocean.

## WORD LIST

| | | |
|---|---|---|
| Cuzco | pale-faces | fountain of youth |
| embassy | Inca | Tenochtitlan |

# XI

## *Part 2:* SPAIN'S HEROIC MISSIONARIES

In the discovery of the New World, Faith had played a vital part. The flagship of the fleet of Columbus was named in honor of the Mother of God, on its sails was emblazoned the cross. In exploration, too, Faith was important. Often the missionary went ahead of the explorer, almost never was he left behind. The most lasting mark that Spain placed upon the New World was the Sign of the Cross of Christ.

SPAIN'S SOLDIERS OF THE CROSS. The amazing accomplishments of Spain in the New World could not have been possible except for the missionaries. The splendid men had left their homes and friends to serve God by serving others. They understood how precious is the immortal soul of every man whether he is rich or poor, white or red. And so the missionaries joyfully gave up comfort, family, and sometimes even their lives in order that Christ might be known. Some were Franciscans, some Carmelites, some were Jesuits, and others were Dominicans. But, alike, they all loved God and God's children in the New World.

THE TASK OF THE MISSIONARIES. The task which the missionaries endeavored to do was to teach the Indians to be good Christians and to lead useful lives. First the missionaries had to learn the Indian languages. There were many Indian languages, and they are all difficult to learn. The Indians were pagans. They did not know about our Saviour. They worshiped false gods. To teach the Indians the catechism required the greatest kindness and patience. Nor could the missionary tell when the Indians might turn against him. Sometimes this happened, and the missionary followed the example of his Master and died for others. Besides teaching the Indians the truths of religion, the missionaries strove to instruct the savages in matters of every day life. They were taught better methods of planting seed and better ways of tilling the soil. The missionaries introduced vegetables and fruits. Thus the orange and lemon, grapes, and olives, and grain were brought to the New World, as well as horses, sheep and cattle.

© Ewing Galloway

**Junipero Serra**

The Franciscan priest, father of the California Missions.

THE SPANISH MISSIONS. The missionaries had their greatest success with the Indians in those places where missions were built. The mission was a series of buildings consisting of a church, a school, a workshop and living quarters. The ruins of many of these missions are still to be seen in the southwestern part of the country, but the best known are those of California. The California missions were founded by the Franciscan Fathers who built, in all, twenty-one missions. These missions extended from one end of California to the other.

Nine of the twenty-one missions were built under the direction of Father Junipero Serra. Some of the missions after all these years are still in use, and one, Santa Barbara, has always been served by the Franciscans. These missions stand as monuments to the zeal of the Franciscans and their superior, Father Serra, but his greatest monument is the fact that he taught the Indians to love God.

THE PLAN OF THE MISSION. When the missionaries reached a spot that they thought would be suitable they established their mission. At first this was a little chapel with a single dwelling attached. After the missionaries had won the confidence of the Indians they planned a larger structure. This was sometimes built of adobe bricks, sometimes of stone. Red tiles covered the roof. Since the missionaries could not build the mission entirely with their own hands, they trained the Indians to make brick and to lay stones. The beauty of the missions was due to the artistic sense of the missionaries.

THE MISSION BUILDINGS. The mission was usually built about an open court or patio. On one side was the Church, always the most beautiful part of the mission. Massive walls, on which rested wooden beams hewn by hand from great trees, supported the tiled roof. From the arches over the door hung the mission bells which called all to prayer and summoned the Indians to work or to rest. In the work-rooms located along the other side of the patio all sorts of activities were carried on. There were shops for baking, candle and soap making, carpentry. There were shops for leather work and for metal crafts. A special hall contained the wine press and the olive press. Another portion of the mission was used for a school. Here the Indians were taught as much as they could master. The missions were the first agricultural schools in America.

*Drawn expressly for the Old World and America.*

## A CALIFORNIA MISSION

There is no episode in American history of which we can be prouder than the story of the Franciscan missions in California.

Some of the Indians learned to read and write Spanish and to sing the Latin hymns and chants of the Church. But most important of all, the Indians learned to pray.

## ORAL DRILL

1. What was the religion of the Indians when the Spanish arrived in America?
2. What religion did many of the Indians later embrace?
3. What is a mission?
4. Who founded the missions of California?
5. Where were the California missions located?
6. Name five things the missionaries brought to California.
7. What mission in California is still served by the Franciscans?
8. What materials were principally used in building the missions?
9. How did the missionaries summon the Indians to their daily tasks?
10. How many missions were founded by the Franciscans in California?

## OBJECTIVE TESTS

TEST 1: Historical Vocabulary.

1. What is adobe?
   a) a Mexican home
   b) a kind of stone
   c) a kind of brick
   d) a Mexican dish

2. Who were the Aztecs?
   a) tribe of Mexico
   b) family of the Inca
   c) people of Canada
   d) people of Peru

3. What is a patio?
   a) a summer home
   b) a Franciscan garment
   c) an open court
   d) the roof of a mission

4. What is a pagan?
   a) one who gives up his faith
   b) one who lives a bad life
   c) a follower of Mohammed
   d) one who believes in false gods.

5. Who are the Jesuits?
   a) all those who believe in Jesus
   b) members of the Society of Jesus
   c) French missionaries
   d) explorers and soldiers

## QUESTIONS THAT MAKE YOU THINK

1. Why were missionaries called "soldiers of the cross"?
2. "The Indians had many different languages." What effect did this have upon the work of the missionaries?
3. Name two different missionary orders that went to America.
4. Why was the work of the missionaries so hard?
5. Show how the missionaries helped the Indians.
6. Why did the Indians welcome the Californian missions?
7. Describe a Spanish mission.
8. Why is Father Serra an important figure in American history?
9. Explain the contribution of the Spanish to education in the New World?
10. How often would you expect the mission bell to ring each day? Name the reasons for ringing the mission bell.

## QUESTIONS THAT TEST YOUR CHARACTER

1. What was the greatest contribution of the Spanish missionaries? Explain your answer.
2. "The Spanish missionaries were real heroes." Give a reason for agreeing or disagreeing.
3. "Father Serra was a lovable figure." Why?
4. In what way could the Spanish have improved their treatment of the Indians?

## ACTIVITIES

1. From wood, clay, or soap, make a model of a Spanish mission.
2. Tell of a visit to a Spanish mission in California.
3. Draw a sketch of a Franciscan missionary, showing his achievements in the New World.
4. Dress a doll as a Spanish missionary (Franciscan).
5. Deliver a short speech at the unveiling of a statue to Father Serra.
6. Dramatize: life in the missions.
7. Draw a cartoon, comparing Spanish and English treatment of the Indian.
8. Make a chart on the Spanish gifts to the New World.
9. Paste in your scrapbook pictures and clippings of missionary life.

# XI

*Part 3:* SPAIN'S GIFTS TO THE NEW WORLD

Spain's possessions in the New World covered a vast territory which included a notable portion of North America and (except Brazil) all of South America, besides the islands of the Caribbean Sea. Throughout this vast region Spain's influence prevailed. The official language was Spanish and it remains the language of the people today. Spanish laws, Spanish customs and the Catholic religion are Spain's gift to a great part of the New World.

THE POPULATION OF SPANISH AMERICA. The native population was, of course, made up of Indians. The Indians belonged to different tribes. Some of them like the Aztecs in Mexico and the Indians of Peru were much more civilized than those Indians who lived in northwestern Mexico or in the jungles of South America. In time perhaps most of these Indians came under the influence of the Spanish priests and so they became more civilized. The rule of the Spanish authorities was generally, though not always, just. The Indians were not exterminated as they were in the English colonies, and to this day the Indians in Mexico form an important part of the population. The Spanish population increased so that within a hundred years after America's discovery, the Spanish population numbered about 200,000. This was large, but not large enough for the size of the territory that Spain was attempting to control.

*Courtesy New York Public Library*

**Education in Spanish America**

Magnificent universities were built by the Spaniards.

EDUCATION IN SPANISH AMERICA. Education to fit the needs of the Spanish people and the more promising Indian youth was provided. The oldest college in the New World was the College of the Holy Cross founded in 1535. Two universities were opened in 1551—one in Mexico City, and that of St. Mark in Lima, Peru. Education was provided for girls also. These colleges were founded many years before the first colleges were established in the English colonies. The kind of education in the University of Mexico generally surpassed that given in the colleges in the thirteen English colonies.

THE SPANISH RECORD. Spain's record in the New World was remarkable not only for education and missionary activity, but also for many other things. The first printing presses in America and the first hospitals were Spanish. The Spaniards introduced plants, trees, vegetables, horses, dogs and cattle to the New World. They had done all this before the other great nations in Europe had made a beginning. Spain was the leader in the New World. Could she retain this leadership? The answer to this question was to be found in Europe.

## ORAL DRILL

1. Which Indians in Spanish America were the more highly civilized?
2. What was the name of the oldest college in the New World?
3. Where were the oldest universities located?
4. Where are the Indians today an important part of the population?
5. Name two animals introduced into the New World by the Spaniards.
6. In what part of the New World were the first printing presses set up?
7. Which European people founded the first hospitals in America?
8. What is the official language of Brazil?
9. About how large was the Spanish population of America one hundred years after discovery?
10. Were the Indian girls given an education?

## OBJECTIVE TESTS

TEST 1: Completion Test.
1. ................. was the oldest College in the New World.
2. The Indians in Spanish colonies were not wiped out as they were in the ................. colonies.
3. Spain's possessions included the islands of the ............. Sea.
4. In 1551 the University of St. Mark was founded in the City of .................

TEST 2: Selecting the Correct Item.
Pick out the contributions of the Spanish:
1. Conquered New England.
2. Explored the St. Lawrence.
3. First College in New World.
4. Converted Mexico.
5. Missions of California.

6. Exterminated the Indians.
7. First hospitals in New World.
8. Introduced horses to the New World.
9. Reached India by new route around Africa.
10. Civilized the Iroquois.

## TOPICS FOR DISCUSSION

1. The Spanish treatment of the Indian was better than the English treatment.
2. Spain founded education in the New World.
3. The rule of the Spanish authorities was cruel.
4. There should be a Californian holiday in honor of Father Serra.
5. Spanish influence in the New World was greater than that of the English.

## WORD LIST

| | |
|---|---|
| pagans | patio |
| catechism | mission |
| missionaries | College of the Holy Cross |
| exterminate | University |

# XII

## RIVALRIES IN EUROPE

## AIM

To see how Protestantism divided Europe.
To understand why the decline of Spain in the Old
World affected the history of the New World.

IN LITTLE more than a quarter of a century after Columbus discovered America the Spanish ruler Charles V was the mightiest monarch in the New World and also in the Old World. Within his dominions were the cities of Mexico, Vienna, Madrid and Amsterdam. Spain lost her position as the foremost power in Europe as a result of wars with rival nations and of the political effects of the Protestant revolt.

# XII

## *Part 1:* THE DIVISION OF CHRISTENDOM

Before the sixteenth century all the Christians in western Europe, and those in America also, believed in one religion. They were all members of the Catholic Church, governed by the Pope as Christ's vicar. In the sixteenth century, a German named Martin Luther persuaded some Catholics in Germany to believe in ideas that he had about religion. John Calvin who lived in Switzerland also led many to give up the Catholic religion.

THE TEACHINGS OF MARTIN LUTHER. Martin Luther was able to persuade many Catholics in Germany to give up their belief in many things which were taught by the Catholic Church. Luther also persuaded them to accept a religion which Luther himself founded. Luther had followers not only in Germany but also in the countries of northern Europe. There were other men who at first followed Luther's ideas and later disagreed with him on many important points. These men also established new religions. They, too, had followers. The teachings of John Calvin impressed many. John Calvin wrote a famous book called the *Institutes of Christianity*. Calvin's follower, John Knox, preached in Scotland where he had many followers.

THE PROTESTANT REVOLT IN ENGLAND. In England King Henry VIII made himself head of the English Church. Henry VIII was able to do this because the king then could do as he liked. The people had lost their freedom. In the reign of Henry's daughter, Queen Elizabeth, most of the people of

England could no longer practice the Catholic religion; indeed the law forbade Catholics to worship according to their conscience. The fact that England became Protestant while Spain remained Catholic caused much bitter feeling between these countries. This was one reason why these countries later went to war.

IGNATIUS OF LOYOLA. In different countries numbers of people were disobeying the Pope and giving up the practice of the Catholic religion. The Church had great need of a specially trained body of teachers. Their work was to bring back those who were giving up the Catholic Church which was established by Christ for churches established by men.

*Courtesy B. F. Williamson*

**St. Ignatius Loyola**

Find out what is the meaning of "Ad Majorem Dei Gloriam."

This need was supplied by the Company of Jesus, or the Jesuits. The Jesuits were organized by a Spaniard nobleman, Ignatius of Loyola. Ignatius had been wounded while fighting, and during the time he was getting well he had a chance to think about the important things of life. Ignatius began to realize that the one important thing is to know, love, and serve

God. Ignatius then gave himself entirely to the service of God and the Church.

THE COMPANY OF JESUS. As Ignatius had been a soldier he organized his followers on military lines, a company of Soldiers of Jesus. In addition to their other vows, the Jesuits took a vow of service to the Pope. The work of the Jesuits was to stem the revolt against the Church and to spread the Catholic Church in foreign lands. The Jesuits did heroic work for the Faith. Many people were saved to the Church through the preaching of the Jesuits. Many Jesuits in saving the Faith died as martyrs.

THE DIVISION OF EUROPE. Europe as a result of the Protestant Revolt soon became an armed camp. Religion was made the excuse for warfare and rebellion. Undoubtedly, the question of religion had much to do with the struggle between the people of the Netherlands and their Spanish ruler. This struggle, like the wars with France, contributed toward the weakening of Spain.

---

## ORAL DRILL

1. Where did Emperor Charles spend his last days?
2. Who was the ruler of the Netherlands when the Dutch revolted?
3. Which country in Europe after 1550 was the most powerful rival of Spain?
4. Who founded the Company of Jesus?
5. Who was a famous follower of John Calvin?
6. Who was Queen Elizabeth's father?
7. What king made himself head of the Church of England?
8. Who persuaded the people in Germany to disobey the Pope?
9. What special vow do the Jesuits take?
10. Which Church did the people of western Europe before 1500 believe in?

## OBJECTIVE TESTS

Test 1: Completion Test.
1. ............... are called the "Company of Jesus."
2. John Calvin wrote a book called ...............
3. The Protestant Revolt was started in the first quarter of the 16th century by a man named ...............
4. ............... wrote a clear description of Protestant beliefs.
5. ............... preached Protestantism in Scotland.
6. ............... was the founder of the Jesuits.
7. King ............... made himself head of the Church of England.
8. England became Protestant during the reign of ...........

Test 2: Matching Test.

| Column A | Column B |
| --- | --- |
| 1. Protestant Revolt in England | Henry VIII |
| 2. Protestant Revolt in France | John Knox |
| 3. Society of Jesus | John Calvin |
| 4. Scotch Protestants | Ignatius Loyola |

Test 3: Order of Time.
Arrange the following events in the order of time:
Lutheran revolt
Founding of Jesuits
Fall of Constantinople
Discovery of San Salvador
Voyage of Leif Ericsson

## QUESTIONS THAT MAKE YOU THINK

1. Compare the extent of the empire of Charles V and that of Charlemagne.
2. Show how the Protestant Revolt helped bring about the decline of Spain.
3. Give two other reasons for the decline of Spain.
4. Which is more correct, Protestant Revolt or Protestant Reformation? Give a good reason for your answer.
5. Point out one thing which Calvin and Luther had in common.
6. Why did Henry VIII break away from the Pope?
7. "The Jesuits did heroic work for the Faith." Explain this statement.

# XII

## *Part 2:* SPAIN'S FRENCH AND DUTCH RIVALS

War is the most costly of human activities. Even the country that wins a war cannot afford it. The wars which Spain fought with the French, Dutch, and English so weakened that country that Spain never fully recovered. Besides, Spain already had sent her best leaders to the New World to explore and to preach the Gospel.

RIVALRY BETWEEN FRANCE AND SPAIN. France was nearly surrounded by the Spanish possessions in Europe. Shortly after Charles V became ruler of the Spanish dominions, Francis, also a young man, became king of France. He was often called the "gentleman King," of which title he was very proud. At first, Francis I, King of France, and Charles V, King of Spain and Emperor, were quite friendly, but this did not last. The rulers, Francis I and Charles V, become involved in a series of wars over territory in Italy and Burgundy to which both laid claim.

FRANCE A UNITED NATION. Francis I, King of France, did not rule over possessions nearly as vast as those of his rival, Charles V. But King Francis I ruled a country which was united in its opposition to Spain. King Francis had an excellent army composed of brave men under the leadership of gallant captains. One of them the Chevalier Bayard, "the Knight without fear and without reproach" who died facing the enemy, was especially famous. With such excellent captains Francis I was able to oppose the armies of Spain.

Eventually the wars between France and Spain were over and no good came to either side. The French, however, became sure of their strength and they were anxious to explore the New World which was Spain's treasure chest. The voyage of John Verrazano marked the beginning of French discovery in America.

DISCOVERERS FOR FRANCE. King Francis I sent John Verrazano in 1524 on a voyage of discovery. This mariner reached the coast of America and seems to have entered what is now New York Bay. Later King Francis I commissioned Jacques Cartier to lead an expedition to China. His orders were to find China or a pas-

**Francis I, King of France**

He was the first king of France to send explorers to America.

sage leading to it. Meanwhile Spain was having a severe struggle with the Dutch. She emerged from this struggle a weaker nation, as she did from that with France. All this had an effect upon the history of the New World.

## THE RISE OF THE DUTCH REPUBLIC

THE NETHERLANDS. The Netherlands, or Lowlands, are located on that part of the coast of Europe that lies just north of France. The land is formed by the deposits of earth brought down by the rivers, the rushing Rhine, the Meuse, and the lazy Scheldt. These rivers leave their earthy deposits at their mouths before they go into the sea. In the north, particularly, the land is low. It is so low, indeed, that the inhabitants had to build walls or dikes to keep out the sea.

THE PEOPLE OF THE LOWLANDS. There is quite a little difference between the people in the north and those in the south. Those in the north resemble the Germans; many of those in the south are more like the French. Each division of the country has its own language. A kind of German is spoken in the north while a French tongue is spoken in the south. After the Protestant Revolt there were differences in religion. The southern provinces were loyal to the old Faith, while many of the inhabitants in the north followed the ideas of Luther or Calvin.

OCCUPATIONS OF THE PEOPLE. In spite of many drawbacks the people in the Netherlands managed to do very well on their lowlands. Some engaged in fishing, others took to seafaring, and as seafaring and trading go hand in hand, they became successful traders. Still others made a living by farming. Where the land was covered with water, the men built windmills which pumped the water from the land into canals. In the south, manufacturing was carried on with great success. For years the products of the cities of Bruges and Ghent were famous all over Europe.

THE BEGINNING OF STRIFE. For many years the Netherlands had been a busy, happy place. Disunion appeared when Protestant ideas began to spread in the northern provinces. While Charles V of Spain was ruler of the Netherlands the situation was kept well in hand. Disunion came later. This occurred after Charles gave up his throne.

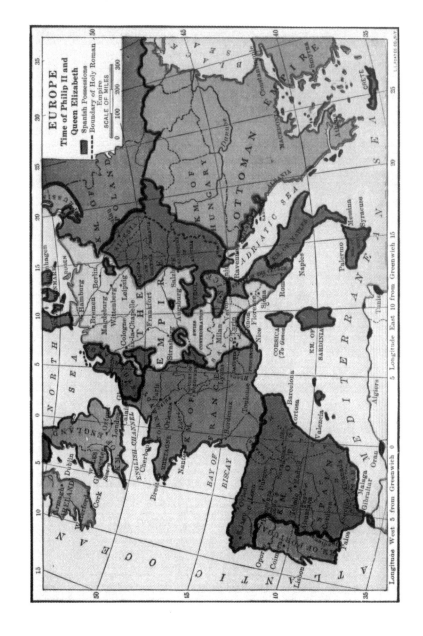

EUROPE
Time of Philip II and
Queen Elizabeth

Spanish Possessions
Boundary of Holy Roman
Empire

SCALE OF MILES
0   100   200   300

## Last Days of Charles V of Spain

Weary of war and strife the old emperor sought peace with the good monks.

Charles was weary of the world. Hoping to spend his last days in peace he gave up his vast possessions and entered a monastery. His son Philip II succeeded him. This was an unfortunate change for the Netherlands. Charles was popular among the people there. He was one of them, for he had been born in Ghent. Philip was a stranger to the people. They knew little about him. The Dutch were ready to revolt, which they did. In 1581 the Dutch proclaimed their independence. Led by William, the Silent, a clever military leader from Orange, in the northern part of the Lowlands, the Dutch were able finally to win their independence from Spain. Once they had become independent, the Dutch developed their trade. Dutch ships sailed to the most distant harbors.

HENRY HUDSON'S DISCOVERY. Henry Hudson, in the employ of Amsterdam merchants, sailed to the New World where he discovered the river which is called after him, Hudson River. As a result of this discovery the Dutch decided to make a settlement in the New World. This settlement, which was really a trading post, they called New Amsterdam. It is now the site of New York City, the greatest commercial city in the western hemisphere. Thus another rival of Spain in Europe tried to share in the wealth of the New World. The Dutch failed because of Spain's most powerful rival, England.

ENGLAND, SPAIN'S NEWEST RIVAL. England meanwhile was growing into a powerful nation. Her island position had kept English soil free from invasion. English industries were increasing in value. English seamen were more and more engaging in profitable trading ventures. A number of Englishmen now had two ambitions, one, the advancement of England, the other, the ruining of Spain. A bitter struggle between these two countries was the natural result. This contest was fought during the reign of Queen Elizabeth. The results coming from it are of great importance in the story of the New World.

---

## ORAL DRILL

---

1. What Spanish ruler was born in the Netherlands?
2. What nationality was Henry Hudson?
3. Who were the original European settlers of New York?
4. What was the language of the people of the Netherlands?
5. Did all the people of the Netherlands belong to the same Church?
6. Who was the leader of the Dutch revolt?
7. Name two important towns in the Netherlands.
8. Who was "the knight without fear and without reproach"?

## OBJECTIVE TESTS

TEST 1: Completion Test.
1. The gentleman king was ...............
2. King ............... of France commissioned John Verrazano to make a voyage.
3. Jacques Cartier was commissioned to make a voyage of discovery by ...............
4. The English mariner ............... sailed to the New World in the service of the Dutch.
5. In 1581 the Dutch revolted under their leader .............
6. The Dutch constructed ............. to keep out the sea.
7. ............... are used to pump water.
8. The first Dutch settlement in the New World was ...............

TEST 2: Matching Test.
1. Meuse              (    )  City in the Netherlands
2. William the Silent (    )  Explorer
3. Ghent              (    )  River
4. Philip II          (    )  Gentleman King
5. Henry Hudson       (    )  Dutch Leader
6. Francis I          (    )  King of Spain

## QUESTIONS THAT TEST YOUR CHARACTER

1. Point out one good and one bad trait of Martin Luther.
2. What lesson should Catholics learn from the Protestant Revolt?
3. Why did the Dutch revolt against Philip II, but not against Charles V?
4. Why did Charles V retire to a monastery?
5. a) Name two people from this chapter whom you admire.
   b) Tell why in each case.

## ACTIVITIES

1. Draw maps showing the difference in size of the lands ruled by Charles V and Francis I.

2. Make a series of "Minute Movies" entitled "Men of the Protestant Revolt."
3. Have a class pageant on "Contributions of the Jesuits."
4. Dramatize: Philip II hears of the Dutch Revolt.
5. Describe an imaginary visit to the Netherlands.
6. Make a model of a Dutch windmill.
7. Give an imaginary speech which Charles V might have given when he retired to a monastery.
8. Suppose you lived in Germany in Luther's time. Write a letter to a friend in England telling of Luther's revolt.

## TOPICS FOR DISCUSSION

1. The Protestant Revolt was one of the causes of the decline of Spain.
2. John Calvin was the greatest of the so-called "reformers."
3. Henry VIII was a tyrant.
4. Charles V was a coward to retire.
5. The Dutch had no right to revolt against Spain.

## WORD LIST

| | |
|---|---|
| "gentleman king" | revolt |
| emperor | rebellion |
| reformation | Jesuits |
| Lowlands | Netherlands |

# XII

## *Part 3:* THE ELIZABETHAN SEA DOGS

Spain had to contend with still another rival, England,
Indeed, England had given assistance to the Dutch in
their revolt against Spain. The English, therefore, had
been in conflict with the Spaniards even before they went
openly to war. So it happened that a few years after the
Dutch claimed their independence, England and Spain
were engaged in a desperate struggle. The outcome had a
most important bearing on American history. The defeat
of Spain in the Old World helped to bring about her final
downfall in the New World. This important conflict between the English and the Spaniards occurred when
Elizabeth was Queen of England.

ELIZABETH, ENGLAND'S QUEEN. Elizabeth became
Queen of England at the age of twenty-five. Elizabeth was a
clever woman. Her education had been thorough. It is said that
she knew several languags, among them Latin and Greek.

Besides her good qualities, she had certain serious defects.
Elizabeth was vain and she was hungry for flattery. By some
of her subjects, however, she was called "Good Queen Bess."
Elizabeth in spite of her faults was wise enough to choose
capable men for her advisers.

WILLIAM SHAKESPEARE. A number of famous writers
lived when Elizabeth was queen. The writings of one of them,
William Shakespeare, are especially fine. William Shakespeare

*Courtesy New York Public Library*

## William Shakespeare

The great poet is shown here in a group of famous writers of his day.

was born in the little town of Stratford-on-Avon where he attended the Guild School. When he was a young man he went to London. Here he supported himself by acting in plays written by other authors. Soon he began to write his own plays. Among Shakespeare's plays are *Hamlet, Julius Cæsar, The Merchant of Venice, Romeo and Juliet*. These are regarded by many as the greatest plays in the English language.

THE ADVENTURERS. Elizabeth's reign was made famous also by the exploits of adventurers who wished to bring glory to England and to put money into their own pockets. The gallant Sir Walter Raleigh, as well as Sir Francis Drake, and Sir John Hawkins made reputations for themselves as seamen and soldiers of fortune.

Sir John Hawkins was an Englishman who looked upon the

*Drawn expressly for "The Old World and America"*

## Queen Elizabeth Knighting the Pirate Drake

Elizabeth handed the sword to a friend of Drake for the accolade.

slave trade as a quick means of becoming wealthy. With this idea in mind he got together a fleet of vessels and set sail for Africa. The fleet was in charge of Francis Drake who acted as pilot. In Africa the Englishmen found little difficulty in obtaining slaves. With a cargo of unfortunate blacks, the fleet sailed for America. There the slaves were sold to the Spanish colonists, although this deal was a violation of the laws of Spain.

In exchange for the slaves, the Englishmen took back quantities of hides, sugar, ginger, and pearls.

DRAKE AS A PIRATE. Drake was a great success as a pirate. In the Gulf of Mexico he captured no less than one hundred small vessels. While on the Isthmus of Panama Drake discovered the trail used by the Spaniards to transport gold and silver which had been mined or captured in Peru. The precious metal was transported on the backs of mules. Drake also learned that only a small force of soldiers protected this precious pack train. Drake's men overpowered the guard and captured the gold and silver. Then having loaded his ships with the plunder Drake set sail for England. The vast quantities of gold in his possession required some explanation but Drake got around this difficulty by saying that by trading he had obtained the gold from the natives.

DRAKE'S FAMOUS VOYAGE. While on the Isthmus of Panama Drake had seen the Pacific Ocean. He declared that he would some day sail on its waters. No doubt he expected to collect booty. With the help of money advanced by Queen Elizabeth and some of her favorites, Drake gathered a fleet of five ships and with these he started his most famous voyage.

Drake sailed across the Atlantic and through the Straits of Magellan, thence along the coast of South America, robbing seacoast towns and trading ships. After plundering the towns along the South American coast, Drake continued along the coast of North America. He sailed farther north than the site of the present city of San Francisco.

AROUND THE WORLD. During the winter Drake encamped on a spot on the west coast of North America which he called New Albion. Albion is a name for England. Drake's stay in this region later gave England a claim to the territory. Realizing that the Spaniards would be waiting for his return, Drake decided to return to England by another route. He, therefore, steered out across the Pacific to the west. Drake reached England after three years of sailing in foreign seas. He was the first Englishman to circumnavigate the world.

Drake had started with five ships. He returned with only

one, but that one ship was laden with gold. The queen who had invested some of her money in Drake's enterprise was delighted. She dined on the ship and later conferred knighthood upon Drake.

TROUBLE WITH SPAIN. Drake's buccaneering expeditions had angered the Spanish king. It was well known that the amount of loot which Drake had seized was divided among close friends of the queen. The Spaniards believed that the outrageous acts of Drake and other English pirates had the approval of the English queen and her advisers. Every time the English captured a Spanish galleon they limited the power of Spain.

The differences of religion between the two countries caused a feeling of bitterness. England's help to the Protestant Dutch in their revolt against Catholic Spain could not be easily overlooked. There was also political rivalry between England and Spain. Spain was jealous of England's growing power and influence with the other nations of Europe. For these reasons war between England and Spain seemed to be unavoidable.

PREPARATION FOR WAR BETWEEN SPAIN AND ENGLAND. As an island, England had a great advantage in wartime. The country that wished to attack England had to have an excellent fleet. England had a splendid navy. The navy consisted of over a hundred ships, some provided by the queen, others by the city of London, while some were hired. Lord Howard of Effingham commanded the fleet. Drake and Hawkins served under him.

THE ATTEMPT TO INVADE ENGLAND. The Spanish king, Philip II, decided that war on England could not be delayed. He, therefore, ordered the admiral of the Spanish fleet to sail for England. The Armada (which means fleet) met with misfortunes from the very outset. Before it

*Courtesy B. F. Williamson*

**The Defeat of the Armada**

The clumsy Spanish troop-ships fell before the smaller but better manned English war-ships.

reached the English Channel a severe storm damaged some of the ships considerably. The damage was repaired, however, and the fleet moved into the English Channel.

The Spanish Armada presented a magnificent sight. The ships were large for that time. A great deal of money had been spent to give the vessels a splendid appearance, but they really were mostly transports and not fighting ships. The English ships were small in size and hardly attractive to look at. But they were real ships. They could weather a gale. Of course, the English captains knew the Channel and the treacherous coasts. The Spaniards were unfamiliar with either the currents or the coast line.

THE DEFEAT OF THE ARMADA, 1588. A gentle breeze was blowing. The breeze suddenly changed to a gale from the southwest. The Spanish ships behaved badly in the storm. The English, taking advantage of the confusion in the Spanish fleet, poured shot into the vessels. The Spaniards tried to get away.

They attempted to sail around the coast of Scotland. Here they met with a series of gales which proved to be their worst enemy. The wind pursued them with terrible ferocity. Ship after ship crashed to pieces on the rock-bound coasts of Scotland and Ireland. More than thirty ships and ten thousand men was the toll of destruction. Thus ended, in 1588, Spain's attempt to conquer England and also her supremacy in the New World. Thereafter the path to the New World was open to the ships of all countries.

## OBJECTIVE TESTS

TEST 1: Completion Test.
1. The Spanish fleet that attempted to invade England in the reign of Queen Elizabeth was called the ...............
2. Queen Elizabeth's subjects sometimes called her ".........
.................''
3. The first Englishman to circumnavigate the globe was
.................
4. Hamlet is a ...............
5. William Shakespeare was a ...............
6. The defeat of the Spanish fleet occurred in ...............
7. Sir John Hawkins was a ...............
8. A galleon is a ...............
9. Albion is the name for ...............
10. Lord Howard of Effingham was ...............

TEST 2: Matching Test.
1. William, the Silent   (   )  Romeo and Juliet
2. Charles V            (   )  Protestant Revolt in Germany
3. William Shakespeare  (   )  enemy of England
4. Queen Bess           (   )  Emperor
5. Philip II            (   )  leader of the Dutch
6. Sir John Hawkins     (   )  sea dog
7. Armada               (   )  famous admiral
8. Lord Howard          (   )  Protestant Revolt in England
9. Martin Luther        (   )  storms
10. Henry VIII          (   )  supported Drake

TEST 3: Selecting the Correct Item.
1. Lord Howard: Dutch revolt, Armada, Carolina, Guild School.
2. Sir John Hawkins: merchant, peace, slave-trade, London.

3. Sir Francis Drake: Romeo and Juliet, Guild School, piracy, Stratford-on-Avon.
4. Queen Elizabeth: humility, kindness, sweetness, vanity.
5. William Shakespeare: Paris, Stratford-on-Avon, Madrid, New Amsterdam.

## QUESTIONS THAT MAKE YOU THINK

1. Why is Drake called a "sea-dog"?
2. Name one thing in common between Drake and Hawkins.
3. Why is Shakespeare regarded as a great man?
4. Was Drake fair to the Spanish? Explain your answer.
5. "Drake was knighted." What does this mean?
6. Give two reasons for the defeat of the Spanish Armada.
7. "The struggle between England and Spain had an important bearing upon American history." Show why this statement is true.
8. Why was the slave-trade important during Queen Elizabeth's time?
9. What is meant by the phrase "Drake's Famous Voyage"?

## QUESTIONS THAT TEST YOUR CHARACTER

1. Why is Drake called a pirate?
2. Name two good traits of Sir Francis Drake.
3. Name two bad traits of Sir John Hawkins.
4. Was Queen Elizabeth a great woman? Explain.
5. a) Mention two people in this chapter whom you admire.
   b) Tell the reason in each case.

## TOPICS FOR DISCUSSION

1. Drake was a scoundrel.
2. The weather defeated the Armada.
3. Queen Elizabeth was a very good ruler.
4. The slave trade was unjust.
5. The Spaniards were poor sailors.

## WORD LIST

| | | |
|---|---|---|
| Elizabethan literature | flattery | New Albion |
| religious animosity | vengeance | Armada |

# XIII

## THE FOUNDATIONS OF AMERICA

### AIM

To realize that many countries in Europe shared in laying the foundations of the United States.

To understand the meaning of THE OLD WORLD AND AMERICA.

SPAIN after the defeat of the Armada no longer had the best navy. After 1588 the mariners of England, France, and Holland felt that they could sail their ships to the New World without fear. Even before the defeat of the Armada, the English had been interested in the New World. It was not until the year 1607, however, that England was able to plant a permanent settlement in America.

# XIII

## *Part 1:* ENGLAND IN THE NEW WORLD

The story of England in North America begins shortly after the discovery of the New World by Christopher Columbus. The voyage of John· Cabot in 1497 gave England a claim to North America. England did not send colonists to the New World after Cabot's voyage, as Spain did after the voyage of Columbus. Nevertheless, the history of England in North America properly begins with the voyage of John Cabot.

JOHN CABOT OF BRISTOL. Although John Cabot had been born in Venice he spent much of his time in England. He was living in Bristol, England, when the news of Columbus's voyage began to be spread abroad. John Cabot was a good business man and equally able as a sea captain. In his younger days he had done a considerable amount of trading with the East; he had invested money in a caravan or two, and had, therefore, a good idea of the value of an all water route to India. Besides, he evidently believed that Columbus had a good plan for getting to India.

CABOT'S DISCOVERY OF NORTH AMERICA. John Cabot was satisfied that he had a workable plan for reaching the East. He therefore sought permission of Henry VII, the English king, to undertake a voyage westward. The permission was given.

John Cabot set sail with a crew of eighteen men in a little

**Cabot's Departure**
Start of the voyage that gave England her claims to what is now the United States.

ship called the *Matthew*, steering his ship to the west. After many weary weeks on the ocean, the *Matthew* reached land at some point on the coast of Labrador (1497). John Cabot took possession of this land for the King of England. After cruising about for a while, John Cabot returned home. He was the first of the explorers actually to reach the North American continent (Columbus touched South America in his later voyages). Upon John Cabot's discovery England based her claim to possession of much of North America.

THE VOYAGE OF SEBASTIAN CABOT. The report of John Cabot's successful voyage created a great stir in English shipping circles. He was urged to undertake a second voyage, which he did. This time he had a fleet of some six vessels. His son,

Sebastian, it seems, accompanied him. The fleet crossed the Atlantic to Labrador and after cruising down the coast returned home. For some time after this England paid little attention to the New World. But during the reign of Queen Elizabeth, some Englishmen began to believe that England must take more interest in America.

ENGLISH PLANS FOR COLONIZATION. Even before the defeat of the Armada, Englishmen had planned colonies in the New World. They saw in colonization a means of limiting Spain's power. As early as 1579 Sir Humphrey Gilbert had made an attempt to settle Newfoundland. The English had already become somewhat familiar with that section of America. During the early years of Elizabeth's reign the Grand Banks of Newfoundland were the favorite haunts of the more daring among the English fishermen. An Englishman, Martin Frobisher, had made three attempts to find gold in Labrador. Although Gilbert's first attempts at colonization had failed, he was willing to try again.

THE SECOND TRIAL OF GILBERT. Sir Humphrey Gilbert had considerable influence in England. He was a prominent member of Parliament. His step-brother, Sir Walter Raleigh, was also influential. Because of his position, Gilbert was able to get the funds to make a second attempt to colonize a portion of America. Gilbert again set sail for the New World, landing at St. John's, Newfoundland. Very much to his surprise, he found there fishermen of different European nations, including a large number of Spaniards, busily engaged in fishing.

SIR HUMPHREY GILBERT'S FAILURE. Much as Gilbert desired it, the settlement which he planned did not prove a success. Indeed it ended in almost complete disaster. Its failure was due to illness and lack of proper preparation among the settlers to live in America. Gilbert, therefore, realized he could not remain in America. Gathering a quantity of rock which the jewelry expert of the party declared contained silver, Gilbert set sail for home. The boat that carried this worthless rock reached England. The vessel carrying Gilbert went down. All hands were lost.

## A VOYAGE TO VIRGINIA.

Gilbert's failure did not discourage the English. Sir Walter Raleigh became interested in the idea of founding a colony in America. Just about the time Gilbert was making his last and unsuccessful attempt to found a colony, Raleigh was planning an enterprise of his own. He sent two vessels to America. The ships cruised along the coast of what is now North Carolina until they reached Roanoke Island. Here they cast anchor.

*Courtesy New York Public Library*

**Sir Humphrey Gilbert**

No attempt was made to found a colony. The voyagers merely contented themselves with a tour of inspection.

The voyagers upon their return to England described the country about Roanoke in the most glowing terms. They declared the country to be "the most sweet, fruitful and wholesome of all the world." The Indians were highly complimented on their good conduct. Sir Walter Raleigh was immensely pleased over the report and so also was Queen Elizabeth. It is said that she named the country Virginia, after herself, since she was the maiden queen.

## THE FIRST ROANOKE COLONY.

Naturally this delightful land of Virginia was the proper place for a colony; so thought

Raleigh and the queen. A fleet of seven vessels under Sir Richard Grenville was fitted out to carry one hundred and eight colonists to Virginia. The party finally arrived at Roanoke Island after first capturing some Spanish galleons on their way to Spain with treasure. Having arrived in the New World, the colonists did not quite know what to do. They had come here expecting to find gold but there seemed to be none about. Within a short time the colonists had made the Indians hate them. When in June, 1586, Sir Francis Drake appeared, the colonists begged to be taken back to England. Drake agreed to take them home.

RALEIGH'S SECOND ATTEMPT. To many men, the business of colonizing seemed to be a most unprofitable enterprise. Sir Walter Raleigh thought otherwise. He still hoped to make a fortune from his venture. In 1587, the English made another attempt to colonize. The venture this time was under the leadership of Captain John White. As on the former occasion, the settlers camped on Roanoke. Shortly after their arrival it became clear that if the colony were to succeed, better equipment must be had immediately. It was decided that White should return to England to procure the necessary supplies.

RALEIGH'S LOST COLONY. White landed in England at that moment when all the energies of the English were bent on beating back the dreaded Spanish Armada. No one had any time to listen to the story of the troubles of the colonists. The colonists were in distant Virginia while the Spaniards were at their very door. Nearly three years passed before White could return to Roanoke.

"CROATAN," THE LOST COLONY. Before White's departure for England, he told his men that if it should be necessary to move the camp, the name of the new location should be cut

Courtesy New York Public Library

## The Lost Colony

What do you think became of the lost white settlers?

into a tree. When he returned to the site of his colony he found nothing but a few kitchen utensils. No colonists were to be seen. Searching for some sign, he at length came upon a tree with "Croatan" cut deep into the trunk. White took courage when on closer inspection he saw no cross over the word. The cross was to be the distress signal.

Croatan is the name of an island. The island is not far from Roanoke. Captain White could not get a boat to reach the island. He never knew what had happened to the colony. Nor has any one ever found out. The colony is called the "lost colony."

JAMESTOWN, 1607. Poor Raleigh's attempts to colonize ended in failure. They were expensive failures, too. They cost Raleigh an enormous sum of money. Although Raleigh failed, he pointed the way for the successful colonization which came later. In the year 1607, what Raleigh hoped for was realized. A band of Englishmen landed in Virginia. They selected a place on the banks of a river which they named James in honor of the king, James I, King of England. A little town called Jamestown was reared. The town consisted of a few log huts. Rude fortifications were built to protect it. Jamestown was the first successful English colony in the New World. In 1620 it was followed by the Pilgrims' settlement at Plymouth, the beginning of the New England colonies.

## ORAL DRILL

1. What mariner first sailed from England to reach the coast of Labrador?
2. Who was the father of Sebastian Cabot?
3. Who first tried to colonize Virginia?
4. Where did Sir Humphrey Gilbert try to plant a colony?
5. What island off the coast of America was settled by the English?
6. When did the Spaniards attempt to invade England?
7. What was the name of the Spanish fleet?
8. When did the English establish their first permanent settlement in the New World? Where?
9. When was the second permanent English settlement made? Where was it located?

## OBJECTIVE TESTS

TEST 1: Character Judgment.
1. Sir Humphrey Gilbert: greedy, stingy, unsuccessful, weak.
2. Martin Frobisher: gold-seeker, doctor, teacher, banker.
3. Sir Francis Drake: saintly, daring, nervous, cautious.
4. Sir Walter Raleigh: persevering, quiet, bloodthirsty, lucky.

TEST 2: Completion Test.
1. ................ was the first successful English colony in the New World.
2. The history of England in America begins with the voyage commanded by ...............

3. The voyage of ............... in 1497 gave England a claim to North America.
4. ................ was the first to reach the mainland of North America.
5. During Elizabeth's reign the Grand Banks of ............. were visited by English fishermen.
6. Martin Frobisher made three attempts to find gold in ................
7. ................ was the English explorer whose ship was lost.
8. Virginia was named in honor of ................
9. The word "Croatan" was found on the island of ...........
10. Gilbert was the step-brother of the famous ...............

TEST 3: Order of Time.
Arrange the following in the order of time:
> First voyage of John Cabot to America
> First voyage of Columbus to New World
> Spanish Armada is defeated
> Jamestown is founded
> Sebastian Cabot reaches Labrador.

## QUESTIONS THAT MAKE YOU THINK

1. a) Did Columbus discover America?
   b) Explain your answer.
2. Name three English explorers.
3. Why is the work of John Cabot important?
4. Give one reason for Gilbert's failure to colonize America.
5. Explain the meaning of the word "Virginia."
6. State one contribution of Sir Walter Raleigh.
7. Give one reason for English interest in the New World.
8. Point out the effect of defeat of Armada upon the New World.
9. Why were Europeans interested in Newfoundland?
10. a) Name two English colonies which did not last.
    b) Give one reason for the failure of each.

## QUESTIONS THAT TEST YOUR CHARACTER

1. Do you admire Sir Francis Drake? Give a reason for your answer.
2. Make a list of five important traits which a good explorer must have.

3. Make a list of three traits which are bad for a colonist to have.
4. Point out a lesson which one might learn from the story of Roanoke Colony.
5. Describe the character of Sir Walter Raleigh.

## ACTIVITIES

1. Make a model of Cabot's ship.
2. Dramatize: Captain White finds "Croatan" carved on a tree.
3. Write a short story of what might have happened to the colonists of Roanoke.
4. Suppose you were John Cabot. Give a report to the English king about your first voyage to America.
5. Suppose you were a colonist of Roanoke. Keep a week's diary, telling what happened to the colony.
6. Draw a "Minute Movies" sketch of Gilbert, Frobisher, Raleigh, John and Sebastian Cabot.
7. Suppose you were one of the settlers at Jamestown. Write a letter to your brother in England telling him of the New World.
8. Paste in your scrapbook pictures and drawings of English explorers.

## TOPICS FOR DISCUSSION

1. The Roanoke Colony intermarried with the Indians.
2. John Cabot was greater than Christopher Columbus.
3. The Armada encouraged English colonization.
4. Gilbert was the greatest of English explorers.
5. Jamestown was a poor location for a colony.

## WORD LIST

| | |
|---|---|
| Labrador | Grand Banks |
| Newfoundland | galleons |
| mainland | colonization |

# XIII

*Part 2:* ENGLAND'S RIVALS IN THE NEW WORLD

The exploits of Spain's discoverers and explorers had made a great impression upon the people of the countries in Europe that were rivals of Spain. It is said that when King Francis I of France heard about the line of demarcation by which Spain and Portugal divided the New World, he was very much annoyed. Soon ships flying the French flag sailed for the New World.

## THE FRENCH IN AMERICA

FRANCE AND ENGLAND. England had rivals among the nations of the Old World. The European rival which caused England most trouble in the New World was France. This happened because both England and France sent settlers to North America where they were neighbors. The English and French who lived in North America after a while became bad neighbors and began to fight. In the end, England was the victor.

THE FRENCH EXPLORERS. Francis I, the King of France, decided that his country should send seamen to find new routes to the East. The king wanted the French traders and merchants to make money by exchanging French goods for the products of the East. Of course, the king hoped to make a fortune for himself through the success of this venture. The first explorer to be sent out by the king of France was John Verrazano. Verrazano was not a Frenchman but a Florentine. On the voyage, which took place in 1524, Verrazano probably reached what is now called New York Harbor. It seems likely that he sailed up Hudson River.

Courtesy New York Public Library

**Jacques Cartier**

In the background the artist shows part of the New World explored by Cartier.

JACQUES CARTIER. The next mariner in the service of the French king to embark upon a voyage of discovery was Jacques Cartier. Cartier was expected to find a short passage to China. In the city of St. Malo, Cartier selected a crew. St. Malo is a fishing city on the French coast. Its seamen are famous for their pluck. When his ship was ready for the voyage Cartier attended Mass and received Communion. All hands went on board, lines were cast off and the ship steered a course to the westward.

After many days, Cartier sighted the coast of Newfoundland. He cruised along the coast until on August 10, 1534, he came upon a gulf he called after Saint Lawrence, on whose feast day Cartier first saw it. Cartier explored the country in the vicinity of the gulf where he captured two Indians. Then he sailed for home taking the two Indians with him.

THE RETURN OF CARTIER. The report made by Cartier to the French court evidently pleased everybody. As a result, a return trip was ordered. Cartier was accompanied on this voyage by several gentlemen, who were rich in titles but poor in money. They hoped to find wealth in the wonderful country they were about to visit. The course taken by Cartier on the second voyage was very much like the first. This time he actually entered the Gulf of St. Lawrence and sailed up the St. Lawrence River. After sailing some distance, Cartier came to the rocky height where the city of Quebec now stands. When Cartier came abreast of this point, he lowered the sails and dropped anchor.

CARTIER AND THE INDIANS. Cartier was met by a delegation of friendly Indians. To show their pleasure over his visit they danced and howled. Cartier tried to show his appreciation. He made a long speech in French of which the redskins understood not a single word. They listened in respectful silence and at its conclusion they howled the louder. Then they showed him by signs that he ought to sail farther until he arrived at a great Indian city.

HOCHELAGA. Just as the Indians declared, some distance up the river on an island stood the Indian village of Hochelaga. But what a disappointment it must have been to Cartier! The Indian village was made up of a number of ugly huts. Each hut was about one hundred and fifty feet long and one third as wide. Several families were housed in a single hut, each family having its own part of the hut with a family fireplace. Dirt and ugliness were everywhere. Bursting with curiosity, the Indians crowded about Cartier's men, touching the beards of the white men and feeling their clothes. It was all very strange to the Indians. To the whites it was even more strange. Cartier decided to explore the country carefully, hoping against hope that he was not far from China, the land of his dreams.

THE EXPLORATION OF THE RIVER. The party set out in small boats. Their tour of inspection did not last long. After a time progress became too difficult for they had reached the rapids. The hopeful Cartier called this stretch of water Lachine (China), thinking he had found the way to China. Then he turned back, for the days were growing shorter and the nights colder. This kind of weather was a new experience for Cartier. Soon winter came.

The poor Frenchmen soon found themselves caught in the icy grip of the Canadian winter. The badly constructed cabins of the explorers were almost buried under snow drifts. Then followed a season of bitter cold. Many of his men were frozen to death, while disease took others. Those who escaped were too weak to bury their dead comrades. When the spring came, the exhausted survivors climbed aboard ship and with weary hearts set sail for France.

CARTIER'S IMPORTANT WORK. Seventy-five years later Cartier's voyages began to have real results. In 1608, Samuel de Champlain made the first lasting French settlement in Canada. Thus we have another of the Old World nations, and a rival of both Spain and England taking her place in the New World. Champlain chose a site for his settlement on the banks of the St. Lawrence, the site the Indians called Quebec, a place which abounded in nut trees. It was a fine location for a town since it was protected by a steep cliff which rose almost from the river's edge. An enemy could scarcely capture the town so well fortified was it by this protecting cliff. The St. Lawrence River, passing in front of the site, protected it on that side. Satisfied with the place, Champlain planned a town.

**Champlain Routs the Iroquois**

It was a costly victory for it made enemies of those powerful Indians. They afterward sided with the English.

THE BEGINNING OF NEW FRANCE. Champlain ordered his men to cut down some trees. Logs hewn from the trees were used for the construction of a storehouse. The storehouse itself was protected by a ditch dug about it. This was the beginning of the city of Quebec.

Champlain then cultivated the friendship of the Indians about Quebec. These Indians were the Algonquins. Unfortunately, Champlain's friendship for the Algonquins was the cause of trouble with another tribe of Indians, the Iroquois. The Iroquois were enemies of the Algonquins.

THE FRENCH AND THE IROQUOIS. Champlain undertook to help his friends, the Algonquins, fight the Iroquois. The Iroquois lived in that part of the country that is now northern New York. Champlain's help in the Indian war was so effective that the Iroquois were defeated. But the Iroquois never forgot this defeat. They hated the French. The French therefore could not settle in the territory held by the Iroquois. The French furthermore could not use the easier route by way of Lake Ontario to the interior of the continent. They were forced to take the longer and more difficult route by way of the Ottawa River. The fierce Iroquois became at times the allies of the English whom later they helped in defeating the French.

THE COMING OF THE MISSIONARIES. Champlain was a devout Catholic. He grieved deeply because the Indians were pagans. To convert the Indians, he sent to France for missionaries. The Franciscan missionaries came first. Later Jesuits and Sulpicians arrived to help preach the Gospel. Schools were established, and in 1635 a college was founded at Quebec. The Sisters also helped. There were communities for nursing the sick and for teaching.

NORTH AMERICA'S SAINTS. Among the early missionaries in the northeastern part of the continent were eight men who died martyrs. Six of this band were priests belonging to the Company of Jesus; two were laymen. The best known of these heroes is Father Isaac Jogues, now known as Saint Isaac Jogues. With his companion René Goupil, a young French surgeon, Father Jogues labored among the Hurons. Many times together they braved the dangers of the trackless forest. Often they were hungry. Twice they were captured by unfriendly Indians and finally both were martyred.

MISSIONARIES AND EXPLORERS. Missionaries continued to go to New France to serve the French settlers and to convert the Indians. To reach the widely scattered Indian villages the missionaries often traveled hundreds of miles. Sometimes they traveled by water, using birch bark canoes or dugouts, rude

**The Death of Father Marquette**
He exhausted himself in the service of his Church and his
Country and died in the wilderness he loved.

canoes fashioned from logs hollowed by burning or cutting.
Sometimes the entire journey was made through the forests on
foot. Besides helping the Indians by preaching and teaching,
the missionaries added to the white man's knowledge of the
continent of North America. One of the early Jesuit missionaries, Father James Marquette, accompanied Louis Joliet
on an expedition to find the Mississippi River.

THE JOLIET-MARQUETTE EXPEDITION. The governor
of New France, Count Frontenac, sent the fur trader Louis
Joliet to find the Mississippi River. Reports of the existence
of this great river had reached the French. Joliet was joined
by Father Marquette. The party paddled down the Fox and
Wisconsin rivers to the Mississippi.

The swift current of the "Father of Waters" bore their
canoes as far as the mouth of the Arkansas River; here the

explorers decided to return. They were convinced that the Mississippi flowed into the Gulf of Mexico.

THE AMBITIOUS LA SALLE. The accounts of the explorations of Champlain and other Frenchmen greatly interested a young man named Robert Cavalier Sieur de la Salle. La Salle possessed the qualities that a successful explorer must have. He had a body that was strong. He was able to withstand cold. He could make long treks through the forests. La Salle was a man of great courage. Besides these qualities, he had a special aptitude for learning languages. Thus he was able quickly to master the Indian tongues.

LA SALLE'S FIRST EXPLOITS. La Salle, soon after his arrival in Canada, learned to know the course of the St. Lawrence River. Later he explored what is now western New York. He noted the abundance of fur-bearing animals in this region. This led him to think about the profits to be made in furs. He, therefore, planned to build a ship of fair size that could sail on the Great Lakes. He also planned a fort at the outlet of the Niagara River, which would serve both as a means of defense and as a trading post.

THE BUILDING OF THE *GRIFFON*. In due time La Salle's ship was built. He called the vessel *Griffon*. He could be very proud of his ship, for it was itself a victory over obstacles. To build the *Griffon* La Salle's men cut down the green trees of the forest and fashioned the logs into planks. Five small cannon were mounted on the ship's decks. The *Griffon* was the first ship to sail on Lake Erie. The first voyage up the Great Lakes to Green Bay was made in 1679. At Green Bay a cargo of furs was put aboard and the ship sent back. But the gallant *Griffon* never reached its destination. Probably a gale sent it to the bottom. La Salle, however, was not on the ship at the time. He was thus saved for further adventures.

LA SALLE AND THE MISSISSIPPI. La Salle had a magnificent scheme. He thought that he could get great riches for himself, and at the same time serve France by building forts and trading posts on the shores of the Great Lakes and along the banks of the rivers flowing into the Mississippi. He decided to explore this great river. With a party of hardy explorers he journeyed down the Mississippi to the Gulf of Mexico (1682). At one of the outlets of the Mississippi, La Salle's party gathered around a wooden pillar and chanted the *Te Deum*. La Salle took possession of the vast region drained by the Mississippi for his king, Louis XIV. He named the region Louisiana in honor of the king.

**La Salle and the Building of the Ship "Griffon"**

Would a ship be built in such fashion today? Explain.

THE RESULTS OF THE FRENCH EXPLORATION. Through the work of the French explorers France laid claims to the vast territories drained by two great waterways, the St. Lawrence and the Mississippi. But France did not, as did the English, follow up her claims by establishing large settlements. Few Frenchmen came to America. Some came to make money by trading with the Indians at the lonely trading posts along the St. Lawrence, the Great Lakes, or the Mississippi. Others, "coureurs de bois," more hardy and venturesome, went deep into the forests to hunt game and to trap fur bearing animals.

THE CONQUEST OF NEW FRANCE. While the French did not come to America in large numbers France claimed an enormous region. However, small in numbers though they were they have left a lasting mark on eastern Canada. Here the Catholic religion flourishes. Countless places are named for the saints, and holy things. The French language is still spoken in the Province of Quebec. Many of the finest of Canada's citizens are the descendants of the old French stock.

Meanwhile English in large numbers were coming to America. They brought their families with them. The English rapidly became numerous, while the French inhabitants increased very slowly. Soon the French and English were fighting each other. Finally a war was begun in 1754 called the French and Indian War. It ended in 1763. At the end of the war the French in America were defeated, and England took Canada. Thus England was the chief power in most of North America.

## ENGLAND'S DUTCH RIVALS

THE DUTCH IN THE NEW WORLD. Some Dutch merchants who lived in the city of Amsterdam hired an experienced English seaman, named Henry Hudson, to sail on a voyage of discovery. Hudson's employers hoped that he would be able to find a short sea route to China. Hudson tried to find this route. He sailed to the north, but the cold and ice of the Arctic seas forced him to change his course. He finally reached the coast of North America. After an examination of the coast he entered what is now New York harbor, in 1609. This is the harbor which Verrazano had previously entered in 1524.

*Courtesy Museum of City of New York*

**Purchase of Manhattan**

> The Dutch and Indian come to a bargain for the sale of what is now the richest part of New York City.

HUDSON AND THE INDIANS. Henry Hudson sailed up the river, now known as Hudson River, until the water became too shallow for safe sailing. He then realized that he had not found the northern passage to China. Hudson was disappointed. One thing, however, cheered him. The Indians he had met were friendly.

Hudson invited a party of Indians to visit him on his ship, the *Half Moon*. Hudson found out from this visit that the Indians had beaver skins to trade for hatchets, knives, and glass beads. Beaver fur was about to become the fashionable thing to wear in Europe. Hudson, therefore, was glad to be able to tell the Dutch merchants about the possibilities of the fur trade.

NEW AMSTERDAM. Henry Hudson wrote a report of his voyage for his Dutch employers. Some of the Amsterdam merchants who had been responsible for Hudson's voyage were

### Saint Isaac Joques in New Amsterdam

The Jesuit saint having escaped from the Mohawks is received kindly by the Dutch settlers and sent back to France.

enthusiastic at the thought of the fur trade. A number of traders came to America. The region which they settled they called New Netherland. Trading posts were established. The most important of these trading posts was located on Manhattan Island. It was called New Amsterdam.

NEW SWEDEN. Another European people to settle in the New World were the Swedes. The Swedes knew about the success of the Dutch merchants in America. A company of Swedish merchants therefore was formed to trade with the Indians. A tract of land located near Delaware Bay was purchased from the Indians. Settlements were made along the Delaware River. These were not successful and in 1655 the

Dutch forced New Sweden, as the whole tract was called, to surrender.

THE END OF THE DUTCH POWER IN AMERICA. However, the power of the Dutch in America soon came to an end. In 1664 the Dutch were forced to surrender their claims to the English. Their province of New Netherland became the English colony of New York. Their trading village, New Amsterdam, became the English village of New York.

THE ENGLISH POWER IN AMERICA. With the Dutch surrender of New Netherland, the English came into possession of the eastern coast of North America from Canada to Florida. The problem of keeping Spain from moving north was being solved by the growth of the English colonies in the south. The New England colonies and the Iroquois Indians kept the French from moving southward along the coast. The French were active in the interior of the continent. In time the French were compelled to surrender Canada and the territory east of the Mississippi to England. This happened at the close of the French and Indian War in 1763.

---

## ORAL DRILL

---

1. What did the King of France think of the line of demarcation?
2. What mariner first entered New York harbor?
3. What land did Jacques Cartier propose to visit?
4. What did Cartier do before sailing?
5. What happened to Cartier's settlement?
6. Which Indians did Champlain help?
7. Who settled Delaware?
8. When did New Amsterdam become New York?
9. Who accompanied Father Marquette?
10. Who was martyred in what is now New York State?

## OBJECTIVE TESTS

TEST 1: Completion Test.

1. The explorer ............. named the region of Louisiana for the French King Louis XIV.
2. Another name for New France was .................
3. The ............... language is spoken in the Province of Quebec.
4. ............... was the companion of Louis Joliet.
5. The enemies of the Algonquins were the ............... Indians.
6. Lachine Rapids is named after the country of .............
7. French fur trappers were called .................
8. At the end of the French and Indian war ............... took Canada.
9. The *Half Moon* was the ship of the explorer .............
10. In 1664 the Dutch surrendered New Netherland to ...............

TEST 2: Matching Test.

| Column A | | | Column B |
|---|---|---|---|
| 1. New Sweden | ( | ) | Jacques Cartier |
| 2. New Netherland | ( | ) | Samuel de Champlain |
| 3. St. Lawrence | ( | ) | Delaware |
| 4. Governor of New | ( | ) | New York |
| France | ( | ) | Verrazano |
| 5. Jesuit missionary | ( | ) | first permanent settlement in |
| 6. Hochelaga | | | Canada |
| 7. Quebec | ( | ) | La Salle |
| 8. Florentine | ( | ) | Marquette-Joliet |
| 9. *Griffon* | ( | ) | Isaac Jogues |
| 10. Arkansas River | ( | ) | Indian village |

TEST 3: Order of Time.

Arrange the following events in the order of time:

English settlement at Jamestown
French settlement at Quebec
Dutch surrender New Netherland
England takes New France
Verrazano enters New York harbor
Cartier sails up St. Lawrence
Dutch take New Sweden
La Salle reaches Gulf of Mexico

## QUESTIONS THAT MAKE YOU THINK

1. Why is Verrazano called a Florentine, instead of an Italian?
2. Why was Cartier disappointed in the Indian village which he saw?
3. a) Mention two French explorers, and b) the work of each.
4. Why were the Iroquois enemies of the French?
5. Explain two contributions of the French missionaries.
6. Why is Father Marquette not called a martyr?
7. Why did the English come to America in such large numbers?
8. Why did the Dutch settle in New York?
9. Name four nations who settled in the New World at this time.
10. Why are there many Catholics today in Canada?

## QUESTIONS THAT TEST YOUR CHARACTER

1. a) Mention two good traits of Cartier.
   b) To what degree do you possess these traits?
2. Why is Isaac Jogues a man to be admired?
3. Explain why Father Marquette is admired by Catholics and non-Catholics.
4. Describe the character of Henry Hudson.

## ACTIVITIES

1. Make a model of the *Half Moon.*
2. Compare the *Half Moon* and the *Queen Mary* with regard to size. Illustrate this difference by two pictures side by side.
3. Dress a doll like a French fur trader.
4. Dramatize: Cartier lands in Canada.
5. Suppose you were Joliet. Write in your diary telling of your journey with Father Marquette.
6. On a large cardboard make a chart of the different colonies in the New World.
7. Give a two-minute talk on Isaac Jogues.
8. Tell of a trip to modern Quebec. Point out French influences.
9. Make a model of an Indian village.
10. Paste in your scrapbook pictures and clippings of explorers and settlers.

## TOPICS FOR DISCUSSION

1. Champlain was a great leader.
2. Father Marquette was more important as a missionary than as an explorer.
3. La Salle had no right to claim the valley of the Mississippi.
4. Hudson's work was more important than Cartier's.
5. The citizens of Quebec are French, not Canadian.

## WORD LIST

| | |
|---|---|
| fur trader | expedition |
| Lachine Rapids | exploits |
| St. Lawrence River | Half Moon |
| New Amsterdam | New France |

HONOR ROLL
DU BOIS
SMITH
O'BRIEN
CEJKA
LEVY
KNUTSON
GONZALES
RVITCH

# SUMMARY

## The Old World and America

THE history of Europe in America we shall study more completely in other books. For the present, we shall remember the course of the story thus far studied as follows:

THE STORY OF EUROPE IN AMERICA.

1. DISCOVERY. The finding of the continents of North and South America and the claims of the various European nations to the New World. We shall remember Columbus for Spain, Cabot for England, Cartier for France, Hudson for Holland.

2. EXPLORATION. The discoverers were followed by explorers who added to the knowledge of the people of Europe concerning the New World. The countries that sent out these explorers claimed territory in America because of their explorations. These claims to territory often conflicted.

3. APPROPRIATION. The governments of the various European countries that claimed territory in the New World followed exploration by colonization. Most of Spain's settlements were located to the south of our present borders. But France, England, the Dutch, and the Swedes made settlements within what is now the United States.

4. ELIMINATION. There was a conflict among these European powers in America. The Dutch eliminated Swedish power. The English eliminated the Dutch. Then, through the victory of the English in the time of the French and Indian War,

France's political power in America was destroyed. Finally, England's mastery of North America, from the Gulf of Mexico to Hudson's Bay, and from the Atlantic Ocean to the Mississippi River, was complete.

OUR STORY'S END. We have almost reached the end of our story, a story that has taken us back many centuries. In the countries of western Asia and Egypt we found the first home of civilization. Thence civilization went to Greece. After the Greeks came the Romans, who preserved Greek civilization and added to it. In time the mighty Roman Empire fell, conquered by the Teutons. Then, but for the Catholic Church, civilization would have been utterly destroyed. The Catholic Church was able to build a better civilization on the ruins of the old. A new Europe was born.

MAKERS OF AMERICA. The various peoples that were to serve America in its discovery, exploration, and settlement slowly formed themselves into nations. We have learned a little about most of these peoples. We have followed the course of Italian traders and navigators. The discoverers and explorers sent out by Spain, Portugal, and France have interested us. We have read about German inventors and geographers. Something about the making of England and the English part in the colonization of America has been told.

THE BEGINNING OF THE UNITED STATES. In the books you will study later you will read the story of the men who settled in the English colonies. Most of the settlers came in search of liberty. They left the mother country because liberty and opportunity were there denied them. At length there were thirteen colonies, all under the rule of England. In 1776 the thirteen colonies declared their independence. Thus was our glorious United States started on her career. But even then Europe did not cease to have its influence upon us.

SUCCESSORS OF THE FIRST SETTLERS. About the middle of the last century, thousands of earnest high-minded men and women began to come to America from Europe in increasing numbers. These people, like the early settlers, came to America in search of freedom and a fair opportunity to better themselves. In return for the liberty America gave them, they gave America in turn toilers for her farms, teachers for her schools, leaders for her legislatures, bishops, priests and religious to preserve and spread the truth. And when the very life of this nation was threatened by civil war there were heroes by the thousands from this stock who gave their lives that America might live.

AMERICANS ALL. After the World War an artist drew a most inspiring picture to encourage people to lend their money and so to help the government. The picture showed a monument over the graves of American soldiers. On the monument were the names of soldier dead. If you looked closely you would see that there were great differences among the names. They belonged to many different nationalities. At one time these names were French and Irish, Slavic and English, German and Italian and many others. Now they are the names of Americans, Americans all—brave men who died that America might fulfill her destiny as a nation fashioned on ideals of liberty, devoted to the service of humanity, and founded upon trust in God.

\* \* \* \* \* \* \* \* \* \* \* \* \* \* \* \*

# PRONUNCIATION

| a at | ã care | ė her | ō more | ou out | ch chip |
|---|---|---|---|---|---|
| ā came | ạ alone | ẹ towel | ö to | u up | g go |
| ä far | ạ̈ opera | i it | ô off | ū use | th thin |
| â all | e end | ī line | ọ actor | ù put | ŦH then |
| à ask | ē be | o on | ȯi oil | y̨ nature | y you |
| | | n as in French bon | | | |

\* \* \* \* \* \* \* \* \* \* \* \* \* \* \* \*

Cyprus, sī'prus
Danelau, dän'lâ
Darien, dä'ri'en
Darius, dạ-rī'us
da Vinci, Leonardo, lä-ō-när'dō dä
   vēn'chē
De Leon, Ponce, pōn'thä dä lä-ōn
Delphi, del'fī
Della robbia, del'ạ rob'bē-ạ
de Montfort, Simon, sī mon dē mont'fọrt
Diaz, dē'äs
Feudal, fū'dạl
Forum, fō'rum
Frobisher, frō'bish-er
Frontenac, frônt-näk'
Gallic, gal'ik
Ghent, gent
Giotto, jōt'to'
Gladiator, glad'i-ā-tọr
Gracchi, grak'i
Granada, grạ-nä'dạ
Gutenberg, gö'ten-berch
Hamilcar, ha-mil'kạr
Hammurabi, ham-mü-rä'bē
Hannibal, han'i-bạl
Hegira, hej'i-rạ
Hengist, heng'gist
Herodotus, he-rod'ọ-tus
Hieroglyphics, hī'ẹ-rọ-glif'iks
Hippocrates, hi-pok'rạ-téz
Hispaniola, his-pan-i-ō-lạ̈
Hochelaga, hō-shel'ạ-gạ̈
Horace, hor'äs
Horsa, hôr'sạ̈
Ignatius, ig-nä'shus
Iliad, il'i-ạd
Inca, ing'kạ̈
Ionic, ī-on'ik
Iroquois, ir-ọ-kwoi'
Isabella, iz-ạ-bel'ạ̈
Isthmus, ist'mus
Janus, jä'nus
Jeremias, jer-ẹ-mi'ạ̈s
Jerome, jẹ-rōm'
Jerusalem, jẹ-rö'sạ-lem
Joan of Arc, jōn ọv ärk
Justinian, jus-tin'i-ạn
Jutes, jöts
Khufu, kö'fö
Koran, kọ-rän'
Kublai Khan, kü'blī kän
Lisbon, liz'bọn

Loyola, Ignatius, ig-nä'shus loi ō'la
Macedonia, mas-ẹ-dō'ni-ạ̈
Magellan, mạ-jel'ạn
Magna Carta, mag'nạ̈ kär'tạ̈
Marathon, mar'ạ-thon
Marquette, mär-ket'
Marseille, mär-sāy'
Mecca, mek'ạ̈
Meuse, mūz
Michelangelo, mī-kel-an'je-lō
Milan, mi-lan'
Mohammed, mọ-ham'ed
Monte Cassino, mōn'ta-käs-sē'nō
Montezuma, mōn-tẹ zö'mạ̈
Mylae, mī'lē
Nabuchodonosor, neb'ū-kạd-ṅez'ạ̈r
Nazareth, naz'ạ-reth
New Foundland, nụ found'land
Nile, nīl
Nineveh, nin'ẹ-vẹ
Obelisk, ob'e-lisk
Odoacer, ō-dō-ā'sėr
Odyssey, od'i-si
Olympia, ō-lim'pi-ạ̈
Olympic, ọ-lim'pik
Orinoco, ō-ri-nō'kō
Orleans, ôr-lä-äṅ
Palermo, pạ-lėr'mō
Palestine, pal'es-tīn
Palos, pä-lös'
Panama, pan-ạ-mä'
Pantheon, pan'thē-ọn
Papyrus, pạ-pī'rus
Parliament, pär'li-mẹnt
Parthenon, pär'the-non
Patriciane, pạ-trish'ạn
Pavia, pä-vē'ä
Pepin, pep'in
Perez, pä'räth
Pericles, per'i-klēz
Petrarch, pē'trärk
Pharaoh, fä'ro
Phidias, fid'i-as
Philosopher, fi-los'ọ-fėr
Phoenicians, fẹ-nish'ạns
Pinta, pin'tạ̈
Pisa, pē'zä
Pizarro, pi-zä'ro
Platea, pla-tē'ạ̈
Plebeians, plẹ-bē'ạns
Poitiers, pwä-tyä'
Polo, Marco, mär kō pō'lō

# xii

PRONUNCIATION

Pompey, pom'pi
Ponce de Leon, pōn'thä-dä-la-on
Poseidon, pọ-sī'dọn
Prague, präg
Praxiteles, praks-it'e-lēz
Pueblo, pweb'lō
Puerto Rico, pwer'tō rē'kō
Quebec, kwẹ-bek'
Raleigh, Walter, râ'li
Raphael, raf'ā-el
Renaissance, ren-ä-säns'
Rheims, rēmz
Rio Grande, rē'ō grän'dä
Romanesque, rō-mạ-nesk'
Rubicon, rö'bi-kọn
Russia, rush'ạ
Saguntum, sa-gun'tum
Saladin, sal'ạ-din
Salamis, sal'ạ-mis
San Salvador, san sal'vạ-dôr
Santa Barbara, sän'tä bär'bạ-rạ
Saracens, sar'ạ-sẹns
Serra, Junipero, sär'rä
Sobieski, sō-bē ès'kē
Socrates, sok'rạ-tēz
Solomon, sol'ọ-mọn

Solon, sō'lọn
Sulpicians, sul-pish'iạnz
Switzerland, swit'zèr-lạnd
Syria, sir'i-ạ
Te Deum, tē dē'um
Tenochtitlan, ten-ōch-tēt-län'
Thames, temz
Thebes, thēbz
Theodosius, thē-ō-dō'shi-us
Thermopylae, thèr-mop'i-lē
Thessaly, thes'ạ-li
Toscanelli, tos-kä nel'lē
Tours, tör
Valens, vä'lenz
Vercingetorix, vèr-sin-jet'ō-riks
Verdun, ver-duṅ
Verrazano, ver-rät-sä'nō
Vesta, ves'tạ
Virgil, vèr'jil
Visigoths, viz'i-goths
Waldseemüller, vält'zä-mül-ler
Woden, wō'den
Xerxes, zèrk'sēz
Zama, zä'mạ
Zeuz, zūs

# NOTES

# NOTES

# NOTES

# NOTES

# NOTES

# NOTES

*If you have enjoyed this book, consider making your next selection from among the following . . .*

Prices subject to change.

Hail Holy Queen (from *Glories of Mary*). *St. Alphonsus* . . . . . . . . . . . . . . . 8.00
Novena of Holy Communions. *Lovasik* . . . . . . . . . . . . . . . . . . . . . . . . . . . 2.00
Brief Catechism for Adults. *Cogan*. . . . . . . . . . . . . . . . . . . . . . . . . . . . . . . 9.00
The Cath. Religion—Illus./Expl. for Child, Adult, Convert. *Burbach* . . . . . . . 9.00
Eucharistic Miracles. *Joan Carroll Cruz* . . . . . . . . . . . . . . . . . . . . . . . . . . 15.00
The Incorruptibles. *Joan Carroll Cruz* . . . . . . . . . . . . . . . . . . . . . . . . . . . 13.50
Pope St. Pius X. *F. A. Forbes* . . . . . . . . . . . . . . . . . . . . . . . . . . . . . . . . . . 8.00
St. Alphonsus Liguori. *Frs. Miller and Aubin*. . . . . . . . . . . . . . . . . . . . . . 16.50
Self-Abandonment to Divine Providence. *Fr. de Caussade, S.J.* . . . . . . . . . . 18.00
The Song of Songs—A Mystical Exposition. *Fr. Arintero, O.P.* . . . . . . . . . . 20.00
Prophecy for Today. *Edward Connor* . . . . . . . . . . . . . . . . . . . . . . . . . . . . . 5.50
Saint Michael and the Angels. *Approved Sources* . . . . . . . . . . . . . . . . . . . . 7.00
Dolorous Passion of Our Lord. *Anne C. Emmerich*. . . . . . . . . . . . . . . . . . 16.50
Modern Saints—Their Lives & Faces, Book I. *Ann Ball* . . . . . . . . . . . . . . 18.00
Modern Saints—Their Lives & Faces, Book II. *Ann Ball* . . . . . . . . . . . . . . 20.00
Our Lady of Fatima's Peace Plan from Heaven. *Booklet* . . . . . . . . . . . . . . . .75
Divine Favors Granted to St. Joseph. *Père Binet* . . . . . . . . . . . . . . . . . . . . 5.00
St. Joseph Cafasso—Priest of the Gallows. *St. John Bosco*. . . . . . . . . . . . . 4.50
Catechism of the Council of Trent. *McHugh/Callan*. . . . . . . . . . . . . . . . . . 24.00
The Foot of the Cross. *Fr. Faber*. . . . . . . . . . . . . . . . . . . . . . . . . . . . . . . . 16.50
The Rosary in Action. *John Johnson* . . . . . . . . . . . . . . . . . . . . . . . . . . . . . 9.00
Padre Pio—The Stigmatist. *Fr. Charles Carty* . . . . . . . . . . . . . . . . . . . . . 15.00
Why Squander Illness? *Frs. Rumble & Carty*. . . . . . . . . . . . . . . . . . . . . . . 2.00
The Sacred Heart and the Priesthood. *de la Touche* . . . . . . . . . . . . . . . . . . 9.00
Fatima—The Great Sign. *Francis Johnston* . . . . . . . . . . . . . . . . . . . . . . . . 8.00
Heliotropium—Conformity of Human Will to Divine. *Drexelius* . . . . . . . . . 13.00
Charity for the Suffering Souls. *Fr. John Nageleisen* . . . . . . . . . . . . . . . . . 16.50
Devotion to the Sacred Heart of Jesus. *Verheylezoon* . . . . . . . . . . . . . . . . . 15.00
Who Is Padre Pio? *Radio Replies Press* . . . . . . . . . . . . . . . . . . . . . . . . . . . 1.50
Child's Bible History. *Knecht*. . . . . . . . . . . . . . . . . . . . . . . . . . . . . . . . . . . 4.00
The Stigmata and Modern Science. *Fr. Charles Carty* . . . . . . . . . . . . . . . . . 1.25
The Life of Christ. 4 Vols. H.B. *Anne C. Emmerich* . . . . . . . . . . . . . . . . . 60.00
St. Anthony—The Wonder Worker of Padua. *Stoddard* . . . . . . . . . . . . . . . . 5.00
The Precious Blood. *Fr. Faber* . . . . . . . . . . . . . . . . . . . . . . . . . . . . . . . . . 13.50
The Holy Shroud & Four Visions. *Fr. O'Connell* . . . . . . . . . . . . . . . . . . . . 2.00
Clean Love in Courtship. *Fr. Lawrence Lovasik* . . . . . . . . . . . . . . . . . . . . . 2.50
The Prophecies of St. Malachy. *Peter Bander*. . . . . . . . . . . . . . . . . . . . . . . 7.00
St. Martin de Porres. *Giuliana Cavallini* . . . . . . . . . . . . . . . . . . . . . . . . . . 12.50
The Secret of the Rosary. *St. Louis De Montfort*. . . . . . . . . . . . . . . . . . . . . 3.00
The History of Antichrist. *Rev. P. Huchede*. . . . . . . . . . . . . . . . . . . . . . . . . 4.00
St. Catherine of Siena. *Alice Curtayne* . . . . . . . . . . . . . . . . . . . . . . . . . . . 13.50
Where We Got the Bible. *Fr. Henry Graham* . . . . . . . . . . . . . . . . . . . . . . . 6.00
Hidden Treasure—Holy Mass. *St. Leonard*. . . . . . . . . . . . . . . . . . . . . . . . . 5.00
Imitation of the Sacred Heart of Jesus. *Fr. Arnoudt* . . . . . . . . . . . . . . . . . . 15.00
The Life & Glories of St. Joseph. *Edward Thompson*. . . . . . . . . . . . . . . . . . 15.00
Père Lamy. *Biver*. . . . . . . . . . . . . . . . . . . . . . . . . . . . . . . . . . . . . . . . . . . 10.00
Humility of Heart. *Fr. Cajetan da Bergamo* . . . . . . . . . . . . . . . . . . . . . . . . 8.50
The Curé D'Ars. *Abbé Francis Trochu*. . . . . . . . . . . . . . . . . . . . . . . . . . . . 21.50
Love, Peace and Joy. (St. Gertrude). *Prévot* . . . . . . . . . . . . . . . . . . . . . . . . 7.00

***At your Bookdealer or direct from the Publisher.***
***Call Toll-Free 1-800-437-5876.***

Prices subject to change.